the Ostrich,
the Eagle,
and the Unborn Child

the Ostrich,
the Eagle,
and the Unborn Child

An In-depth Biblical and
Legal Exposé on Abortion

Loren W. Brown J.D. and Taylor J. Brown Th.M.

the Ostrich,
the Eagle,
and the Unborn Child

An In-depth Biblical and Legal Exposé on Abortion

by
Loren W. Brown J.D.
Taylor J. Brown Th.M.

Published by
LoveUnborn Publishing,
Yorba Linda, California
www.LoveUnborn.com

First Edition

Copyright © 2017

ISBN-13: 9780997785906
ISBN-10: 099778590X
Library of Congress Control Number: 2017905483

Cover Design by Loren W. Brown, Jr.,
PlanView Communications, Austin, Texas • www.planviewco.com

About the Authors...

Loren W. Brown, J.D., holds a bachelor of science degree from the University of Arizona as well as a law degree from Western University, State College of Law. He has practiced in the legal areas of contracts and estate planning for many years, and he became a full-time instructor of legal studies at the University of Houston-Downtown in 2011. An avid Bible scholar, Loren enjoys speaking at events on legal and moral issues—specifically abortion and its impact on society. Loren has been married for more than four decades and is the father of three adult children.

Taylor J. Brown, Th.M., holds a bachelor's degree in economics and business with a prelaw emphasis from Westmont College. He has a master's degree in biblical theology from Fuller Seminary and has completed advanced master's studies in practical theology at Holy Cross Greek Orthodox School of Theology.

What began as a personal Bible study on abortion led this father-and-son team to combine their legal and theological expertise to coauthor *The Ostrich, the Eagle, and the Unborn Child*.

Table of Contents

An Introduction to the Abortion Debate

ABORTION. THE VERY sound of the word is for many of us enough to tug at the emotions and trigger extreme reactions, regardless which position we take. It is one of *the* great battlegrounds of our time. Across America demonstrations have been held, people have been willingly arrested, abortion clinics have been bombed or set on fire, and doctors have been killed for their involvement. An annual March for Life is carried out in Washington D.C. each January on the anniversary of the Supreme Court's *Roe v. Wade* decision. Recently, as we were preparing this book for publication, another attack has taken place at a Planned Parenthood clinic in Colorado Springs. But why is abortion such a passionate and volatile issue?

It is now more than 40 years since the Supreme Court announced in the case of *Roe v. Wade* that a pregnant woman has a fundamental right under our Constitution to decide whether to carry her baby to term or abort it without governmental intervention into what the Court deemed to be a matter of privacy and not a matter of criminality.

In the years since that decision was rendered, the debate has not diminished. The Catholic Church has been a most vocal opponent of abortion practices, but certainly not the only one.

Other churches and denominations and a host of secular organizations have strongly opposed abortion-on-demand, and the combined efforts of the pro-life community, Christian or otherwise, have brought about changes in the law that has narrowed this so-called fundamental right.

Not all Christians are anti-abortion, nor are all non-Christians pro-abortion, as some may believe. Whether Christian or not, however, it is important that we know and are able to share with others the basis for our beliefs and the positions we take. This book will endeavor to set forth a consistent biblical view while also systematically analyzing the legal status of abortion in the United States. We also carefully consider other important factors surrounding the abortion issue, including medical science, abortion statistics and others. Following our own personal journeys to discover how this important issue fits into the Christian worldview, it has been our intention to assist others in their own pursuit of the Truth and to bring understanding concerning the dominant positions taken in our society.

While the battle over abortion is generally couched in terms of either "Pro-Choice," representing the view that women rightfully have an unfettered right to an abortion under *Roe v. Wade*, or "Pro-Life," the position that the unborn have a God-given right to life, Christians must not stop their query with mere analysis of current laws and social trends. While God has given us free will so that we have choices in how we live our lives, the real objective for followers of Christ is to be centered on making certain our choices honor and glorify God. Does it matter to Him if we choose to continue a pregnancy or terminate it? Do our current circumstances make a difference in how God views our choice of whether or not to abort? These are the kinds of questions that must be asked and answered with God's Word as our spiritual Guide.

Before going any further, it would certainly be a fair question to ask why the Bible should be consulted at all about the abortion issue. There is no Hebrew, Aramaic or Greek equivalent of the word "abortion" anywhere in Scripture. Although Exodus 20:13 says, "You shall not murder," one of the Ten Commandments, it is strongly asserted by pro-choice advocates that abortion is not murder because until a child is born alive, or at least until the fetus has developed to a stage of "viability" (a term normally used to mean that point in the process of fetal development when it could survive outside the womb), it is either not considered a living human being (that is, a "person" in constitutional terms) or it is argued that the mother's right of choice supersedes all consideration for fetal life.

If we believe, as the Bible says, that God is our Creator and the One to whom we must ultimately answer, we must also remember that He knows all of the choices we make and that we may be called to give an account to Him for our choices, whether good or bad. If God is to judge us fairly, or if our rewards for eternity will be based on how we have handled the issues of earthly life, it stands to reason that He would reveal to us exactly what He expects.

The legal system in the United States works on the same principal. We cannot be held to have broken laws that do not exist. Until a law is enacted and made public, no one can be held to have violated it. Once it has become law, however, we are all presumed to know what the law requires. This is what is meant by the well-known adage: "Ignorance of the law is no excuse."

The great and wonderful significance of the Bible is that it claims to have been given to us by God Himself for that very purpose – to let us know who God is and what He expects of us. In the book of Romans, the Apostle Paul wrote:

Yet if it had not been for the law, I would not have known sin...For apart from the law, sin lies dead. (Ro. 7:7-8)

Unless and until He made His will known to us, God could not justly condemn our actions. In Paul's second letter to Timothy, we find that:

All Scripture is breathed out by God and profitable for teaching, for reproof, for correction, and for training in righteousness, that the man of God may be complete, equipped for every good work. (2 Tim. 3:16-17)

The Apostle Peter tells us:

Knowing this first of all, that no prophecy of Scripture comes from someone's own interpretation. For no prophecy was ever produced by the will of man, but men spoke from God as they were carried along by the Holy Spirit. (2 Peter 1:20-21)

We cannot convince another man or woman that these statements are true. They must be taken on faith. But if God truly exists and if the Bible really is His communication to us, then we are without excuse when we come face to face with Him, for we are held accountable to know what it says and to comply with its teachings.

With respect to abortion, one thing is clear: there can be only one correct position from God's point of view. Doing what is right in our own eyes is not enough. King Solomon in his Proverbs wrote:

> There is a way that seems right to a man, but its end is the way to death. (Prov. 14:12)

Our guide, therefore, must be based on better things than human reasoning. Relying upon what seems right to us may have dire consequences.

On the important issues of life, which must include abortion, there should be no division in the church. As Christ said in Mark 3:25, "If a house is divided against itself, that house will not be able to stand." In Philippians 2:2 we are called as a body of believers to be "of the same mind, having the same love, being in full accord and of one mind." We are reminded of the Apostle Paul's exhortation when he was faced with potentially conflicting views within the church at Corinth. Paul was upset that Christians were quarreling and separating into factions, some saying, "I follow Paul," another claimed, "I follow Apollos," another said, "I follow Cephas," and still another boasted, "I follow Christ" (1 Cor. 1:12). To this Paul said:

> I appeal to you, brothers, by the name of our Lord Jesus Christ, that all of you agree, and that there be no divisions among you, but that you be united in the same mind and the same judgment. (1 Cor. 1:10)

Paul then asks, "Is Christ divided?" The question demands a resounding *no*. Neither should His church be divided. Divisions within the church are a destructive force. At a minimum, they tend to render the church impotent and cause the message of the Gospel to lose power. Unless the church body is united, how can we expect those outside the church to be persuaded? Where Christians disagree, Christ is ridiculed. This was what Jesus meant when He taught us:

> You are the salt of the earth, but if salt has lost its taste, how shall its saltiness be restored? It is no longer good for anything except to be thrown out and trampled under people's feet. (Matt. 5:13)

Even the differences among the various Christian sects and denominations should be restricted to insignificant matters. Whether one is Orthodox, Catholic, or Protestant of any persuasion, all should be united in the critical issues of life that concern our salvation and God's eternal purposes.

Saltiness is lost when Christians are divided. Our effectiveness in reaching those who need Christ and in making positive changes in the world around us is greatly diminished where unity is lacking. How then can the church remain salty? We all need to take our direction from one source. We must all sing from the same songbook to make music worth hearing, and our songbook can only be the Word of God. The music we make must come from the harmony of collective obedience to God. And we can trust God because "God is not a man that he should lie, or a son of man, that he should change his mind" (Num. 23:19).

The body of Christ labors through the outworking of the Holy Spirit in each individual member. Accordingly, the Apostle Paul gives us strong admonition:

> According to the grace of God given to me, like a skilled master builder I laid a foundation, and someone else is building upon it. Let each one take care how he builds upon it. For no one can lay a foundation other than that which is laid, which is Jesus Christ. Now if anyone builds on the foundation with gold, silver, precious stones, wood, hay, straw – each one's work will become manifest, for the Day will disclose it, because it will be revealed by fire, and the fire will test

what sort of work each one has done. If the work that anyone has built on the foundation survives, he will receive a reward. If anyone's work is burned up, he will suffer loss, though he himself will be saved, but only as through fire. (1 Cor. 3:10-15)

We realize that in writing this book we are attempting to teach others the will of God concerning abortion. This we take very seriously. When tested by fire, it is our desire that our work will survive. James, the brother of Jesus, reminds us that "Not many of you should become teachers, my brothers, for you know that we who teach will be judged with greater strictness" (James 3:1). We have made every effort to search the Scriptures carefully and report to you honestly and in all humility what we have found there. As best we could, we have shelved our own emotions and preconceived notions while we searched for Truth. We urge each of you to diligently search the Word for yourselves. As you read this book and compare its teaching with God's Word, focus on the central question that we have done our best to answer: What is God's will with respect to abortion? We cannot rely on our own fallible wisdom. As Paul cautioned the believers at Corinth:

Let no one deceive himself. If anyone among you thinks that he is wise in this age, let him become a fool that he may become wise. For the wisdom of this world is folly with God. For it is written, "He catches the wise in their craftiness," and again, "The Lord knows the thoughts of the wise, that they are futile." (1 Cor. 3:18-20)

Our earnest prayer is that Christians will unite in their convictions concerning abortion, all in accordance with God's will. And having united, we will, with one voice, speak out in truth and in love. Although Christians, those who are truly born-again, may be a bona-fide minority not only in the United States but throughout the world, a united minority can make a positive difference.

There is no middle ground. President John F. Kennedy is credited with saying, "The hottest places in Hell are reserved for those who in period of moral crisis maintain their neutrality."[1] Those who know and trust Jesus Christ as their Lord and Savior should be enthusiastic about the things of God. And biblical truths must not be compromised.

Abortion, however, is not just a religious issue. It is thoroughly a legal and moral one from top to bottom. Under our federal system of government in the United States, authority is divided between the states and the federal government, which requires a systematic means of sharing powers. This sharing of powers, however, often creates struggles between the federal government (whose laws are deemed superior to State laws) and the states. It is the U.S. Constitution that must resolve these conflicts and provide peaceful means to harmony among the various levels of government.

Interpretation of the various Constitutional provisions is where problems often arise and the abortion issue falls squarely within that area of concern. The U.S. Supreme Court is the final arbiter of all Constitutional issues. But the Court is not infallible. A substantial portion of this book is concentrated, by necessity, in discussion of abortion rights and the constitutional interpretations that provide those rights and the limitations on them.

Abortion law, as we will see, has created a tremendous clash among the stakeholders involved; it pits federal government against State rights, women's rights against the rights of the unborn, and even mother's rights against the father's rights. It also causes conflict among doctors, theologians, philosophers, and all those who have a financial interest in the abortion industry. Conflicts exist even within the same level of government. This is a balancing act that is very difficult, indeed impossible, to accomplish to everyone's satisfaction. While we consider these very challenging issues, we attempt always to involve God and seek His guidance through the Word and His Holy Spirit who leads us to the Truth.

---

1 This statement was reportedly made by JFK on June 24, 1963 at Bonn, Germany at the signing of a Charter Establishing the German Peace Corps. Kennedy attributed this quotation to the poet, Dante (although it does not appear that Dante ever truly penned these words). *Public Papers of the Presidents of the United States: John F. Kennedy*, 1963. Retrieved from http://www.jfklibrary.org/Research/Research-Aids/Ready-Reference/JFK-Quotations. aspx Accessed on 3/23/2016

The abortion issue represents a great moral crisis that will not be resolved by straddling the proverbial fence. Now is the time for Christians and the pro-life community to unite and take their stand for what they profess to believe. But in so doing, we must not lose sight of the fact that many who are searching for answers, and many who may read the words of this book, have personal issues that require and deserve our sincere understanding. And so, we desire to be helpful rather than a hindrance. Let us assure anyone who takes the time to study God's Word on this important issue that His provision for us is sufficient no matter what our past has been. Just as the Bible says:

> If we confess our sins, he is faithful and just to forgive us our sins and to cleanse us from all unrighteousness. (1 John 1:9)

We do not condemn anyone. Our purpose is to reveal, as best we can, the Truth as we have discovered it. We trust that God will bring healing wherever needed.

1

The Beginning of Life – God's Overall Plan

NO BIBLICAL STUDY of the abortion issue could be complete without carefully considering the intended relationship between God and mankind. Abortion almost always results in the destruction of a human fetus in the womb, and it is God's will concerning the unborn that we, as Christians, need to discover. Unless we have as a solid foundation God's design and purpose for mankind in general, we cannot begin to understand His will regarding the human fetus. To truly comprehend God's purpose for us and our children, it is necessary that we trace our roots, so to speak. These roots are found in the account of Creation and the sinful fall of man as recorded in the first three chapters of the book of Genesis. It is there that we discover God's deliberate design for all that would follow.

The Six Days of Creation

The very beginning is usually the best place to start, and that is particularly true when we approach the Bible and its teachings. The first three chapters of the Bible are foundational to our faith and that is where we must begin as we explore the matter of abortion.

In Chapter 1 of Genesis we find a capsule view of God's great creative work. We are told in the first two verses that it was God who created the heavens and the earth, and the earth was "without form and void." What follows is an account of six magnificent days of God's Creation in which the earth is given form and the vast emptiness is filled with wondrous life. The Bible is a book of life and the significance of life in all its forms. All that has been created was created during those six days. In Chapter 2 of Genesis, we find:

> And on the seventh day God finished his work that he had done, and he rested on the seventh day from all his work that he had done. (Gen. 2:2)

Before delving further in this study of Creation as presented in the book of Genesis, it is important to note that the Bible is not, by and large, a science book. There are, of course, many factual and historical writings contained within it, and the Bible is an authoritative and truthful revelation from God. Its intended purpose is to instruct mankind in God's ways. But within the factual and literal narratives revealed in its pages, we also find a variety of other literary genres. Much of the Bible's insights come to us in the form of awe-inspiring parables and poetry, proverbs, allegories, and the like.

When Genesis speaks, then, of the six days of creation, we must acknowledge that the "days" of Creation may not have been literal 24-hour days as we know them. They may have been, but no one knows for certain just how lengthy in time those days were in which God created all. The Apostle Peter tells us in his second epistle, that "with the Lord one day is as a thousand years, and a thousand years as one day,"[2] perhaps echoing Psalm 90:4 where we find, "For a thousand years in your sight are but as yesterday."

God is all-powerful, omniscient. He was certainly capable of doing anything He desired and He could have created it all in an instant. But He could just as certainly have accomplished His creative work over a much longer period of time. God is not bound by time or space. Science has discovered evidence from which it is proposed that the creation process could have extended

---

2 2 Peter 3:8

for many millennia, and such evidence should be carefully considered in the search for truth.[3]

Concerning those six days of God's creative work, however long that may have been, the Genesis account provides a narrative of those miraculous events. On the first day, God spoke and light appeared and He separated the light from the darkness.[4] On the second day, He spoke and divided the waters on the earth from the waters above the earth, and the waters on the earth were confined so that the seas and dry land were divided.[5] From the earth God then caused plants and trees to grow and produce fruit on the third day, each with seeds so they would reproduce, each "after its kind."[6] Next, we are informed that God placed the sun and moon in the heavens, one to rule the day, the other to govern the night.[7] On the fifth day, God created the fishes of the sea and birds that fly over the earth, and He commanded that they should "Be fruitful and multiply."[8] During the sixth day, animals that live on the land were created. At the end of each of these days, God pronounced that what He had created was "good."[9]

God's final act of Creation was mankind. But unlike the accounts of the Creation of everything that came before, we are told:

> Then God said, "Let us make man in our image, after our likeness. And let them have dominion over the fish of the sea and over the birds of the heavens and over the livestock and over all the earth and over every creeping thing that creeps on the earth." (Gen 1:26-27)

---

3 For more information, read the article written by Temper Longman III: "What Genesis 1-2 Teaches (and What It Doesn't)," *Reading Genesis 1-2: An Evangelical Conversation* (Edited by J. Daryl Charles, Hendrickson, 2013), 103-28.

4 Gen. 1:3-4

5 Gen. 1:6-10

6 Gen. 1:11-13

7 Gen. 1:14-19

8 Gen. 1:20-23

9 Gen.1:3, 10, 12, 18, 25

From this single passage, we learn that God intended mankind to be unique in all of His Creation. Mankind alone was created in God's *image and likeness*, and God intended for humanity to be dominant over the rest of His Creation. Humanity was placed in the highest position of honor among all earthly things and given enormous responsibility to rule over and care for that which God had created. It is a position of great honor and trust. King David expressed his awe and wonder of this very special relationship in the whole of Creation when he said:

> When I look at your heavens, the work of your fingers, the moon and the stars, which you have set in place, what is man that you are mindful of him, and the son of man that you care for him? Yet you have made him a little lower than the heavenly beings and crowned him with glory and honor. You have given him dominion over the works of your hands; you have put all things under his feet, all sheep and oxen, and also the beasts of the field, the birds of the heavens, and the fish of the sea, whatever passes along the paths of the seas. O LORD, our Lord, how majestic is your name in all the earth! (Ps. 8:3-9)

It was no accident that mankind was God's final creation. Everything God made before creating humanity was necessary for mankind's well-being, sustenance, enjoyment and comfort. Can we imagine, for example, what our lives would have been like if there had been no light to illumine our way, if the waters on the earth and those above it were not divided, if there were no fruit trees, or no birds that sing, no horses to ride, no beasts of burden to help us with our work? Everything God made was in some way beneficial to humanity. He intended it that way. He declared that everything He created prior to Adam was "good," partly because it was all designed to benefit the crowning jewel of His creative works—mankind. When He finished creating mankind, the Bible says:

> And God saw everything that he had made, and behold, it was *very good*. (Gen. 1:31)

It was not just "good" any longer. Now, after humanity was created, it was "very good."

No doubt God had many reasons for describing the whole of His Creation as very good. It was, for example, complete. Nothing more was needed, and everything that had been created was made in such a way as to ensure its perpetual existence. The plants and trees produced seeds for reproduction, virtually the entire animal kingdom was created male and female and equipped for reproduction, and day and night were set in cyclical motion.

At the end of the sixth day, nothing more was needed for God's marvelous Creation to continue and thrive. God could now rest from all His creative work, knowing that everything necessary and beneficial had been done. Everything was in harmony—in perfect order. Nothing was out of place, and every created thing joined with every other to comprise a comprehensive, cohesive working system with each part dependent in some manner upon each of the others and with mankind as caretaker over it all. The divine Watchmaker had completed His Creation, wound it to run perpetually, and entrusted it to our care.

Though His relationship with us could have ended there, He chose to remain very personally and intimately involved in our lives. Continued existence of the earth and everything in it, including mankind, is totally dependent upon Him.

> He [Christ] is the image of the invisible God, the firstborn of all creation. For by him all things were created, in heaven and on earth, visible and invisible, whether thrones or dominions or rulers or authorities—all things were created through him and for him. And he is before all things, *and in him all things hold together.* (Col. 1:15-17)

Our very existence is a precious gift from God. There is nothing that is self-existent in all of Creation. If, at any moment, God decided to withhold His infinite grace, everything that exists could suddenly vanish.

God's Command to "Be Fruitful"

Reproduction of every species was the key to God's plan. It was to His plea-sure and for His purposes that the earth should be fully populated. Without the ability to reproduce each species of plants and animals after their own kind, the filling of the earth would require continuing acts of His creative work, meaning that God could never have "rested" from His work. Only through His design for reproduction could God cease His creative work with the assurance that His plan to fill the earth would be accomplished.

> So God created man in his own image, in the image of God he cre-ated him; male and female he created them. And God blessed them. And God said to them, *"Be fruitful and multiply* and fill the earth and subdue it, and have dominion over the fish of the sea and over the birds of the heavens and over every living thing that moves on the earth." (Gen. 1:27-28)

Humanity plays a very important role in God's plan. Scripture tells us that only mankind was delegated the responsibility to rule over God's Creation. Adam is God's agent, so to speak, His trustee on the earth to whom was given a duty of the highest order to oversee and protect that which is God's. The authority and responsibility given to us is like a signet ring that a king might bestow upon his trusted servant, endowing that servant with the power of the throne over the king's possessions. Whatever the servant would cause to be sealed with the ring would carry the same authority as if personally ordered by the king. This speaks of great authority and corresponding responsibility. If the king were to discover that his trusted representative had taken actions contrary to his wishes or sealed orders in violation of his express instructions, he would have every right to be displeased and take whatever corrective action he felt appropriate. That is the kind of relationship that is to exist between God and humanity with respect to how we are to deal with His Creation. God is our king, the earth and everything in it are His. We are the caretakers of His possessions on the earth.

The earth is the LORD's and the fullness thereof, the world and those who dwell therein...Who is this King of glory? The LORD of hosts, he is the King of glory! (Ps. 24:1-2, 10)

The problem is that we have, in great measure, abdicated the rights and renounced the responsibilities entrusted to us, thus failing miserably to rule in the manner God intended. As written in Isaiah 53:

All we like sheep have gone astray; we have turned—every one—to his own way. (Isa. 53:6)

Worse yet, mankind has at times done true evil while claiming it was done by the authority of God and for His glory. This is why God commanded, "You shall not take the name of the LORD your God in vain" (Ex. 20:7).

Creation of Man by God

Having summarized all of God's creative acts in the first chapter, Chapter 2 of Genesis then focuses directly on mankind. Here we are told:

Then the LORD God formed the man of dust from the ground and breathed into his nostrils the breath of life, and the man became a living creature. (Gen. 2:7)

Humanity's existence was no accident. According to the Bible, God personally *formed* Adam and gave him the "breath of life." These are intentional acts done with noble purpose and design. God made man separately and distinctly from all of His other creative acts. There is much controversy over just how God carried out His creative works. And the truth of the matter is that no one knows for certain just how He did it all. The Bible does not explain God's creative processes in detail. With respect to most of his Creation, it says very simply that God "spoke" and things were created.

Many have proposed that everything that exists came about through evolution over a very long period of time. With respect to mankind, however, and if Chapters 1 and 2 of Genesis are taken literally, a convincing biblical argument can be made that mankind could not have come about through evolution, for Genesis 2:7 says plainly that the first man, Adam, was created directly by God who *formed* him of "dust from the ground and breathed into his nostrils the breath of life, and the man became a living creature." Again, literally speaking, if Adam was formed directly from the dust and infused with life by the breath of God, then Adam could not have been a product of random genetic mutations.

On the other hand, those who support the theory of evolution do so from a great spectrum of positions and persuasions. At one extreme, some have taken the position that the biblical creation narrative of Genesis 1 and 2 is a fable, a fairytale, and that if God existed at all, He had nothing to do with Creation. In essence, they propose that everything happened by accident and without any form of intelligent design. The authors of this book soundly reject that proposition. At the other end of the spectrum, however, there are those who are convinced by their scientific inquiry that while evolutionary means may have been used to produce life as we know it, the fingerprints of an intelligent designer and creator are undeniable.[10]

No one can, with absolute authority, tell us categorically just how God chose to accomplish it all. The biblical account of the six days of Creation cannot be proved empirically by scientific demonstration. It must to some degree be accepted by faith.

But it is also true that the theory of evolution lacks convincing proof in many of its various claims, particularly where creation is viewed as a purely random phenomenon. By the nature of all that exists, Genesis 1:1 rings true: "In the beginning God created the heavens and the earth." *He* did it all – a purposeful, intelligent, miraculous work. Exactly how long that took and precisely which methods He used are simply beyond our present knowledge.

---

10 For more on the theistic evolution position, we refer you to The BioLogos Foundation (biologos.org).

God's purposeful involvement, as opposed to accidental creation, is fundamental to understanding our place in this world and our responsibilities to God. For if humanity's existence was not by God's express purpose and design, as the Bible says it was, then our species is in no better position than any of the other animals, meaning that we have no special relationship to God, no special duties, and no special promises from God. We then have no hope of life after physical death and need not be concerned about what we do or say while we live. Life is ultimately meaningless unless the Bible is truthful in its teaching that we were created to have a deeply loving relationship with our Creator. King Solomon summarized this relationship and our responsibilities before God, saying,

> Fear God and keep his commandments, for this is the whole duty of man. For God will bring every deed into judgment, with every secret thing, whether good or bad. (Ecc. 12:13-14)

The Apostle Paul also acknowledged the meaningless nature of life, whether in this world or the next, unless God's Word can be trusted:

> If in Christ we have hope in this life only, we are of all people most to be pitied. (1 Cor. 15:19)

If, contrary to biblical instruction, God was not our Creator and the special relationship between humanity and God does not really exist, then we are truly without hope, and the issues with which we concern ourselves simply do not ultimately matter. Home and family, careers, goals, good and evil become non-issues in the eternal sense, and every choice then becomes acceptable, because there is no one with a right to judge our actions. This life, then, is all there is and there is no reason to deny ourselves anything while it lasts. Why be saddled with unwanted responsibilities or limit ourselves in any way in our short life, particularly if there is no hope for life ever after?

The truth is, of course, that God is our Creator and His guidance and instructions to us are not given simply to spoil our fun or load us down with unnecessary responsibilities. The God who created us and loves us also provides us with His guidance in order that we may live life to its fullest as He intended. Life in tune with His will is the secret to true joy. It is when we attempt to unburden ourselves from God's yoke that we are most destructive, both to ourselves and to everything around us. Christ offers a far better way.

"Take my yoke upon you, and learn from me, for I am gentle and lowly in heart, and you will find rest for your souls. For my yoke is easy, and my burden is light." (Matt. 11:29-30)

The Garden and the Helper

Having purposefully created humanity, we are then told in Genesis 2:8-9 that God put Adam in a garden within Eden, a garden that contained all kinds of trees that were "pleasant to the sight and good for food." The garden was a gift. It was beautiful ("pleasant to the sight"), and it was life sustaining ("good for food"). In Genesis 2:15, we find humanity placed in the garden to work it and care for it, another illustration of our unique responsibility to carefully manage and protect what God has created on the earth. But after all of this, God recognized Adam's need for a companion.

Then the LORD God said, "It is not good that the man should be alone; I will make him a helper fit for him." (Gen. 2:18)

As interesting and wonderful as all of the other creatures were, none were suitable as a helper for Adam. Within the whole of His Creation, this was the only thing declared to be "not good." Adam needed a mate.

So the LORD God caused a deep sleep to fall upon the man, and while he slept took one of his ribs and closed up its place with flesh. And the rib that the LORD God had taken from the man he made into a woman and brought her to the man. (Gen. 2:21-22)

It is again important to recognize that the woman was created from a "rib" taken from Adam, another biblical statement contrary to the theory of accidental creation. Like the man, the woman was created by the expressed intent of God. Those who claim that creation came about by accident have never been able to explain the phenomenon of the sexes.

If everything came into being without intelligent purpose, how can we then explain the existence of both male and female throughout the animal kingdom, both genders produced from the same womb according to its species? Since the sex of every person is determined by the sperm from the male, how can accidental evolution explain the presence of both male and female sperm coming from only one of the sexes? Only by accepting the fact that God created us male and female with the ability to reproduce both sexes can this phenomenon be explained.

The Rev. Dr. Pentiuc points out that the term "rib," as translated above, is the Hebrew word *sela'* and is perhaps more appropriately translated "side," as opposed to "rib." He finds, for example, that the same word is used to describe the side of a hill or mountain in 2 Samuel 16:13 and the side of a building in 1 Kings 6:5 and 8. He concludes that Genesis 2:21-22 should be viewed as describing the creation of woman by taking from Adam one side of his humanity which God then made into the woman.

As a result, Adam was no longer complete in and of himself since a "side" of him had been removed for the creation of woman. The two sides of humanity are now male and female, each of them different from—but complementary to—the other, and they are uniquely designed so that only together are they fully equipped to fulfill the divine imperative to "be fruitful and multiply" and rightly perform our work as God's faithful representatives and trustees on the earth.[11]

---

11 Eugen J. Pentiuc, *Jesus the Messiah in the Hebrew Bible* (Mahway, NJ: Paulist Press, 2006), p. 10

Marriage and Family Are Ordained

Once God finished forming the woman, He presented her to the man:

> Then the man said, "This at last is bone of my bones and flesh of my
> flesh; she shall be called Woman, because she was taken out of Man."
> (Gen. 2:23)

The verse that follows after this is absolutely key to our understanding of
God's plan for the family unit. Remember that in Genesis 1:28, God had
commanded the man and woman to "Be fruitful and multiply and fill the
earth and subdue it." Now, after the woman was created and presented to
Adam, the Bible tells us:

> Therefore a man shall leave his father and his mother and hold fast to
> his wife, and they shall become one flesh. (Gen. 2:24)

This relatively short verse has immense and far reaching implications. It holds
the secrets of God's divine plan for marriage and the family. Before we look
closely at the core of this verse, it should be noted that it begins by saying,
"therefore," and we must then ask what the "therefore" is there for.

Look back to the preceding verse for the answer. It is because the woman
is "bone of my bones, and flesh of my flesh" that "a man will leave his father
and mother and hold fast to his wife, and they shall become one flesh." The
two of them, male and female, are God's perfect match. As we are told in verse
18, she is "a helper fit for him," but she is much more than that.

God's intention was that she complement the man, that she would complete the man, and that she be his helper in ruling over God's Creation.
Because she was taken from the man, she is necessary to complete that which
is missing in him, for he is indeed incomplete without her. She is to become
"one flesh" with the man. The two of them become truly whole only as they
cling together as one flesh.

How is it possible that the man and woman shall become one flesh? And
what is meant by the term "hold fast"? To hold fast to one another is in great

measure the process of becoming one flesh. Although it encompasses the idea of uniting the woman and man sexually, it is far more than a physical connection; it denotes a unifying of the feelings and emotions of a husband and wife, their spirits, their goals, and their reliance upon their Creator. It signifies a closeness both strong and healthy in every sense.

The two of them, man and wife, are to be devoted to one another so they will not separate. In short, the words, "hold fast," as used in this context, set forth an all-encompassing plan for the family unit: one man, one woman, having the ability to reproduce, and unified in every sense of the word so they become inseparable. They not only love one another deeply, but they cling to one another and work together to accomplish God's will for their lives. They unite spiritually, mentally, emotionally, and physically, and in their physical union they achieve the resulting reproduction that fulfills God's command that they "Be fruitful and multiply and fill the earth."[12] It is God's intention that their union be enveloped in selfless, true love. They are to give of themselves and help one another become everything they are capable of being, all for their common joy and to the glory of God their Creator.

> Love is patient and kind; love does not envy or boast; it is not arrogant or rude. It does not insist on its own way; it is not irritable or resentful; it does not rejoice at wrongdoing, but rejoices with the truth. Love bears all things, believes all things, hopes all things, endures all things. Love never ends. (1 Cor. 13:4-8a)

Jesus used Genesis 2:24 to illustrate the sanctity of marriage and God's purpose for the continuity of the family unit. In Matthew 19, He was asked by some religious leaders, "Is it lawful for a man to divorce his wife for any cause?"

> He answered, "Have you not read that he who created them from the beginning made them male and female, and said, *'Therefore a man*

---

12 Gen. 1:28

*shall leave his father and his mother and hold fast to his wife, and the two
shall become one flesh*'? So they are no longer two but one flesh. What
therefore God has joined together, let not man separate."

They said to him, "Why then did Moses command one to give a
certificate of divorce and to send her away?"

He said to them, "Because of your hardness of heart Moses
allowed you to divorce your wives, but from the beginning it was
not so. And I say to you: whoever divorces his wife, except for sexual
immorality, and marries another, commits adultery." (Matt. 19:3-9)

In the Old Testament masculine mindset, adultery was something that could
only be committed against a husband because wives were considered to be a
possession of their husband. If a husband had relations with another man's
wife, the man's act of adultery was not a sin against his own wife, but against
the adulteress's husband.[13] Here, in Matthew 19, Jesus corrects the obvious
hypocrisy, giving the wife equal standing in the relationship with her husband and declaring that the man's infidelity must likewise be condemned as
adultery.

Just as marital fidelity is demanded by both spouses in Genesis 2:24,
sexual immorality in any manner is likewise denounced. In 1 Corinthians
6, Paul further amplifies the meaning of Genesis 2:24 by going a step further and categorizing all sexual immorality—including a man having sexual
relations with one other than his wife—as a sin against one's own body and
against God in the person of the Holy Spirit who dwells within the believer.

Do you not know that your bodies are members of Christ? Shall I
then take the members of Christ and make them members of a prostitute? Never! Or do you not know that he who is joined to a prostitute
becomes one body with her? For, as it is written, *The two will become*

13 See e.g., M'Clintock, R., D.D., & Strong, J., S.T.D. (1891). Adultery. In *Biblical,
Theological and Ecclesiastical Literature* (Vol. I-A,B, p. 84). New York City, NY: Harper &
Brothers.

one flesh." Flee from sexual immorality. Every other sin a person commits is outside the body, but the sexually immoral person sins against his own body. Or do you not know that your body is a temple of the Holy Spirit within you, whom you have from God? You are not your own, for you were bought with a price. So glorify God in your body. (1 Cor. 6:15-20)

Again, in the book of Ephesians, Paul commands us by the authority of Genesis 2:24 that husbands are to go even further and submit their own interests to those of their wives. The marriage of a man and wife is intended to create a spiritual picture, a graphic representation of the relationship that exists between Christ and His church.

Husbands, love your wives, as Christ loved the church and gave himself up for her, that he might sanctify her, having cleansed her by the washing of water with the word, so that he might present the church to himself in splendor, without spot or wrinkle or any such thing, that she might be holy and without blemish. In the same way husbands should love their wives as their own bodies. He who loves his wife loves himself. For no one ever hated his own flesh, but nourishes and cherishes it, just as Christ does the church, because we are members of his body. *"Therefore a man shall leave his father and mother and hold fast to his wife, and the two shall become one flesh."* This mystery is profound, and I am saying that it refers to Christ and the church. (Eph. 5:25-32)

It is clear from these passages, therefore, that the unification of the man and woman spoken of in Genesis 2:24 is one of very broad meaning, and it includes, without doubt, a sexual quality that cannot be denied. There is to be a unification and a commitment that culminates in the two becoming "one flesh." The act of sexual intercourse is a unifying of the flesh of the man with the flesh of the woman, and the result of that union is designed to produce "one flesh" in the sense that a child is conceived, literally combining the attributes of the man and woman into one new human being—one flesh.

This verse demonstrates God's stamp of approval on the sexual relations of a husband and wife and the reproductive act it encompasses. Through marital and sexual relations and the reproductive process sanctioned by Genesis 2:24, God's plan to populate and fill the earth is to be accomplished. God can rest in the knowledge that all of His personal, creative work is complete. God's creation can survive and flourish and the earth will be filled.

Although we made note above that the Bible is not, by and large, a science book, it is quite interesting to see how accurate the Bible is about very scientific matters. When it speaks of the two (the man and the woman) becoming "one flesh," this is a very accurate scientific fact. The sperm of the male combines with the egg (ovum) of the female to bring about conception of a new individual. The fertilized egg itself (called a zygote) is comprised of forty-six chromosomes, the full complement required to make a human being. Twenty-three of these chromosomes are provided by the sperm and twenty-three by the ovum. Conception is the combination of the attributes of the sperm and the egg together, which only then constitutes a new living being, "one flesh," the end result of the union of male and female. (See Chapter 10 of this book for more discussion of these scientific facts)

Sin Enters God's Creation

In Chapter 3 of Genesis, we find recorded the Fall of mankind from grace through sin: the disobedience of mankind to God. It is once again difficult to determine exactly how this narrative is to be viewed, whether each statement should be taken literally or in some other manner. What is clear is that mankind is shown manifestly to have failed and fallen short of the divine ideal, and the consequences of disobedience were severe. When He placed Adam and Eve in the Garden of Eden, God commanded:

> "You may surely eat of every tree of the garden, but of the tree of the knowledge of good and evil you shall not eat, for in the day that you eat of it you shall surely die." (Gen. 2:16-17)

But Eve was deceived by the serpent and enticed to eat the forbidden fruit which she then took and gave to her husband, who, just as disobedient, willingly accepted it. Though God had specifically told them not to eat from that tree, they ate it anyway. As a result of this sin, verse 22 says their eyes were opened so that they knew both good and evil. God then announced the consequences that would result from their disobedience.

To the woman He said:

"I will surely multiply your pain in childbearing; in pain you shall bring forth children. Your desire shall be for your husband, and he shall rule over you." (Gen. 3:16)

And to Adam He said:

"Because you have listened to the voice of your wife and have eaten of the tree of which I commanded you, 'You shall not eat of it,' cursed is the ground because of you; in pain you shall eat of it all the days of your life; thorns and thistles it shall bring forth for you; and you shall eat the plants of the field. By the sweat of your face you shall eat bread, till you return to the ground, for out of it you were taken; for you are dust, and to dust you shall return." (Gen. 3:17-19)

According to this account, both the pain of childbearing and the necessity of painful, hard work are a direct result of sin. Mankind had fallen from grace, and their disobedience produced serious consequences, just as the Lord had warned them. Their physical lives on earth would not continue forever, but would end with a returning to the dust from whence they came.

The Life Continuum

Despite their disobedience, God's plan for the man and woman to reproduce and fill the earth was not changed. Although the perfect fellowship with their Creator had been broken through sin and childbearing would now be painful, it was assumed without question that they would reproduce and carry life forward. Genesis 3:20 says:

> The man called his wife's name Eve, because she was the mother of all living. (Gen. 3:20)

This again is a very profound statement with direct implications for our study. Eve, according to the Bible, is *our* mother, "the mother of all living." The woman's name, "Eve," literally means "living." Through her, all people everywhere have been given life. We are then told in Chapter 4 of Genesis that:

> Now Adam knew Eve his wife, and she conceived and bore Cain, saying, "I have gotten a man with the help of the LORD." And again, she bore his brother Abel. (Gen. 4:1-2)

Thus began the filling of the earth with humanity. God was now resting from His creative works. Mankind and all of His Creation had begun to reproduce, to populate and fill the earth with His creatures, each "according to its kind." The life cycles were set in motion and all that exists today is directly descended from what God created "In the beginning."

In a very real sense, therefore, our lives are directly linked to Adam and Eve. We, as their descendants, are no different than Cain and Abel. We are their sons and daughters, all of us the result of God's plan from the beginning. Our very lives are the result of an unbroken genealogy that extends all the way back to the first man and woman. Their lives were the direct result of God's creative design, and by that design each of us has inherited life as it is passed on from one generation to the next.

In the broad sense, therefore, the beginning of life for every person who has ever lived was there at the Creation. Life is literally a *continuum* that had its beginning, its "genesis," at Creation and will continue until God brings it all to an end. God infused life into the man and woman, and that life continues forward through the reproductive plan established in the beginning. Had there been any break in the genealogy concerning any of us, we, as the unique individuals we are, would simply not exist today. Likewise, those who would follow after us and into the future could not exist without our own reproduction. And this brings directly to the purpose of our study, to determine the effect of abortion on God's plan for mankind.

Abortion Breaks the Life Continuum

Abortion is, very literally, a deliberate and man-initiated break in the life chain, a termination of all life that would normally have followed but for the abortion. It is a direct assault on God's plan for mankind to fill the earth and subdue it. Like murder, which is prohibited by the command "You shall not murder,"[14] abortion is an intentional act, consciously performed in order to destroy a very precious and integral part of God's Creation. Destruction of a human fetus is, in literal truth, the destruction of future generations of human beings created in the image and likeness of God Himself. Consider the following passage that clearly illustrates this concept of the life continuum.

> And Isaac prayed to the LORD for his wife, because she was barren. And the LORD granted his prayer, and Rebekah his wife conceived. The children struggled together within her, and she said, "If it is thus, why is this happening to me?" So she went to inquire of the LORD. And the LORD said to her,
>
> "Two *nations* are in your womb,
>   and two *peoples* from within you shall be divided;
> the one shall be stronger than the other,
>   the older shall serve the younger."
>
> When her days to give birth were completed, behold, there were twins in her womb. (Gen.25:21-24)

---

14 Ex. 20:13; Dt. 5:17

Notice first that Rebekah's pregnancy was the result of God's answer to Isaac's prayer. It was the Lord who opened her womb and allowed her to conceive children where she was once barren. As will be covered in detail later in this book, God is involved in every step of the reproduction process, including conception. In Rebekah's case, God's plan was that she should bear twin boys. But more than that, by God's design, these twins were destined to become "two nations" and "two peoples," future generations that would follow from these yet unborn children.

The fact that none of those future generations had even been conceived was of no consequence to the Lord. He saw them clearly into the future. Furthermore, these two future nations and peoples were the direct result of an unbroken genealogy extending all the way back to Adam and Eve. Rebekah's children would not have existed but for Rebekah and Isaac. They, in turn, would not have existed but for their parents, and so on. With the exception of the first man and woman who received life directly from God, human life has forever been dependent upon its transfer and continuation from the previous generation.

Note the fact that the babies "struggled together" within Rebekah, denoting purposeful acts that were done while still within the womb. Even before birth, the two boys were striving against each other, struggling to get the better of the other, a struggle that would continue in later life. This description of pre-birth activity in the womb helps us to see the complete humanity of the unborn and God's foreknowledge of their future lives.

If we truly want to do God's will, we must be willing to view things the way God does. We may look into the womb and see a single unborn child, but God looks into the womb and sees human life into the infinite future and all the way back to Creation in one grand panoramic view.

Adam and Eve were only the beginning of the human life continuum. That is why Genesis 3:20 tells us Adam named his wife Eve, "because she was the mother of all living." To the Lord, Eve is still "our mother." And women today are the mothers of all human life that will be in the future. Every individual is a critical link in the human life chain. The destruction of a single individual, whether before physical birth or afterwards, brings about a break in the life chain and literally destroys "nations" of future generations. Had

Rebekah terminated her pregnancy by abortion, Jacob and Esau would never have been born, and the entire Israelite and Edomite nations and all who have descended from them would never have existed.

A further example of this continuum concept is presented in Hebrews where we find:

> One might even say that Levi himself, who receives tithes, paid tithes through Abraham, *for he was still in the loins of his ancestor when Melchizedek met him.* (Heb. 7:9-10)

Abraham was the ancestor who met Melchizedek, as told in Genesis 14. Abraham was Isaac's father, Isaac was Jacob's father, and Jacob was Levi's father. Abraham, then, was Levi's great-grandfather. Here the writer of Hebrews makes the case for the life continuum by asserting that Levi (the priest) was there in his great-grandfather's body even before Abraham's son, Isaac (Levi's grandfather), was yet conceived. In other words, the point is abundantly made that the essence of Levi's life was, in fact, present in Abraham three generations before Levi came into physical existence in his mother's womb! By extension, we can see that Levi's life actually existed from the very beginning when God infused the life-giving spirit into the first man and woman. It follows from this illustration that life for each of us, we who are living today, was also present from the very beginning. Eve is our mother just as the Bible has clearly taught.

The life God created in the beginning has continued from generation to generation. Each generation simply continues from the previous and into the future and each person is charged with responsibility for the "nations" of individuals that should follow after them.

The life continuum as presented here is not a new concept. It has been an accepted truth by Jews and Christians for many centuries. As one example of its early acceptance, dating back prior to the birth of Jesus Christ, the Jews took very seriously the application of the continuum principle in their instructions to witnesses who were called upon to give testimony in capital cases in which a person would be put to death if convicted. In their Mishnah (writings of Jewish law), in what is known as the Sanhedrin writings, we find the following admonition (English translation) that was read aloud before the witness was allowed to testify in a capital case:

> [What you say may be merely your own opinion, or hearsay, or sec-ondhand, or derived from a trustworthy person. Perhaps you do not know that we intend to question you by examination and inquiry. Know, moreover, that capital cases are not like non-capital cases: in non-capital cases a man may pay money and so make expiation; but in capital cases the blood of the accused *and of his posterity* may cling to him (the witness) to the end of the world.[15]

In other words, the witness was admonished in the strongest possible terms that if he or she testified falsely or without true knowledge of the matter, and if the accused was then wrongfully convicted and put to death, the witness who aided in the wrongful conviction would not only be answerable for the blood of the one unjustly put to death, but also for the blood of that person's descendants (his posterity) that should have otherwise been born to him; this included not only the blood of his immediate children, but also the blood of all future, yet unborn generations, even "to the end of the world."

This was very serious business! Through this instruction, we readily see that to the Jews and early Christians the death of a person by any means resulted in a break in the life continuum, a halting of the life chain that otherwise should have continued indefinitely. It is not difficult to understand from this that abortion brings about the very same result.

God's Plan Will Succeed

In Chapter 9 of this book, we will deal directly with the issue of whether God considers abortion to be murder. From Genesis 4, we will look carefully at the

---

15 Danby, H. (1919). Tractate Sanhedrin. Retrieved from http://www.sacred-texts.com/jud/tsa/tsa13.htm Accessed 3/24/2016.

very first murder recorded in the Bible, which was committed by Cain, the oldest son of Adam and Eve. Because of his jealousy and hatred, Cain plotted and killed his younger brother despite the fact that God had warned Cain not to allow the sin in his heart to master him.

For his actions, Cain was driven from the presence of God, away from his home and family, and the ground was cursed so that it would no longer produce its fruit for Cain. God's judgment was swift and sure. But His plan to populate the Earth was still intact, despite Cain's attempt at sabotage. After the death of Abel, we are told that:

> And Adam knew his wife again, and she bore a son and called his name Seth, for she said, "God has appointed for me another offspring instead of Abel, for Cain killed him." (Gen. 4:25)

God's ultimate plan cannot be thwarted. He will accomplish His desires regardless of our actions. The real question is whether we, as His people and His agents on earth, will be obedient to His will and receive all that He intends for us to have. Will we use our God-given ability to reproduce and fill the earth to His glory, bringing up godly children, and loving and caring for our spouses such that we become one flesh? Or will we, through our own selfish actions, cut off the blessings God intends for us? Because of the free will God has given us, the *choice* may be ours, but the intended blessings can only come through our obedience. Wrong choices will bring serious consequences.

When Did Abortion Rights Begin?

If women truly have a fundamental right to choose an abortion, as asserted by the U.S. Supreme Court in the infamous case of *Roe v. Wade*, then Eve, the first woman, had that right as well. If she had made that choice, however, the question must be asked whether God would have been any more pleased with her than He was with Cain who murdered Abel. Could Eve have pleased God by aborting any of her children after God commanded her and her husband to "Be fruitful and multiply and fill the earth and subdue it"? Would she have fulfilled her duty to become the mother of all the living as God had planned?

At which generation can we say that God's command to "Be fruitful and multiply" was no longer valid? Did Mary have a fundamental right to abort Jesus? And what of Elizabeth, the mother of John the Baptist? Jesus said of John in Matthew 11:11, "Truly, I say to you, among those born of women there has arisen no one greater than John the Baptist." Did Elizabeth have that fundamental right to abort John?

Did your grandmother have a fundamental right to abort your mother? Or did your mother have any right to abort you? Who decides whether or not a fundamental right exists or where it comes from? God is the One who created us and the One who has the ultimate right also to judge us. And just as Eve was to be the mother of all the living, God intends women today to be the mothers of all future generations, allowing the earth to be filled. Life is a gift from God alone. Human judges have no business interfering in God's plan for human life.

It cannot be doubted that the destruction of even "potential life" (a term used in *Roe v. Wade* to describe a developing fetus) results in a termination of all future generations that would come through that unborn child if it were allowed to develop fully, be born, and to reproduce. Through abortion, future generations are eliminated just as certainly, regardless whether we call it "murder" or not. The continuum of life set in motion by God through Adam and Eve is halted by abortion in precisely the same way. The label we give it is immaterial because the result is the same. And if the result is the same, does it stand to reason that God will judge the two acts, abortion and murder, by different standards? Both actions interfere with His divine plan. Both are an attempt to render Him irrelevant.

By any reckoning, the difference between "potential life," as that term is used in *Roe v. Wade*, and "actual life" is really nothing more than semantics— the difference between the present and the near future concerning the unborn. To say it another way, given a few months in the womb, what the Supreme Court deemed to be mere "potential life" will be seen for what it truly is: "actual life." In that regard, there is no distinction at all.

As we will see when we discuss the ostrich in Chapter 3 of this book, the Bible makes no distinction whatsoever between the born and unborn. From the moment of conception, they are living beings, the offspring of their parents, and are worthy of love and protection.

In Summary

- Mankind's existence was not accidental. God created mankind in His image and likeness, crowned them with glory and honor above all other creatures, and gave them dominion and responsibility over everything He had made.
- God ordained marriage and family. The husband and wife are to be united together in every way—spiritually, mentally, emotionally, and physically—so that they become "one flesh."
- A man and a woman are created different from and complementary to each other. They are uniquely designed so that, together, they are fully equipped to fulfill the divine imperative for humanity to reproduce and be God's faithful representatives and trustees on the earth.
- Reproduction was the key to God's plan. God commanded mankind to be fruitful and multiply and fill the earth.
- Marital fidelity is commanded and sexual immorality is denounced by God.
- Life is literally a continuum and each generation is dependent upon the previous generation for its continuance. Killing a human being, either before or after birth, whether by abortion or any other means, breaks the life chain and destroys "nations" of future generations.

2

The Beginning of Individual Life

IN CHAPTER 1, the issue of when life begins was discussed in the context of God's overall plan for mankind, specifically His divine plan for a life continuum that would populate the earth through the family unit. In this chapter, we will explore God's Word for the narrower answer to the question regarding the beginning of life for the individual person. Our determination that abortion violates God's overall plan should be sufficient of itself, but for those who choose to confine the issue to the individual, this chapter will look at life from that prospective.

The Mystery of Life

The Bible, as we have seen, says that human life began on the sixth day of Creation with God forming the first man called Adam.

> Then the LORD God formed the man of dust from the ground and breathed into his nostrils the breath of life, and the man became a living creature. (Gen. 2:7)

What is this "breath of life" that God breathed into the man? When Genesis 2:7 says God "breathed into his nostrils the breath of life, and man became a living creature," this was far more than a thrusting of air into the man's lungs. Life is not mere air. Air only helps sustain the body's life once life itself is present. The "breath of life" in this verse refers to God's infusion of His life-giving spirit into mankind.

In fact, the phrase *nephesh hayyah* in verse 7 (usually translated "a living creature" or "a living being" or "a living soul") linguistically parallels the Hebrew *nishmat hayyim* ("breath of life"), also in verse 7, and therefore the verse could be rendered "and the man became a living breath."[16]

The poetry of the Creation account is remarkably telling. Until the creation of humanity on the sixth day, God had been depicted as sitting upon his throne, directing His creative work by divine fiat: God spoke and things were created. But when it came time to create humanity, God descended from the throne and entered into the scene of His Creation so that He could become intimately and directly involved in the forming of Adam ("mankind") with His own hands and with His own Spirit. And whereas the lower creatures were simply *given* living breath, God, face to face with Adam, intimately breathes His life-giving Spirit into the man, and Adam is said to have *become* "a living breath."[17]

In Dr. Pentiuc's words, "Humanity is the living breath within God's creative breathing...Thus, humanity is a part of God in this world, his representative, and is therefore called to take an active part in God's creative and providential activities."[18] It is by virtue of this unique endowment, with humanity as God's breath and His divinely appointed representative, that God is able to retire to His throne and "rest."

Individual Life Begins

When we consider the beginning of each new individual life, therefore, we must ask ourselves just how and when the Spirit enters the new life, the "Adam" being formed in the womb. A complete understanding of the precise mechanism by

---

16 Eugen J. Pentiuc, *Jesus the Messiah in the Hebrew Bible* (Mahway, NJ: Paulist Press, 2006), p. 10

17 *Id*. at p. 11-12

18 *Id*. at p. 11

which a new individual life begins with the infusion of God's Spirit cannot be had through observation with any of the human senses. It is a mystery, in that sense, by God's design. In the book of Ecclesiastes, we find this:

> As you do not know the way the *spirit* comes to the bones in the womb of a woman with child, so you do not know the work of God who makes everything. (Ecc. 11:5)

The New International Version of the Bible substitutes "wind" for "spirit" and translates the passage as follows:

> As you do not know the path of the *wind* or how the body is formed in the womb, so you cannot understand the work of God, the maker of all things. (Ecc. 11:5, NIV)

The words "wind" and "spirit" in the original Hebrew language are precisely the same word. The word "pneuma" in New Testament Greek is used in the same identical way. Wind (or breath) and spirit are invisible things to the human sense of sight, yet they are dynamic and energetic forces, and those who spoke the Hebrew or Greek languages viewed them as conceptually synonymous. Being the same word, they may be interchangeable in English.

Nevertheless, given the context of the passage, speaking as it does concerning the formation of a child in the womb, it appears certain that "spirit" rather than "wind" is the better choice for the translation of Ecclesiastes 11:5. In short, God says that we simply cannot know how the life-giving spirit enters the forming body within a mother's womb to animate it and produce its life. It is God's secret, like many others, that our human minds cannot fully comprehend. The works of God are truly mysterious and simply beyond human understanding, especially concerning the giving of life. The best we can find to explain it is there in Genesis where we find that Adam's life was received directly from God.

Life itself cannot be adequately defined with words. We can only describe life in terms of what we can observe when it is present or not present. Only the One who creates life is able to fully comprehend it. And just as we are powerless to control either the wind or the spirit, God alone is the One who created the means by which life is infused into the developing child and He is the One who controls it all.

We can, of course, observe with our senses that, when a baby is born alive, it is indeed living. The baby breathes, cries, eats, sleeps, and has all the vital signs that adults have. Through modern scientific methods, we are now able to graph thought waves from the baby's brain, even during the early weeks of development in the womb. We can hear the pulse of its heart. In recent years, we have developed ways of watching the fetus grow and develop. We have observed the very process of conception itself, that moment when the sperm penetrates the ovum. Fertility doctors have learned how to bring about conception by means of what we call "In Vitro Fertilization," and other methods to promote pregnancy. All of these activities are indicators of life and the reproductive processes.

But there is no method known to man whereby we can positively view and appreciate the precise process and mechanism by which the spirit of life is infused into the body being formed. We can only speculate as to the answer. The inspiration of new life remains invisible to our senses and our most sophisticated scientific instruments, just as the wind is invisible to our eyes. We can observe what it does, but never where it comes from or where it goes.

Jesus used the invisible qualities of the wind and spirit to teach spiritual truths. In Chapter 3 of the book of John, a religious leader named Nicodemus came to Jesus at night and said:

"Rabbi, we know that you are a teacher come from God, for no one can do these signs that you do unless God is with him." (John 3:2)

In reply Jesus declared:

"Truly, truly, I say to you, unless one is born again he cannot see the kingdom of God." (John 3:3)

This reply did nothing to dispel Nicodemus' confusion. He asked:

> "How can a man be born when he is old? Can he enter a second time into his mother's womb and be born?" (John 3:4)
>
> Jesus answered, "Truly, truly, I say to you, unless one is born of water and the Spirit, he cannot enter the kingdom of God. That which is born of the flesh is flesh, and that which is born of the Spirit is spirit. Do not marvel that I said to you, 'You must be born again.' The wind blows where it wishes, and you hear its sound, but you do not know where it comes from or where it goes. So it is with everyone who is born of the Spirit." (John 3:5-8)

Through this passage, Jesus shows us that spiritual truths are only discernable by those who have God's Holy Spirit living within them. Spiritual truths cannot be grasped by the unspiritual mind, one that has not been "born of the Spirit." Paul taught the same truth saying:

> These things God has revealed to us through the Spirit. For the Spirit searches everything, even the depths of God. For who knows a person's thoughts except the spirit of that person, which is in him? So also no one comprehends the thoughts of God except the Spirit of God. (1 Cor. 2:10-12)

The same truth applies to the infusion of life into a new human being. Our human senses cannot observe the spirit entering the forming body in the womb any more than we can observe the Holy Spirit entering a new Christian believer. Since that is true, how then are we to understand the deep things of life that God has set in place? If God has hidden certain things from us, will we by any means be able to uncover them? Through the Spirit of God that is available to us through faith, we only begin to comprehend the mind of God.

> As it is written, What no eye has seen, nor ear heard, nor the heard of man imagined, what God has prepared for those who love him"

– these things God has revealed to us through the Spirit. For the Spirit searches everything, even the depths of God. (1 Cor. 2:10-12)

For us who believe, it must be enough that God has determined to keep hidden precisely how the spirit of life enters the body forming in the womb. His divine purpose, whatever it is, is being fulfilled through His withholding of that knowledge from us. Perhaps it is because He wants our actions to be taken by faith, and not simply by what we can fully understand.

Conception: Life Comes from the Father

It is commonly understood that individual life begins at conception, defined as that point in time when the sperm from the man penetrates and is implanted into the ovum (or egg) of the woman. Conversely, some (including the Supreme Court) have speculated that life must enter the body being formed at some later point after fertilization and before eventual birth.[19] But if life is not present at the moment of conception, how then is it possible for the fertilized egg, the zygote, to multiply cells and grow? And where does an individual's life come from if it is not immediately present at conception?

Although it is difficult to imagine that life could begin before the egg has been fertilized by the sperm, even there we cannot limit God's power or His wisdom. In God's great plan, it is possible that determination of life could begin even before what we call conception. For example, who can say what power drives and directs the sperm toward the ovum? Who can say why one particular sperm succeeds while the rest fail? Some sperm are made male and some female; who chooses which one this child shall be? Does it all happen by sheer chance? Or is it possible that the life-giving Spirit of God brings all these things about? In Jeremiah 1:5, God says,

---

19 In the *Roe v. Wade* case, the Supreme Court chose to accept what it called "new embryological data that purport to indicate that conception is a 'process' over time, rather than an event." See 410 U.S. 113, 161.

Before I formed you in the womb I knew you; and *before* you were born I consecrated you; I appointed you a prophet to the nations.

As we attempt to understand the beginning of new life, we cannot help but observe that the sperm from the male is itself a form of living organism that is able to move and find its way to the ovum and then work its way inside to bring about what we call conception. The sperm must have some form of life in it or it could not do these things. For those who would argue that life is not present at conception (that is, the moment of fertilization), how then can they explain and account for the power ("the life") within the sperm that makes it possible to move and swim, find the ovum, and penetrate it? And where did that life, that driving force within the sperm, go if it is not still present after fertilization and conception?

The answer is inescapable that the life which animates the sperm is still present after fertilization of the ovum. Logic demands that conclusion. The life that directed and propelled the sperm with energy to find and penetrate the ovum simply remains and continues in a new and possibly different form following conception. The resulting life of the fertilized ovum is then fully observable in its ability to multiply cells, grow and develop into a vital, functioning, and complete human being. It is the presence of life itself that makes all of this possible. Inanimate things, things without life in them, have no ability to swim, unite with another thing, then grow and develop into animate living beings. Clearly, the sperm is a bearer of life in some form. That much we can positively observe. And the fertilized egg (what we call the zygote) is only able to grow and develop after it has been fertilized by the sperm from the father, again confirming the presence of new life within it. This conclusion is borne out by Scripture. Proverbs 23:22 declares the following:

Listen to your father who gave you life, and do not despise your mother when she is old.

We cannot escape the logical conclusion: The sperm from the father carries the essence of life to the ovum so that human life is present in the fertilized egg from the very moment of conception onward. We may not be able to fully comprehend all that entails and just how life is made possible, but there can be no other conclusion from these observations.

Once the ovum has been fertilized, the mother then carries this process forward to the time of birth. The sperm and its unification with the ovum is, by what we can observe, the physical means by which *life* is carried forward and continued from parents to children at each generation.

It must also be observed that the unification of the sperm and ovum initiates a continuum of its own: from the moment of conception onward, the life of the individual has begun and simply continues in ever changing physical form right up to the eventual moment of bodily death. It may experience various identifiable stages or phases, whether before or after the birth event, but the life itself is the same throughout. By the authority of the Bible, we know that even at the death of our bodies, our lives continue on in a new and different form and with a new and different body.

> So it is with the resurrection of the dead. What is sown is perishable. It is sown in dishonor; it is raised in glory. It is sown in weakness; it is raised in power. It is sown a natural body; it is raised a spiritual body. (1 Cor. 15:42-44)

In his book, *Jesus the Messiah in the Hebrew Bible*,[20] Rev. Dr. Eugen J. Pentiuc discerns from Genesis 1:20-30 that animals, birds, and reptiles have souls, just as humans have souls, defined as "the principle of life that sets all living creatures in motion (distinguished from plants which lack mobility and thus a soul)." Accordingly, sperm can be understood to be driven by a soul that directs them toward their goal of giving this life principle to the ovum. Everything that is necessary, then, for complete humanity is present at conception: twenty-three chromosomes from each parent in combination with the miraculous essence of life carried within the sperm. All that is lacking

---

20 Eugen J. Pentiuc, *Jesus the Messiah in the Hebrew Bible*, (Mahway, NJ: Paulist Press, 2006), p.6

is time and nourishment. Every foundational building block necessary for the fertilized egg to develop and become a fully-functioning human being is present at that moment. It has, from the very instant of conception, become a living human being.

It must also be observed, however, that the sperm has no ability to reproduce on its own any more than the ovum can reproduce alone. Only in combination can reproduction occur—the making of a new individual and the combining of attributes of the man and woman, from which the sperm and the ovum came. Just as God had taken one "side" of man to form the woman, as we discovered from Genesis 2, so that one individual had become two, the reproduction process brings the two of them, male and female, back together to form one unique new individual. Only by joining together do they produce "one flesh."

Unless the sperm unites with the ovum, it simply dies. If the ovum is not fertilized by the sperm during ovulation, it also becomes useless. It is only by combining the sperm with the ovum that life survives, making it possible for cells to multiply and produce a living, human being. To halt the continued growth and development of those human cells in the womb is to destroy human life itself, a unique, fully developed individual that would otherwise ultimately result.

Who can truly understand those things that cannot be observed by natural senses? Whether we like it or not, the answers to these questions are not ours to obtain. Some things must be left to God's wisdom. The Bible says:

> But God chose what is foolish in the world to shame the wise; God chose what is weak in the world to shame the strong; God chose what is low and despised in the world, even things that are not, to bring to nothing things that are, so that no human being might boast in the presence of God. (1 Cor. 1:27-29)

If we could uncover the incredible secret of life, it is certain that we would "boast in the presence of God." Our inability to do that, however, helps keep us humble before Him and allows Him to be God.

The Virgin Birth

We are limited; God is not limited. With God all things are possible. (Matt. 19:26) Many have disbelieved the virgin birth of Christ Jesus. But the biblical account of His miraculous conception and birth through Mary is unmistakable. We refer to it as a miracle because such things are, once again, far beyond our understanding. In the first chapter of Luke, we are told that an angel appeared to Mary and said to her:

"Do not be afraid, Mary, for you have found favor with God. And behold, you will conceive in your womb and bear a son, and you shall call his name Jesus. He will be great and will be called the Son of the Most High. And the Lord God will give to him the throne of his father David, and he will reign over the house of Jacob forever, and of his kingdom there will be no end."

And Mary said to the angel, "How will this be, since I am a virgin?"

And the angel answered her, "The Holy Spirit will come upon you, and the power of the Most High will overshadow you; therefore the child to be born will be called holy—the Son of God. And behold, your relative Elizabeth in her old age has also conceived a son, and this is the sixth month with her who was called barren. For nothing will be impossible with God." And Mary said, "Behold, I am the servant of the Lord; let it be to me according to your word." And the angel departed from her. (Luke 1:30-38)

Never before and never since has such a story been told. A virgin is with child and the son to be born will be the Son of the Most High. The one and only Son of God Almighty would be born of a human woman—not a child conceived by the ordinary uniting of a man's sperm with the ovum, but a child created directly as a result of the Holy Spirit having "overshadowed" Mary. Could anyone argue that Jesus' life spirit was not present at the very moment of his conception by the power of God Almighty?

Precisely how the immaculate conception of Christ was accomplished is truly beyond our comprehension. But it was clearly the result of the almighty power of

God Himself. This single event, more than any other in history, provides us with unmatched testimony to the fact that God alone is the author of life and that He alone is in charge of all things reproductive among the living. As we have seen from our study in Genesis, mankind was created in God's own image and likeness and equipped with the ability to reproduce according to our human nature. We have limited understanding of the mechanics of that process, as discussed above, but we truly have no understanding of just how God accomplishes it all.

With the miraculous conception of Christ Jesus, the mysteries of life increase in infinite proportion. For we now see that a physical union, which is required for our own human reproduction, is totally unnecessary where God determines to bring it about. Jesus' conception and birth was made possible simply by the power of God, the author of life. This divine action broke all the rules and allowed us to see the limitless power of our Creator God. This was the same power by which God spoke and created all things "In the beginning."

This child, called Jesus, was the Christ, the Son of God. And His miraculous entry into the physical world was foretold by the prophet Isaiah, approximately seven hundred years before His birth.

> Therefore the Lord himself will give you a sign. Behold, the virgin shall conceive and bear a son, and shall call his name Immanuel. (Isa. 7:14)

As noted above, Luke 1:26-38 records that the angel Gabriel announced this incredible event to Mary before she had conceived, and before she had been with her husband. The important facets of this child's life were set forth in considerable detail in that announcement:

- Mary would have a son.
- His name would be Jesus.
- He would be great and would be called the Son of the Most High.
- The Lord would give him the throne of His father David.
- He would rule over the house of Jacob forever.
- His kingdom would never end.

While the birth of Christ was entirely unique, it was not the first or the only time recorded in the Bible that God knew a man fully even before conception or birth. In Isaiah we read:

> Listen to me, O coastlands,
>   and give attention, you peoples from afar.
> The LORD called me from the womb… (Isa. 49:1)

God spoke similarly of the prophet Jeremiah:

> "Before I formed you in the womb I knew you,
> and before you were born I consecrated you;
> I appointed you a prophet to the nations." (Jer. 1:5)

King David also testified:

> For you formed my inward parts;
>   you knitted me together in my mother's womb.
> I praise you, for I am fearfully and wonderfully made.
> Wonderful are your works;
>   my soul knows it very well.
> My frame was not hidden from you,
> when I was being made in secret,
>   intricately woven in the depths of the earth.
> Your eyes saw my unformed substance;
> in your book were written, every one of them,
>   the days that were formed for me,
>   when as yet there was none of them. (Ps. 139:13-16)

Note here again that David's conception occurred in "secret," and that God had written down all of his days before one of them came to be. This "secret" place refers to a place hidden from us, not from God. Nothing is hidden from

Him. He is the one who brings hidden things to light. Daniel 2:22 says, "He reveals deep and hidden things; he knows what is in the darkness, and the light dwells with him."

God's foreknowledge of man should not surprise us. Nor should we question His involvement in the reproductive process. As David said, "For you formed my inward parts; you knitted me together in my mother's womb" (Ps. 139:13). God is the master of all life. And His Son, Jesus Christ, is literally the power that binds everything together!

> He [Jesus Christ] is the image of the invisible God, the firstborn of all creation. For by him all things were created, in heaven and on earth, visible and invisible, whether thrones or dominions or rulers or authorities—all things were created through him and for him. And he is before all things, *and in him all things hold together.* (Col. 1:15-18)

Is there life even before conception? Or does the life of an individual, as we know it, begin at the moment of conception? These are God's secrets. But from His Word, we know that He is fully familiar with us even before we are conceived. God controls the womb. He controls every step in reproduction. The following verses leave no doubt of this:

> Then Abraham prayed to God, and God healed Abimelech, and also healed his wife and female slaves so that they bore children. For the LORD had closed all the wombs of the house of Abimelech because of Sarah, Abraham's wife. (Gen. 20:17-18)

> When the LORD saw that Leah was hated, he opened her womb, but Rachel was barren. (Gen. 29:31)

> Then God remembered Rachel, and God listened to her and opened her womb. She conceived and bore a son and said, "God has taken away my reproach." (Gen. 30:22-23)

And the LORD will make you abound in prosperity, in the fruit of your womb and in the fruit of your livestock and in the fruit of your ground, within the land that the LORD swore to your fathers to give you. (Deut. 28:11)

But to Hannah he gave a double portion, because he loved her, though the LORD had closed her womb. And her rival used to provoke her grievously to irritate her, because the LORD had closed her womb. (1 Sam. 1:5-6)

Is anything too hard for the LORD? At the appointed time I will return to you, about this time next year, and Sarah shall have a son. (Gen. 18:14)

Moreover, it is the very power of God, His supernatural power, through which the body is formed in the womb.

For you formed my inward parts;
    you knitted me together in my mother's womb. (Ps. 139:13)

Thus says the LORD who made you,
    who formed you from the womb and will help you:
Fear not, O Jacob my servant,
    Jeshurun whom I have chosen. (Isa. 44:2)

Thus says the LORD, your Redeemer,
    who formed you from the womb:
"I am the LORD, who made all things,
    who alone stretched out the heavens,
    who spread out the earth by myself." (Isa. 44:24)

And now the LORD says,
    he who formed me from the womb to be his servant,

to bring Jacob back to him;
 and that Israel might be gathered to him—
for I am honored in the eyes of the LORD,
 and my God has become my strength. (Isa. 49:5)

Since God is intimately involved, controlling every detail of reproduction, even before conception, do we have any right to interfere? If we cannot fully comprehend how life exists, isn't it appropriate to call it a miracle each and every time a new life is conceived? Is it permissible for us to do anything that would stand in the way of such a miracle? Knowing that life itself is required for growth and development once conception has occurred, how can we destroy the forming body without destroying life that has been given by the very Author of Life? The answer is clear that we simply cannot.

As we will see from the illustration of the ostrich in the following chapter, taken from Job 39, once conception has occurred, once the sperm has penetrated the ovum, God declares the fertilized egg to be our young, a child's new life created in the image and likeness of God. He is the one who has brought about this miracle, a new creation in His own image and likeness.

A Plan for Every Life

After declaring in Psalm 139 his wonder and awe of the miraculous way in which God knits us together in the womb, David then acknowledges that God's purpose and plan for each of us is already determined, even in advance of live birth.

Your eyes saw my unformed substance;
in your book were written, every one of them,
the days that were formed for me,
when as yet there was none of them. (Ps. 139:16)

Because Christ was God's own Son, it makes sense that Jesus' birth and life might be foretold. But does God also consider every individual important enough to devise plans for their lives? He truly does consider each of us that important.

The life plan for John the Baptist, for example, was foretold despite the fact that he was only human. Luke 1:11-17 tells of the visit of an angel of the Lord to Zechariah, the father of John the Baptist, during the year prior to John's birth. There Zechariah was given advanced knowledge of the future life of his son, a son that was to be born to his aged wife.

- His wife, Elizabeth, would bear a son.
- His son's name would be John.
- John would be a joy to them.
- Many would rejoice because of his birth.
- He would be great in the sight of the Lord.
- He would not take wine or other alcoholic drink.
- He would be filled with the Holy Spirit even from birth.
- He would bring many people back to the Lord their God.
- He would go before the Lord in the spirit and power of Elijah.
- He would turn the hearts of fathers to their children.
- He would turn the disobedient to the wisdom of righteousness.
- He would make people ready for the coming of the Lord.

This was God's plan for John, but again, the revelation of John's life plan was not unique, even among mere mortals. God announced in Scripture His plans for many others. As noted above, Isaiah was called by God before birth (Isa. 49:1), and Jeremiah was similarly known by God and called and set apart for ministry before God formed him in the womb (Jer. 1:5). Rachel's children were known fully before birth. It was announced in advance that they would each become separate "nations" of people with one stronger than the other and with the older serving the younger (Gen. 25:21-23). Ishmael, the son of Hagar, the concubine of Abraham, was described in detail while still in the womb. An angel said to Hagar:

"Behold, you are pregnant
    and shall bear a son.
You shall call his name Ishmael,
    because the LORD has listened to your affliction.

He shall be a wild donkey of a man,
> his hand against everyone
> and everyone's hand against him,
and he shall dwell over against all his kinsmen." (Gen. 16:11-12)

We are fully known, before birth and after. God is the One who forms us in the womb, He has a plan for each of us, and He is the One who holds all things together. He cares about each and every person, young or old, and children receive special attention. In Matthew 18, in response to a question of who would be the greatest in the kingdom of heaven, Jesus called for a child and placed him in the midst of His disciples, saying, "Whoever humbles himself like this child is the greatest in the kingdom of heaven." He then made clear that children deserve and are afforded exceptional attention in heaven.

"See that you do not despise one of these little ones. For I tell you that in heaven their angels always see the face of my Father who is in heaven." (Matt. 18:10)

In Summary

- God is the One who gives life to every living creature.
- A complete understanding of the precise means by which a new life begins and God's Spirit is infused cannot be observed by any of the human senses or by any other means known to mankind.
- Only the One who creates life is able to fully comprehend it – where it comes from and why it even exists.
- The virgin birth of Christ is powerful testimony to the unlimited power and involvement of God as the Author of life.
- The fact that growth begins immediately after the moment of conception is proof that life has begun. In God's great plan, it is possible that life begins even before conception.
- The "seed" of every living thing was present at Creation.

- The sperm of the father is what carries the seed of life forward from each new generation.
- God controls the womb. He controls every step in reproduction.
- Every new life is a miracle. God knows us completely even before we are conceived in the womb.

3

The Ostrich

OTHER THAN THE fact that God created them all, what possible connections can exist among the ostrich, the eagle and the unborn child that provided the title for this book? It is neither immediately obvious nor self-explanatory, but a common thread binds these things together, all pertaining to the abortion issue. In this chapter, we will examine abortion in light of scriptural teachings from the book of Job where God uses the ostrich as an example of how not to treat our own children, particularly our unborn children.

The Ostrich

The book of Job in the Old Testament presents the classic case of a man named Job who came to know much misery. The first verse of the first chapter describes Job as "blameless and upright" because he feared God and shunned evil. We are told in verses 9 to 11, however, that Satan accused Job before God, arguing that Job was righteous only because it was profitable for him. Indeed, God had blessed Job with great wealth and excellent health for himself and his family. Take away those things, said Satan, and Job would surely curse God to His face. So God accepted Satan's challenge and, in time, permitted Satan to destroy all of the good things with which Job had been blessed: his family, his wealth, and then his health. The only thing Satan was ordered not to take was Job's life.[21]

In the course of all that follows, Job agonizes. His friends argue that he brought the curse upon himself. Even Job's wife proposes that he should curse God and die.[22] In misery, Job loathes the day of his birth[23] and eventually chides God for treating him unjustly, bemoaning the fact that God is not a man that Job might face his accuser in court and that there existed no mediator to bridge the infinite gap between Creation and its Creator (foreshadowing the solution God would eventually employ, the sending of His Son, the 'theanthropos' or 'God-Man'), "who might lay his hand on us both."[24] Praying for such a mediator, Job insists, "Then I would speak up without fear of him, but as it now stands with me, I cannot" (Job 9:35, NIV).

In Job 38, God answers Job and demands, "Dress for action like a man; I will question you, and you make it known to me."[25] In the discourse that follows, God poses questions to Job that no man could answer, questions that forced Job to realize that, despite all of his suffering, God's divine purpose was being fulfilled, and all of Job's suffering had meaning and value beyond Job's limited understanding. In the midst of His discourse to Job, God speaks of the Ostrich:

> The wings of the ostrich wave proudly,
> > but are they the pinions and plumage of love?
> For she leaves her eggs to the earth
> > and lets them be warmed on the ground,
> forgetting that a foot may crush them
> > and that the wild beast may trample them.
> She deals cruelly with her young, as if they were not hers;
> > though her labor be in vain, yet she has no fear,

---

21 Job 1:12
22 Job 2:9
23 Job 3:1-16
24 Job 9:33
25 Job 38:3

because God has made her forget wisdom
    and given her no share in understanding.
When she rouses herself to flee,
    she laughs at the horse and his rider. (Job 39:13-18)

Although perhaps obvious, the first observation that must be made concerning this passage is the fact that God did not say these things in the hope that the ostrich would mend her ways. God created the ostrich to be what she is, perhaps with the very purpose of teaching us the lessons these verses contain. The message is for us and is given for the express purpose of instructing men and women in the ways of righteousness.

> All Scripture is breathed out by God and profitable for teaching, for reproof, for correction, and for training in righteousness, that the man of God may be complete, equipped for every good work. (2 Tim. 3:16-17)

Before we attempt to unravel the details of this very interesting passage of Scripture in Job, we should first learn something about that unusual creature, the ostrich. Naturalis Historia[26] provides the following observations about the ostrich that will help us better understand the biblical narrative in Job 39. Ostriches are native to hot, dry regions of the African continent, although they have now been dispersed to many areas of the world. They are very large birds, often more than six feet in height and sometimes weighing up to 300 pounds. And while their wings are among the largest of all birds, they are disproportionately small in relation to the ostrich's enormous body, which partially explains why the ostrich is flightless. Nevertheless, the ostrich has powerful legs and can run more than 40 miles per hour for considerable periods of time, a very useful and important means of escape from its predators.[27]

---

26 Naturalis Historia (February 4, 2013). Consider the Ostrich: Job 39 and God's Commentary on His Creation – Part I. Website: http://thenaturalhistorian.com/2013/02/04/consider-the-ostrich-book-job-creation-wisdom/
27 *Id.*

During the reproductive season, it is the male ostrich that prepares the dirt nest where the eggs will be deposited by several females. The last of these females to lay her eggs is typically the dominant one who will then move most, if not all, of the other eggs away from the central nest before depositing her own. The male and the dominant female will then alternately incubate her eggs, abandoning the eggs of other females that now surround the central nest and which will likely never hatch for lack of proper care.[28] Instead, these unprotected eggs, left by non-dominant females, will often be scavenged by predators and may even provide food for the dominant female's chicks that eventually hatch. It is noteworthy that the male ostrich, not the female, will be the one to nurture the chicks once they finally hatch from the properly incubated eggs. The female shows little interest in their upbringing.

With this background in mind, we can now consider in more detail our biblical passage in Job and its bearing on abortion.

The word-picture of the female ostrich that is painted in Job 39 is one of careless abandon. She waves her wings "proudly" and "laughs" as she races past the mighty horse and rider. She has not a care in the world beyond experiencing the thrill of putting down that noble horse with her great speed. Motherhood is not her main concern.

When the Bible observes that the ostrich drops her eggs and abandons them in the dirt "as if they were not hers," this is most clearly a reference to the non-dominant females whose eggs will be moved away from the center of the communal nest and abandoned. The females that deposit these deserted eggs give no thought at all to the fact that their eggs may be crushed and destroyed. They have no time to gather their eggs under them for warmth and protection until they are hatched. They leave that to chance and the actions of the dominant female who cares nothing for them. The warmth needed for incubation of the eggs that have been cast aside is limited to whatever might be available from the sun and sand where they have been left, rather than by the ostrich's body warmth as would be typical with most birds. The warmth provided is not sufficient and it is unlikely those eggs will ever hatch.

---

28 *Id.*

In another biblical reference to the ostrich, God's people are compared to the ostrich and chastened for their lack of caring, which is a consequence of their sin:

Even jackals[29] offer the breast; they nurse their young, but the daughter of my people has become cruel, like the ostriches in the wilderness. (Lam. 4:3)

It is this heartlessness, this cruelty of the ostrich of which God speaks when He says, "Though her labor be in vain, yet she has no fear."[30] It is this same heartlessness that shamed God's people so they were viewed as worse than jackals, for there is no higher calling in life than motherhood and the love it demands and deserves.

"Her Young"

In the Job passage, the ostrich's eggs are referred to as "her young." When she drops her eggs in the dirt or sand and leaves them there, she is treating *her young* cruelly, "as if they were not hers." The word interpreted "cruelly" is variously translated in other Bible versions as "hardened" or "harshly." The King James Version says, "She is hardened against her young ones."

As with the human eggs (ova) in a woman, a bird's eggs do not produce offspring unless they are first fertilized by the sperm of the male. It is clear from our passage in Job that these eggs are deemed to be fertilized, otherwise it would make no sense to refer to them as "her young." They could never develop into young ostriches unless the eggs were fertilized. It is because the

---

29 It should be noted here that the King James Version substitutes "sea monsters" in place of jackals; the Septuagint finds it to be "serpents"; and Young's Literal Translation uses "dragons." These are terms associated with the primordial chaos (sea monsters), the tempter in the Garden of Eden (serpent), and the Devil/Satan in the book of Revelation (dragons); all of these powerful references indicating just how degenerate the people had become in the eyes of the LORD. They are viewed as even more evil than these various creatures.

30 Job 39:16

eggs are fertilized that God considers them to be her young, for everything necessary for their complete development is present at that moment. If the eggs are then trampled by a wild animal, it is not the mere loss of eggs; it is the loss of her young, her children.

This speaks directly to the issue of when an individual life has its beginning, an issue that has been strongly debated and has been discussed in detail in Chapters 1 and 2 of this book. Here, through the example of the ostrich, we see that individual life has begun at least by the time of conception, for even though the eggs are newly fertilized and freshly laid, and although they will not hatch for some time, they are promptly deemed to be the ostrich's offspring, which carries with it the clear declaration that they are living creatures from the moment of fertilization onward.

Since God considers the ostrich egg to be *her young*, we must also acknowledge that He views the fertilized human egg in the same way. Why else would God include this illustration in his Word? This passage is speaking directly to us, giving insight into the mind of God Himself concerning our unborn children.

The Hebrew word interpreted as "her young" is used interchangeably in the Hebrew language to describe the offspring of humans and animals alike. In Genesis 3:16, the word is translated as "children" where God told Eve that "with pain you will give birth to children." In Genesis 5:4, it is translated as "sons and daughters" that Adam begat. It is used in Genesis 18:7 to refer to the offspring of animals when Abraham ran to his flock and picked out a "calf, tender and good." While the very same word is used to refer to both humans and animals, notably it also refers to both the born and unborn (as with the ostrich eggs). So, when this word is used in Job 39:16 in connection with the ostrich eggs, the meaning is unmistakable. Even though the eggs are newly fertilized, freshly laid, and will not hatch for some time, they are the offspring, the children, the sons or daughters of the ostrich parents.

God views the fertilized eggs as her young because the eggs have "life" in them as a result of fertilization. By calling the eggs her young, God has acknowledged that unless crushed by some wild animal, or abandoned as in the case of the discarded eggs, the life inside the eggs will grow and develop according to their DNA as young ostriches, which, without life in them, the eggs could not do. Lifeless, inanimate things simply do not grow and develop into animated living beings. It is the presence of life that differentiates the animate from the inanimate.

Once an egg is fertilized, whether ostrich or human, life has begun, an offspring or child has been created, and having begun its development, anything that halts its advancement destroys the life of that offspring. Whatever the stage of development—from conception until live birth or from infancy to adulthood—it matters not at all to God. He sees the end of the process even before it has begun. Regardless of the stage of development, the unborn is acknowledged as His Creation and the object of His deep love. His plan for each person has been set long before they come into physical existence outside the womb.

As will be discussed more fully in later chapters, the 1973 case of *Roe v. Wade*[31] held that during the first 24 weeks of pregnancy, the mother has a "fundamental right" to terminate or destroy without governmental interference what the Court labeled the "potential life" of an unborn human fetus.[32] Under the terms of the *Roe* decision, it was envisioned that only after the fetus had been allowed to develop to a point of "viability" at approximately 24 weeks, or during the third trimester of development, that a State could claim any meaningful interest in the protection of the prenatal life, and even then, the mother could abort her child if she claimed her own "health" (very broadly defined) would be in any way compromised.[33]

This trimester concept was dependent upon the time element involved in the gestation process following fertilization, which, as we have seen, is entirely irrelevant to God. In contrast to *Roe v. Wade*, the Bible poses no requirement that the fetus reach a point of "viability" or any other arbitrary stage of development to attain the status of the parent's offspring. From the moment

---

31 410 U.S. 113

32 *Id.* at 163-164

33 *Id.*at 163

of conception, the fertilized egg is simply the *young* of its parents, deserving of great love and nurturing and protection.

Wisdom and Good Sense

Since the eggs are the ostrich's own young, her offspring, why then does she treat them so cruelly? Why is she so hardened against them? The answer given in verse 17 is that "God has made her forget wisdom and given her no share in understanding." If ever there was a direct and unequivocal biblical indictment of the practice of abortion, this is surely it. Without wisdom or understanding the ostrich treats her young harshly, abandoning them without protection from any evil that may come along. Without wisdom or understanding, we do the very same. Through the example of the ostrich, God shows us how foolish and ignorant we are when we fail to nurture and protect our young in the womb.

The ostrich, however, has an excuse. If God has withheld from her the necessary wisdom and understanding, as acknowledged in Job 39:17, then she bears no blame of her own. But the same is not true for human beings. Unlike the ostrich, man was created in the image and likeness of God[34] and was not only endowed with far greater intelligence than animals like the ostrich, but are invited by God to receive wisdom and understanding that are available to any man or woman who diligently seeks them.

In 2 Chronicles 1:7, God made an offer to King Solomon: "Ask what I shall give you." Solomon answered in verse 8, "Give me now wisdom and knowledge to go out and come in before this people, for who can govern this people of yours, which is so great?" In response God promised:

> "Because this was in your heart, and you have not asked for possessions, wealth, honor, or the life of those who hate you, and have not even asked for long life, but have asked for wisdom and knowledge for yourself that you may govern my people over whom I have made

---

34 Gen. 1:26

you king, wisdom and knowledge are granted to you. I will also give you riches, possessions, and honor, such as none of the kings had who were before you, and none after you shall have the like." (2 Chron. 1:11-12)

Endowed with wisdom and knowledge from God and writing under the inspiration of the Holy Spirit, Solomon recorded numerous proverbs for the benefit of all who will take the time to study them. Much of his writing is devoted to instructions about the attaining of wisdom and knowledge with which God had greatly blessed him. In fact, the first four chapters of the book of Proverbs speak of little else. Proverbs 2:1-15 is especially instructive:

> My son, if you receive my words
> and treasure up my commandments with you,
> making your ear attentive to wisdom
> and inclining your heart to understanding;
> yes, if you call out for insight
> and raise your voice for understanding,
> if you seek it like silver
> and search for it as for hidden treasures,
> then you will understand the fear of the LORD
> and find the knowledge of God.
> For the LORD gives wisdom;
> from his mouth come knowledge and understanding;
> he stores up sound wisdom for the upright;
> he is a shield to those who walk in integrity,
> guarding the paths of justice
> and watching over the way of his saints.
> Then you will understand righteousness and justice
> and equity, every good path;
> for wisdom will come into your heart,
> and knowledge will be pleasant to your soul;

discretion will watch over you,
>understanding will guard you,
delivering you from the way of evil,
>from men of perverted speech,
who forsake the paths of uprightness
>to walk in the ways of darkness,
who rejoice in doing evil
>and delight in the perverseness of evil,
men whose paths are crooked,
>and who are devious in their ways.

This passage holds the key to understanding the illustration of the ostrich with its lack of wisdom and understanding, compared with God's view of unborn motherhood. Without wisdom, the proverb says we have nothing to save us from the "way of evil," from those whose words are "perverted," who "rejoice in doing evil and delight in the perverseness of evil," and from "men whose paths are crooked and who are devious in their ways." It is only with wisdom from God that Scripture says we will find "every good path," where discretion will protect us and understanding will guard us.

These verses show us a progression that is vital to understanding God and his design for each of us.

First, to obtain wisdom and understanding, we must all start by accepting God's instruction ("receive my words"). Believe what it says. Even before you fully understand, you must start by accepting the truth of God's Word by faith.

Second, study God's Word ("treasure up my commandments with you"), and as you do, ask God earnestly ("call out") for insight and understanding.

Third, if you do these things, the Bible promises that "you will understand the fear of the Lord" which brings with it the knowledge of God. That is His promise to us. It is the formula for attaining true wisdom that is unavailable by any other means.

Fourth, once that wisdom is found, understanding will lead you in "every good path" and away from crooked, evil paths.

Proverbs 3:5-6 provides a summary of these teachings:

> Trust in the LORD with all your heart,
>   and do not lean on your own understanding.
> In all your ways acknowledge him,
>   and he will make straight your paths.

It is by our failure to follow this formula, to trust in the Lord with all our heart, leaning not on our own understanding, that we do foolish and perverse things, like destroying our own young in the womb. Those who do such things are, according to the Bible, unwise. They act imprudently, without wisdom or understanding like the ostrich and are more foolish than the jackal, because God offers wisdom and understanding for the taking and they refuse to take it. James, the brother of the Lord Jesus, put it this way:

> If any of you lacks wisdom, let him ask God, who gives generously to
> all without reproach, and it will be given him. (James 1:5)

We have a personal responsibility to obtain wisdom. We are not born with wisdom, neither do we obtain it just by living. Rather, we are invited to ask God for it. He will give us wisdom "without reproach." Only through His wisdom will we learn to do those things that are acceptable to Him and receive His blessings.

Psalm 111 says:

> The fear of the LORD is the beginning of wisdom;
>   all those who practice it have a good understanding.
> His praise endures forever! (Ps. 111:10)

Without fear of the Lord (an exceeding reverence for Him), we cannot begin to possess true wisdom. But because He has made wisdom available to us, God is fully justified in holding us responsible to act wisely in everything, including how we deal with our unborn children. They are our young, our children, living beings created in God's own image, and are worthy of our love and protection. They are not to be abandoned or allowed to be destroyed while we race off like the ostrich to pursue our own selfish pleasures.

Special notice must be taken of the fact that even the unwise ostrich that abandons her eggs does not do so with actual intent to harm her young. Her actions are merely those of ignorant neglect. Yet God calls her heartless, worse than jackals. What then can be said of us when we purposefully destroy our own young?

Lessons from Job

In addition to the lessons learned from the Ostrich, the book of Job offers other important insights concerning abortion and the spiritual aspects of the abortion decision. It is interesting, and worthy of our attention, to note that God's personal covenantal name, *YHWH* (usually rendered "LORD" in English translations) is used throughout the Job epic. This name relates to the covenant established between the ancient Hebrews and *YHWH*, a promise that guaranteed blessings to those who were faithful to Him and curses to those who were not.[35]

Accordingly, Job's friends assumed and insisted that Job was being justly reproached, and that he stood in need of repentance.[36] Job, on the other hand, knew that he had been a faithful servant of the LORD, and the LORD had so commended him in Job 1:1, finding him to be "blameless and upright." Job could only conclude, then, that the LORD was cursing him unjustly.

When Job's friends had exhausted their accusations, *YHWH* appears and answers Job "out of the whirlwind" (Job 38:1). Through Chapters 38 and 39, He majestically illustrates His absolute omnipotence as Lord over all creation, concluding with a challenge: "Shall a faultfinder contend with the Almighty?"

---

35 See Deuteronomy, especially chapters 5 (the giving of the Ten Commandments) and 28 (blessings for obedience and curses for disobedience).
36 See, e.g., Job 5:17; 8:13; 11:14,18-19

(Job 40:2). Still, Job fails to understand. So *YHWH* continues His instruction with even more challenges, demanding:

> Adorn yourself with majesty and dignity;
> clothe yourself with glory and splendor.
> Pour out the overflowings of your anger,
> and look on everyone who is proud and abase him.
> Look on everyone who is proud and bring him low
> and tread down the wicked where they stand.
> Hide them all in the dust together;
> bind their faces in the world below.
> Then will I also acknowledge to you
> that your own right hand can save you. (Job 40:10-14)

Finally, Job begins to understand the sovereignty of *YHWH* and that His ways are far above our own, His thoughts far above our thoughts, and His purposes are for Him alone to determine. Job then testifies:

> "I know that you can do all things, and that no purpose of yours can be thwarted... Therefore I have uttered what I did not understand, things too wonderful for me, which I did not know." (Job 42:2-3)

The same lesson concerning the sovereignty of God was made yet clearer by Christ Jesus as recorded in the ninth chapter of John's Gospel:

> As he passed by, he [Jesus] saw a man blind from birth. And his disciples asked him, "Rabbi, who sinned, this man or his parents, that he was born blind?" Jesus answered, "It was not that this man sinned, or his parents, but that the works of God might be displayed in him." (John 9:1-3)

Jesus declares that the blind man's suffering was not the result of sin, but was allowed by God in order to fulfill a greater purpose – that Jesus might heal him as a testimony to others, which, of course, He did.

But just as Job had accused God of wrongdoing, the Pharisees of the New Testament accused Jesus of sin in John 9:16 after Jesus miraculously healed this blind man on the Sabbath, a supposed "act" forbidden by Jewish law. Upon interrogating the healed man later, the Pharisees pressed him, saying, "We know that this man [Jesus] is a sinner" (John 9:24). The man answered, "Whether he is a sinner, I do not know. One thing I do know, that though I was blind, now I see" (John 9:25).

After learning that Pharisees had dealt harshly with the man who had been healed, Jesus sought the man out once more and asked:

> "Do you believe in the Son of Man?" He answered, "And who is he, sir, that I may believe in him?" Jesus said to him, "You have seen him, and it is he who is speaking to you." He said, "Lord, I believe," and he worshiped him. Jesus said, *"For judgment I came into this world, that those who do not see may see, and those who see may become blind."* Some of the Pharisees near him heard these things, and said to him, "Are we also blind?" Jesus said to them, "If you were blind, you would have no guilt; but now that you say, 'We see,' your guilt remains." (John 9:35-41)

So it is with the ostrich. It is because she is blind (God has given her no share in wisdom or understanding) that she is not held accountable for dealing cruelly with her young. But where one continues in known sin, the guilt remains and that person will be held accountable for it.

The Pharisees of Jesus' day made the same mistake Job had made. Their perspectives were earthly and humanly based, not spiritually centered. They were convinced that they had true understanding and had need of no one to instruct them. As a result, they rejected their own Jewish Messiah and forfeited the blessings that would have come through their faith as *YHWH* had promised from ancient days.

Job had likewise failed to fully appreciate the sovereignty of God. He could not see the end of his calamity nor understand its meaning. But unlike the Pharisees, Job recognized his error, repented and confessed to God:

"I have heard of you by the hearing of the ear; but now my eye sees you; therefore I retract, and I repent in dust and ashes." (Job 42:5-6)

In honoring Job's repentance, God blessed him:

The LORD blessed the latter days of Job more than his beginning. (Job 42:12)

A woman faced with an unwanted pregnancy may be likened to Job, not understanding why such a thing should be happening to her. Or, she may be like the Pharisees who were blinded to the truth by their own errant ideas. But despite the seeming calamity of the moment, God intends her child to be a wonderful blessing.

Behold, children are a heritage from the LORD,
the fruit of the womb a reward.
Like arrows in the hand of a warrior
are the children of one's youth.
Blessed is the man
who fills his quiver with them!
He shall not be put to shame
when he speaks with his enemies in the gate. (Ps. 127:3-5)

The one who is able to accept God's sovereignty and yield to His wisdom and perfect timing will receive the great blessing a child is meant to be. How tragic it is that so many choose to forfeit that lifelong reward.

In Summary

- God has given us the ostrich as an example of how not to treat our unborn children. Children are formed by God Himself in the womb and are to be nourished and protected.

- From the moment of conception, the unborn are deemed to be "her young," deserving of love and care.
- There is no difference between the born and unborn except time, and time is irrelevant to God who sees the end of it all even before we have seen it begin.
- Those who fail to nurture and protect the unborn are declared to be unwise and have no share in understanding. The Bible says they are heartless and act cruelly toward their own children.
- Even the foolish ostrich does not intentionally harm her young; her actions are merely negligent. But abortion is intentional, making those involved "worse than jackals."
- God intends children, even those unplanned and unwanted, to be an immense blessing.

4

The Eagle

IN CHAPTER 3, we saw that God calls us to wisdom and understanding in dealing with our unborn. The example of the ostrich reveals God's desire that one's "young," whether born or unborn, receive a mother's protection and loving nurture. In this chapter, we consider the circumstance of another bird as we compare the legal status of the eagle and the eagle's egg with that of the unborn human child under U.S. federal laws.

An Imperfect Nation in an Imperfect World

Man's laws can vary dramatically from time to time, from place to place, and from culture to culture, but biblical principles are universal and eternal.

> The law of the LORD is perfect,
>   reviving the soul;
> the testimony of the LORD is sure,
>   making wise the simple;
> the precepts of the LORD are right,
>   rejoicing the heart;
> the commandment of the LORD is pure,
>   enlightening the eyes;

the fear of the LORD is clean,
    enduring forever;
the rules of the LORD are true,
    and righteous altogether.
More to be desired are they than gold,
    even much fine gold;
sweeter also than honey
    and drippings of the honeycomb.
Moreover, by them is your servant warned;
    in keeping them there is great reward. (Ps. 19:7-11)

The fickle, ever-changing views and philosophies of mankind stand in stark contrast to the timeless, unchanging dependability of Scripture. Early in American history, the preamble to our Declaration of Independence proclaimed that "all men are created equal" and that certain "unalienable Rights" flow to man from the One called "their Creator."[37] Among these rights are "Life, Liberty, and the pursuit of Happiness." If a right is "unalienable," that means it cannot be taken away; it has been given by God Himself, and mankind must not attempt to deny such a right. But it is a fair question to ask if these high ideals have truly mirrored reality in the United States. While it is government's duty to preserve and protect those "unalienable Rights" for all Americans, our government, especially including the Supreme Court, has at times found the means to justify denial of fundamental rights to some people, often in irrational, and occasionally in violent ways.

Women, for example, were denied the right to vote until 1920 when the Nineteenth Amendment to our Constitution was ratified (even former slaves were declared to have the right to vote under the Fifteenth Amendment which was ratified in 1870, fifty years in advance of women's rights).

During World War II, innocent Japanese-American citizens were herded by government forces into U.S. internment camps without the slightest legal justification and without a hint of the due process required by the Fifth and

---

37 Declaration of Independence [¶ 2] (1776)

Fourteenth Amendments. This action was later declared to be constitutional by the Supreme Court on grounds of national security,[38] an obvious rationalization in its interpretation since those people had done nothing to deserve such treatment. Their "crime" was the fact of their Japanese ancestry at a time when America was at war with Japan. But they were Americans, legally entitled to due process and equal protection under the law. Forty years later, President Ronald Reagan signed into law the Civil Liberties Act of 1988, known as Public Law 100-383, in which a formal apology was made along with an offer of $20,000 in reparations for each of those who had been interned against their will.

But in all of this country's history, and excepting the current debate over abortion, the most glaring violation of human rights was certainly the slavery of black Americans. Here, in the United States, the "Land of the Free," black people were enslaved and harshly mistreated. In the infamous case of *Dred Scott v. Sandford*,[39] our highest federal court boldly proclaimed in 1857 that negroes are

> "an inferior order, and altogether unfit to associate with the white race, either in social or political relations; and so far inferior, that they had no rights which the white man was bound to respect."[40]

It was not until after the American Civil War that formal amendments to our Constitution[41] finally established the fact that black Americans were and are

---

38 Korematsu v. United States, 323 U.S. 214 (1944)

39 10 U.S. (19 How.) 393 (1857)

40 Id. at 407

41 Following the War Between the States, the "Civil War Amendments" to the Constitution were ratified (also called "The Reconstruction Amendments"). These included the Thirteenth Amendment that abolished slavery anywhere in the United States. The Fourteenth Amendment redefined American citizenship and included the privileges and immunities clauses, the due process clause and the equal protection clauses. The Fifteenth Amendment granted voting rights to American citizens regardless of "race, color, or previous condition of servitude."

truly "persons" and "citizens" entitled to the same unalienable rights previously reserved for the exclusive benefit of the white race within the United States. It is not difficult today to recognize the Supreme Court's appalling and disastrous error that has left a lasting scar.

We could look back at these historical events and argue that such illogical, self-serving, elitist attitudes are behind us. We suppose that callous inequities like those have now been rectified by laws designed to protect those who cannot adequately protect themselves. But the abortion issue confronting us today would bring that evaluation into serious question.

Certainly, laws have been passed to guard against discrimination and protect civil liberties. Attitudes regarding minorities, women, and other previously oppressed groups have also changed significantly. But the same Constitution that was interpreted to deny basic rights to blacks, Japanese-Americans, and women is now interpreted in a way that denies the most basic of human rights to millions of unborn children: the unalienable right to Life. Under *Roe v. Wade,* the unborn were denied status as "persons" as the Supreme Court has interpreted that Constitutional term within the Fourteenth Amendment, and are, therefore, refused protection of their unalienable rights—in much the same way as were former black slaves.

The American Eagle

Americans take great pride in the notion that our system of justice is one of the best in the world. But on the issue of abortion, there is an incongruity of our laws which is perhaps best illustrated by a comparison of the status of unborn children to that of the bald and golden eagles. On June 8, 1940, Congress enacted a statute, which is generally classified as 16 U.S.C. section 668, which may be called the "Eagle Law." It provided:

WHEREAS the Continental Congress in 1782 adopted the bald eagle as the national symbol; and
WHEREAS the bald eagle thus became the symbolic representation of a new nation under a new government in a new world; and

WHEREAS by that act of Congress and by tradition and custom during the life of this Nation, the bald eagle is no longer a mere bird of biological interest but a symbol of the American ideals of freedom; and

WHEREAS the bald eagle is now threatened with extinction: therefore

Be it enacted . . .

The statutory language which follows makes it a criminal offense, punishable by a fine up to $5000, imprisonment up to one year, or both a fine and imprisonment, to act knowingly or with wanton disregard to:

Take, possess, sell, purchase, barter, offer to sell, purchase or barter, transport, export or import, at any time or in any manner, any bald eagle commonly known as the American eagle, or any golden eagle, alive or dead, or any part, nest, or *egg* thereof.[42]

This statute is still valid federal law today, as is the now infamous case of *Roe v. Wade*[43] that was handed down only 33 years later. But a comparison of these two federal laws raises many legitimate questions. The legal reasoning of either law defies explanation of the other. While *Roe v. Wade* considered the unborn as mere "potential life," undeserving of governmental protection, at least until they have developed to a stage of "viability"—and then only if the woman claimed no detriment to her own "health"—the Eagle Law goes far beyond the protection of "viable" unborn eagles, protecting under penalty of criminal punishment even the "potential life" that is within the eagle egg.

The Eagle Law does not qualify its prohibition against tampering with the egg at any particular stage of gestation or incubation. It makes no difference under the statute whether the eagle egg is freshly laid or is ready to

---

42 16 U.S.C. 668(a) (1940)
43 410 U.S. 113 (1973)

hatch; the law applies uniformly throughout the entire gestation period, literally from the moment the egg is produced. Once the eagle has laid its egg, that egg is absolutely protected by federal law from all human tampering. Under this federal statute, the eagle's egg is afforded the same status as a hatched and living eagle, and is given complete protection under penalty of criminal prosecution and punishment.

By contrast, *Roe v. Wade* mandated that government could intercede on behalf of the fetus and for its protection only after approximately the 24th week of development, the point at which the Court judged the fetus to be "viable." But regulation, even after the 24th week of development, was illusive since any possible "detriment" to the woman's health (very broadly defined) would override any form of governmental intervention to protect the fetus. The only real restriction contained in *Roe* was the requirement that the fetal destruction must be completed before the child was fully expelled from the womb, because once born alive, completely expelled from the womb, the newborn baby would be guaranteed full constitutional protection as a "person." To kill after a live birth would constitute murder, even if the killing was done within seconds following the completed birth event. The Supreme Court saw no problem in allowing a child to be killed even during the final minutes prior to a complete live birth.

An eagle is not a human, and an eagle's egg is not even potentially human. Yet the Eagle Law criminalizes even the taking, possessing, or transporting an eagle egg "at any time or in any manner." It makes no difference whether or not an eagle chick is eventually hatched from the egg after the tampering. The only qualification for criminal prosecution is that the tampering act must be done with the necessary mental intent, that is "knowingly or with wanton disregard." Again, by contrast, *Roe* declares that a woman has the fundamental right, *even knowingly or with wanton disregard*, to destroy the unborn human child within her womb. She could do this with absolute impunity and authority. Unlike the act of tampering with the potential life of an eagle, the destruction of a human fetus by its mother is unquestioned, not punishable in any manner. There was to be no censure, no shame, no fine, no imprisonment, and no accountability whatsoever.

In its wisdom, Congress recognized that the value of the eagle's egg is, in fact, in its potential to become an eagle. And because the American eagle is to be valued and preserved, it is not only prudent, but necessary, to protect its egg because that is the process by which eagles come into being. Whether due to a religious conviction or not, the human fetus must be seen as far more valuable and worthy of protection than an eagle egg because it has even greater potential—potential to become a living human being in the likeness and image of God, a productive member of our society, and one able to continue the propagation of our species into the future. If the potential life of an eagle is considered so valuable as to warrant legal protection, how much more should the life of the unborn human be valued and protected?

A Symbol of Freedom

As acknowledged in the Eagle Law, Congress determined that the bald eagle had by tradition and custom become "a symbol of the American ideals of freedom," a direct reference to the greatly treasured personal freedoms enjoyed by the American people. And because Congress noted that a primary reason for the Eagle Law was that "the bald eagle is now threatened with extinction," it is unquestionable that the intent of the statute was to preserve and protect that symbol of freedom, not only for the benefit of Americans living at the time the statute was enacted in 1940, but also for the benefit of future generations of Americans yet unborn. But if the reference to freedom in the preamble to the Eagle Law does not include the right of a child to be born, then the preservation of the symbol of freedom for the benefit of future generations must be viewed as a very tentative and shallow endeavor.

Both laws, *Roe v. Wade* and the Eagle Law, are intended to govern the conduct of people. It is people, not eagles or any other creature, that are forbidden by the statute to tamper with an eagle egg, and it is to people that *Roe v. Wade* gave permission to destroy their own unborn children. Congress passed the law protecting eagles from people because it was either known or feared that some people might otherwise harm the eagle or its eggs, and Congress placed a high value on preventing that harm. But what can be said of the reasoning behind *Roe v. Wade*? Can we say that our Supreme Court acted with similar concern for the human species?

It is both necessary and proper that we protect animals like the eagle from harm. But when Congress elevated the eagle from its former status as a "mere bird of biological interest" to "a symbol of the American ideals of freedom," surely Congress did not intend to elevate the eagle above human beings for whom the eagle was to be that symbol of freedom. In the face of such glaring contradiction, one must ask how our Supreme Court assessed the relative value of eagles and humans. It would appear that the eagle, because of its value as a symbol of the ideals of freedom for the *people*, was considered irreplaceable and of great worth. But future generations of people, those for whom the symbol of freedom exists, were judged unworthy of similar protection. As of the publication of this book, nearly 60 million American children have been denied their "unalienable right to Life" by that ruling of the Supreme Court.

The Eagle Law specifically recognized that aside from the eagle's value as a symbol of freedom, it is a "mere bird of biological interest." The Bible teaches that God created both the birds and humans, but the Bible makes no mistake as to which is more valuable in God's eyes. Jesus taught:

> Are not two sparrows sold for a penny? And not one of them will fall to the ground apart from your Father. But even the hairs of your head are all numbered. Fear not, therefore; *you are of more value than many sparrows.* (Matt. 10:29-31)

Other Laws Protecting Animal Life

Paradoxically, during 1973, the same year the Supreme Court handed down its decision in *Roe v. Wade,* Congress was busy enacting another law in stark contradiction. It was the Endangered Species Act of 1973[44] which declared it a crime, punishable by up to a $50,000 fine, or 1 year in prison, or both a

---

44 16 USC § 1531 et seq. The United States Fish and Wildlife Service and the National Oceanic and Atmospheric Administration are both charged with administration of the Act.

fine and imprisonment, to do any act that might harm any endangered "fish or wildlife" species, its habitat, or its egg. Under the statute, the term "fish or wildlife" is defined as:

> Any member of the animal kingdom, including without limitation any mammal, fish, bird (including any migratory, nonmigratory, or endangered bird for which protection is also afforded by treaty or other international agreement), amphibian, reptile, mollusk, crustacean, arthropod or other invertebrate, and *includes any part, product,* **egg***, or offspring thereof, or the dead body or parts thereof.*

The law further protects any species that may so closely resemble an endangered species that it could be mistaken for the endangered species.

Humans are not an endangered species, at least not yet. But the Endangered Species Act shows plainly that Congress understands the unborn of any species is a living organism and that failure to protect it can result in the destruction of life and become a hindrance to the propagation of that species. If the goal is to foster life, it is necessary to protect the unborn; destroy the unborn and you destroy life.

In Summary

- God's laws are perfect, unchanging, and in keeping them there is great reward. Man's laws are fickle and unreliable and often violate the will of God.
- The Eagle Law and the Endangered Species Act protect unborn animal species under threat of criminal punishment, because that is the process by which they are able to continue their existence, but *Roe v. Wade* denies that protection to unborn humans.
- The Bible makes it clear: Human beings, whether born or unborn, are worth far more than birds or any other animal species.

5

The Privacy Right to Abortion

LTHOUGH VIRTUALLY ALL adult Americans recognize *Roe v. Wade* as the case that eliminated the rights of governmental authorities to regulate abortions as they saw fit, few have ever actually read the written decision, and fewer still have a clear understanding of what the case really means. In this and the following three chapters, we will take a critical look at various aspects of *Roe v. Wade* and subsequent cases and the U.S. Supreme Court's stated reasons behind its decisions. You may be surprised at what is discovered when these important cases are placed under close scrutiny.

Roe v. Wade and Its Predecessors

In 1973, the Supreme Court of the United States decided the issue of whether unborn children are worthy of protection from abortion harm under our federal Constitution. In this now infamous case entitled *Roe v. Wade*,[45] the Court took what might be called the "Wine Connoisseur's Approach," judging that fetal life becomes more valuable with age. Dividing the 38-week average gestation period into three trimesters of approximately twelve weeks each, the Court ruled that during the first trimester of preg-

---

45 410 U.S. 113 (1973)

nancy the fetus, like very new wine, has very little value worth protecting and the mother should have an unfettered right to abort it without any form of governmental regulation.[46] The Court reasoned that no regulation of abortions during this early stage should be allowed because of what the Court called a "now-established medical fact...that until the end of the first trimester mortality in abortion may be less than mortality in normal childbirth,"[47] a statement that totally disregarded the life of the infant and focused solely on a comparison of mortality rates among pregnant women themselves during the birth process as compared to abortions. For the pregnant woman, the Court proclaimed that an abortion may be less likely to cause death to the mother than natural childbirth, so it is better to allow women to abort their pregnancies.

During the second trimester, the fetal wine is still fermenting and clarifying and deemed of little value so that a State may then regulate abortions only "in ways that are reasonably related to *maternal health*."[48] Here, again, the focus was still entirely on the woman – the health and well-being of the fetus was of no concern—so that permissible State regulation during the second trimester included only such measures as establishing licensing requirements for abortion facilities and the persons performing abortions.[49]

Under the *Roe* decision, it was only when the fetus had been adequately "aged" and allowed to develop to a point of "viability" that it would become worthy of some protection and a State could then "go so far as to proscribe abortion during that period, *except* when it is necessary to preserve the life or health of the mother."[50] The Court determined this point of "viability" to be the beginning of the third trimester or after approximately twenty-four weeks. The fetal development was then presumed to be sufficiently "full bodied," like adequately aged wine, and deserving of some attention.

---

46 *Id.* at 163
47 *Id.*
48 *Id.* (emphasis added)
49 *Id.*
50 *Id.* at 163-64

The problem at this late stage of fetal development was that the phrase "health of the mother" was defined so broadly that virtually any concern the mother might have about her pregnancy or childbirth could be a sufficient detriment to her health (physically, spiritually, mentally or emotionally) so that the child could be lawfully aborted, even in the very late stages of the pregnancy—literally at any time before the child was fully expelled from the womb. In actual practice, no one demands to know why a woman has chosen to abort because that would intrude upon her right to privacy.

By virtue of the *Roe* decision, it was only after the child had been born alive, fully expelled from the womb, that it would acquire the status of a "person" deserving protection under our Constitution. The Court said it was persuaded that, "the word "person," as used in the Fourteenth Amendment, did not include the unborn."[51] We discuss that issue regarding fetal personhood in detail in following chapter of this book.

Because of this live birth rule, many full-term babies have been intentionally killed while they were being born, even though they were full-term, and so long as the killing was accomplished before the child was fully expelled from the womb, there was no violation of the law.

It is important to understand the fact that wine, even when freshly crushed and pressed and before the fermentation, clarification and aging processes have begun, is truly worthy of proper care and protection from the beginning to the end of the wine-making process. Unless it is allowed to age and mature, it will never become the fine wine that may be its destiny. And so it is with unborn children. They also are worth the wait and deserve to be protected.

As will be discussed in considerable detail in the Chapter 8, the Supreme Court later found it necessary to reevaluate and modify certain aspects of the *Roe* case that proved to be entirely unworkable and clearly in error.

---

51 *Id.* at 158

Privacy Is Supreme

As a basis for its decision in *Roe*, the Court chose to expand significantly the concept of the right to "privacy,"[52] even though it had to admit that "the Constitution does not explicitly mention any right of privacy."[53]

In an effort to understand this "privacy" right upon which *Roe* was decided, it is useful to examine that right in light of its historical development. Privacy matters in earlier cases were rooted in various constitutional provisions, including the First, Fourth, Fifth, Ninth, and Fourteenth Amendments and in what the court called the "penumbras" of the Bill of Rights.

One early case in 1923, called *Meyer v. Nebraska*,[54] determined that the due process clause of the Fourteenth Amendment was violated where an ordinance prohibited the teaching of modern languages other than English. It held that the right of liberty, guaranteed by the Fifth and Fourteenth Amendments, "denotes not merely freedom from bodily restraint but also the right of the individual to contract, to engage in any of the common occupations of life, to acquire useful knowledge, to marry, establish a home and bring up children, to worship God according to the dictates of his own conscience, and generally to enjoy those privileges long recognized at common law as essential to the orderly pursuit of happiness by free men."[55]

Two years later, *Pierce v. Society of Sisters*[56] nullified an Oregon statute requiring children between eight and sixteen years old to attend only public schools. The Court determined that the statute "unreasonably interferes with the liberty of parents and guardians to direct the upbringing and education of children under their control."[57]

Skinner v. Oklahoma,[58] a 1942 case, was cited in *Roe* for its connection with rights of people to procreate. That case involved an Oklahoma statute

---

52 *Id.* at 153

53 *Id.* at 152

54 262 U.S. 390 (1923)

55 *Id.* at 399

56 268 U.S. 510 (1925)

57 *Id.* at 534-535

58 316 U.S. 535 (1942)

that imposed compulsory sterilization (neutering or castration) on a person after three convictions of a felony "involving moral turpitude." In striking down this sterilization law, the U.S. Supreme Court stated:

> We are dealing here with legislation which involves one of the basic civil rights of man. Marriage and procreation are fundamental to the very existence and survival of the race. There is no redemption for the individual whom the law touches. Any experiment which the State conducts is to his irreparable injury. He is forever deprived of a *basic liberty.*[59] (emphasis added)

What is particularly interesting about the *Skinner* case—at least in the context of the later *Roe v. Wade* case—is the fact that *Roe* effectively accomplished a very similar result that was found so constitutionally objectionable in *Skinner*. Since under *Roe* and later cases dealing with the abortion issue, a pregnant woman alone has a fundamental right to choose whether or not to carry her baby to term without interference from anyone or any entity, the father of the child "is forever deprived of a basic liberty" (as declared by the *Skinner* case) to procreate, because he is now left with absolutely no lawful influence in the matter. *Roe v. Wade* and its progeny declared a mother's fundamental right in the procreation process to be eminently superior to the father's rights so as to provide a complete veto over a father's interest in the unborn child,[60] thus depriving the father of the "basic liberty" to procreate, a result openly condemned in *Skinner*.

In fact, although the *Roe* Court cited *Skinner* to support its privacy theory, a case that had guaranteed a person's right to procreate, whether man or woman, the decision in *Roe* completely repudiated any such right of a father, stating flatly at footnote 67 that "Neither in this opinion nor in [a companion case], do we discuss the father's rights, *if any exist* in the constitutional context, in the abortion decision." The same footnote 67 also avoided discussion of parental

---

59 *Id.* at 541

60 See, e.g., *Planned Parenthood of Central Missouri v. Danforth*, 428 U.S 52 (1976)

rights with respect to a pregnant minor by stating that the issue had not been raised in the *Roe* case. In the thirty-one years between *Skinner* and *Roe*, a man (a father) had somehow lost his constitutional "basic liberty" to procreate in favor of a woman's right to abort her child without the father's involvement, and the parental rights espoused in the *Pierce* and *Meyer* cases were also forfeited, as we will see when we examine subsequent cases in Chapter 8 of this book.

So, what difference might exist between a man's constitutional "basic liberty" to procreate that had been declared in *Skinner* and a "fundamental right" of a woman to abort her child that was announced in *Roe*? Is a "fundamental right" weightier than a "basic liberty"? Do women have greater rights under the Constitution than men? Except for Footnote 67, no direct answer was provided in *Roe* to these questions (The Court responds to those issues in later cases which we discuss in Chapter 8). But it is evident that the holding in *Roe* actually violates (by historical legal standards) both the equal protection and due process clauses of the Fourteenth Amendment. The due process clause is offended because a father's "basic liberty" to procreate has been denied without the required due process safeguards of notice and a right to a fair and impartial trial, and the equal protection clause by its flagrant favoring of the rights of women over the rights of men to procreate. Within the same paragraph with the discussion about "basic rights" in *Skinner*, the Court acknowledged that, "Marriage and procreation are *fundamental* to the very existence and survival of the race," indicating clearly that such matters are of equal interest to both sexes. These very critical issues somehow escaped the attention of the 1973 Supreme Court.

Privacy rights were again expanded in 1965 when the Court rendered its decision in *Griswold v. Connecticut*,[61] overturning a Connecticut law that banned the use and dissemination of information concerning the use of contraceptives by married people. The court found that the statute impermissibly invaded the "zone of privacy" of married couples to use contraceptives.[62]

---

61 381 U.S. 479 (1965)

62 *Id*. at 484. The Court stated, "Would we allow the police to search the sacred precincts of marital bedrooms for telltale signs of the use of contraceptives? The very idea is repulsive to the notions of privacy surrounding the marriage relationship."

While *Skinner* had preserved the fundamental right of people, whether male or female, to procreate, *Griswold* now declared that the right to prevent procreation is also a fundamental right in marriage.

The 1967 *Loving v. Virginia* case[63] concerned a law which prohibited the intermarriage of races, thereby denying them the right to privacy in that regard. In striking down the statutes, the Court stated:

> These statutes also deprive the Lovings of liberty without due process of law in violation of the Due Process Clause of the Fourteenth Amendment. The freedom to marry has long been recognized as one of the vital personal rights essential to the orderly pursuit of happiness by free men.[64]

Then, a year before *Roe*, in a case called *Eisenstadt v. Baird*,[65] the Court struck down a Massachusetts statute which allowed the dispensing of contraceptives to married couples but not to singles. The Court stated:

> If the right to privacy means anything, it is the right of the individual, married or single, to be free from unwarranted governmental intrusion into matter so fundamentally affecting a person as the decision whether to bear or beget a child.[66]

The *Eisenstadt* case, dealing again with contraception, held that the right of privacy included the *individual's* right, whether married or single, *male or female*, to use available means to prevent pregnancy. In retrospect, it now appears that the *Griswold* case in 1965, followed by *Eisenstadt* in 1972, set the stage for *Roe v. Wade*. Once the right to prevent conception was deemed "fundamental" for both married and single persons, the issue concerning a right to terminate a pregnancy after conception was sure to be raised to the Supreme

---

63 388 U.S. 1 (1967)
64 *Id.* at 12.
65 405 U.S. 438 (1972)
66 405 U.S. 438, 454

Court. And for those who found little or no value in prenatal life worth protecting, including the Supreme Court, *Roe* was merely a logical extension of the earlier privacy cases.

Note again, however, that *Eisenstadt* discussed this right of privacy as relating to both sexes and declared that, whether male or female, an *individual* should be "free from unwarranted governmental intrusion into matter so fundamentally affecting a person as the decision to bear or beget a child." But in the following year, the *Roe* Court would completely emasculate that right as to the fathers of unborn children, ignoring altogether its own recent precedents. The Court found no reason at all why the government should not intrude into a father's part in the decision to bear or beget children, all of which was contrary to existing legal precedents. It must be noted that there had been no change in the membership of the Supreme Court during 1972 and 1973. The very same justices were responsible for both *Eisenstadt* and *Roe,* despite their contradictory results.

Limits on the Right to Privacy

The right to privacy is cherished and fervently protected in America. But that does not mean that everything we do involves a right to absolute privacy. When our rights impinge on the rights of others, they begin to find their limits. Our Bill of Rights in the Constitution, contained in the first ten amendments, sets forth very important individual rights that restrict government from overreaching into our private lives. But even those rights are not absolute.

The First Amendment, as an example, declares that the people shall have the right to free speech. The government may not silence the voices of its people just because it finds their message disagreeable or unpopular. But, as the Supreme Court has determined, even that right has its limits. Free speech does not encompass the right to insight a riot or to yell "fire" in a crowded auditorium when there is no fire. Neither are businesses allowed to promote their products or services by the use of deceptive speech or outright falsehoods.

The Supreme Court has acknowledged the right to privacy in many ways, as discussed earlier in this chapter. But the very legitimate question surrounding the right to an abortion as a privacy right is whether the Court has gone too far. Does one person's right to privacy exceed another's right to life? How far does one person's right extend once it begins to adversely affect another? Asked in a different way, this critical question demands a thoughtful answer: Does a woman's right to privacy outweigh her own child's right to be born and experience life for itself? Just how fundamental and absolute is this asserted right to privacy?

There is almost always a need to balance the rights of individuals. Sometimes this comes in the form of protecting one person from the actions of another, like the statutes which declare theft to be unlawful and subject to punishment. Sometimes it means that we attempt to protect a person from potentially harmful effects of their own actions. For instance, we have laws that forbid the private use of unauthorized drugs. The law has determined that our right to privacy does not exceed the government's right to control some substances that we may ingest into our bodies. Alcohol usage is limited to adults and drug usage is limited to those whom the government has authorized through prescriptions issued by licensed physicians. And, although some have argued that a person should have the right to take one's own life under certain circumstances, it is beyond argument that one individual should have the unfettered right to take another's life for one's own purposes, absent the need for self-defense or the immediate defense of others. This fits squarely into the issue surrounding abortion.

In this limited context concerning abortion, the Supreme Court made a stark exception. A pregnant woman, and the pregnant woman only, has been given the right to destroy another human being, her own unborn child, and that right is not limited by the need for self-defense or threat of death or serious health concerns, but would apply under any circumstances she determined *privately* to be sufficient. The right to an abortion was proclaimed by the Court to be so important that the individual states within U.S. jurisdiction were effectively denied any authority whatsoever to interfere in that decision. The woman's privacy right to destroy her baby was, in fact, deemed by our most honored legal thinkers to be more important than life itself for her child.

The Woman Called "Roe"

The woman fictitiously named "Roe," Norma McCorvey, was from Dallas County, Texas. She was single and pregnant in 1970 when she brought her federal class action lawsuit, seeking to have criminal abortion statutes declared unconstitutional. Through her attorneys, she claimed she wanted to terminate her pregnancy by means of an abortion "performed by a competent licensed physician, under safe, clinical conditions,"[67] but was prevented from doing so under Texas law because her life was not threatened by the pregnancy and she could not afford to travel to another State for the desired abortion.[68] She specifically challenged the abortion statutes as unconstitutionally vague and asserted that they impermissibly abridged her right of privacy.

The lower federal court found in favor of *Roe* on the basis of the Ninth Amendment because the Texas statutes deprived single women and married couples of their right to choose whether or not to have children.[69] On appeal to the U.S. Supreme Court, this decision was affirmed, although the Supreme Court felt that the right of privacy which governed the case was to be found in the Fourteenth Amendment rather than the Ninth Amendment. The reader should note again that neither amendment deals directly with the issue of privacy.

It is important to understand that Norma McCorvey never aborted her baby. Rather, she gave birth and then allowed her daughter to be adopted. She was, in fact, an outspoken opponent of abortion rights for many years, stating publicly that she deeply regretted her role in *Roe v. Wade* and had dedicated the rest of her life to undoing the harm done by that decision. Norma died on February 18, 2017 at the age of sixty-nine.

---

67 410 U.S. at 120

68 *Id.*

69 Roe v. Wade (1970) 314 F.Supp. 1217 at 1221. The Ninth Amendment provides: "The enumeration in the Constitution, of certain rights shall not be construed to deny or disparage others retained by the people."

Abortion on Demand

Especially disturbing about *Roe v. Wade* is the fact that, although the Court confessed that it had not determined the point at which unborn life begins, it would allow abortion on demand even if it meant human life would be destroyed in the process. After presenting a very lengthy history of abortion, going back to the Persian Empire and including extensive discussion on ancient thoughts about when fetal life begins, but avoiding any in-depth analysis of religious positions taken by the Catholic Church and others on the subject,[70] the Court made this remarkable declaration:

> We need not resolve the difficult question of when life begins. When those trained in the respective disciplines of medicine, philosophy, and theology are unable to arrive at any consensus, the judiciary, at this point in the development of man's knowledge, is not in a position to speculate as to the answer.[71]

As we will see, Congress and other federal courts have had no problem at all in determining the unborn to be living beings from the moment of conception. The Supreme Court, however, claimed ignorance in that very important matter. To acknowledge the existence of life would have greatly curtailed the Court's determined ruling.

Having listed prior privacy cases, including the cases discussed above, noting that "the right [of privacy] has some extension to activities relating to

---

70 The opinion states flatly at page 130 that "Ancient religion did not bar abortion." But the Catholic Church's position on abortion, as well as the Orthodox churches and others, is particularly relevant for a number of important reasons. Theses churches and faiths have existed for approximately twenty centuries and their position on abortion has been steadfast. The Catholic and Orthodox faiths have also had widespread acceptance in many parts of the world during their entire existence. But their teaching runs counter to the Court's decision, which may at least partially explain the Court's determination to relegate any mention of that position to footnote 61, which states only that "For discussions of the development of the Roman Catholic position, see D. Callahan, Abortion: Law, Choice, and Morality 409-447 (1970); Noonan 1."

71 410 U.S. at 159 (emphasis added)

marriage, procreation, contraception, family relationships, and child rearing and education,"[72] and having declared that they need not determine whether an unborn child was living or not, the Court matter-of-factly announced its decision:

> This right of privacy…is broad enough to encompass a woman's decision whether or not to terminate her pregnancy.[73]

When the Supreme Court said, as we quoted above, "We need not resolve the difficult question of when life begins," and then declared without reservation that a woman should have an absolute right to abort the child in her womb, it showed to the world that it did not care whether the child's life had begun or not. The Court was going to do what it had determined to do regardless. The life of the child was irrelevant.

The Justification

The Court found its justification for its ruling in the possible *detriment* to the mother if she were denied the choice to abort her pregnancy. Following the above announcement that the privacy issue was broad enough to encompass the decision for abortion, the Court continues:

> The *detriment* that the State would impose upon the pregnant woman by denying this choice altogether is apparent. Specific and direct harm medically diagnosable even in early pregnancy may be involved. Maternity, or additional offspring, may force upon the woman a distressful life and future. Psychological harm may be imminent. Mental and physical health may be taxed by child care. There is also the distress, for all concerned, associated with the unwanted child, and there is the problem of bringing a child into a family already unable,

---

72 *Id.* at 152 (citations omitted)

73 *Id.* at 153

psychologically and otherwise, to care for it. In other cases, as in this one, the additional difficulties and continuing stigma of unwed motherhood may be involved. All these are factors the woman and her responsible physician necessarily will consider in consultation.[74]

That's it. That is the full extent of the Court's legal justification for declaring a "fundamental right" for women to destroy literally millions of unborn children. It was an exercise of raw judicial power. It was the preeminent example of "legislation from the bench," where the judiciary branch of government usurps constitutional powers reserved to Congress alone. Justice Rehnquist argued against such judicial action in his dissenting opinion, saying that the majority opinion "partakes more of judicial legislation than it does of a determination of the intent of the drafters of the Fourteenth Amendment."[75]

In fact, if it had been known in the mid-1860s that the Supreme Court would later interpret the Fourteenth Amendment as it did in *Roe*, there is little doubt the drafters of the Amendment would have worded it far more succinctly so as to avoid its eventual mischaracterization by the Court. The *Roe* decision was not, by any stretch of the imagination, a reasonable interpretation of the Fourteenth Amendment in the abortion context. The problem is, of course, that there is no other authority under our Constitution having the power to overrule the Supreme Court in its chosen direction.

Take special notice that the Court cited in its reasons for the necessity of abortion rights the *possibility* of "specific and direct harm medically diagnosable," even though that issue was not presented at all by the facts in *Roe v. Wade*. Neither was "psychological harm" alleged as a basis for Roe's appeal. In fact, none of the concerns listed by the Court were presented by the facts of the case. Norma McCorvey's case argued simply that she was unmarried and pregnant; that she wished to terminate her pregnancy by an abortion

---

74 *Roe*, 410 U.S. at 153 (emphasis added)
75 *Id.* At 174.

"performed by a competent, licensed physician, under safe, clinical conditions"; that she was unable to get a "legal" abortion in Texas because her life did not appear to be threatened by the continuation of her pregnancy; and that she could not afford to travel to another jurisdiction in order to secure a legal abortion under safe conditions."[76]

She claimed none of the possible "detriments" that the Court had used to justify its position.

In an obvious attempt to make the right to an abortion appear imminently more necessary than actually existed under the facts, the Supreme Court went far beyond the issues presented by the case in making its decision. The Court became, in fact, a most ardent proponent of abortion rights, inventing on its own this marketing approach designed to sell (or justify) the concept to the public.

This was entirely inappropriate under our system of laws. If a lower court had taken action like this, the Supreme Court would have been obligated by legal standards and professional ethics to overrule it. Just as the majority opinion had made note in Footnote 67 (discussed above) that the issue of parental rights in the abortion context was not presented by the facts of the case and could not therefore be considered in the *Roe* matter, the potential detriments listed and relied upon by the Court in *Roe* as justification for its decision were likewise entirely outside the parameters of the case.

No one denies that pregnancy can cause "detriment" to a woman or a man—if you define detriment in terms of an imposition of unwanted responsibility, inconvenience, or the trials associated with parenthood. Few could fail to have sincere sympathy for a woman faced with an unplanned or unwanted pregnancy. Parenthood does impose considerable responsibility, and the potential for hardships for a mother or father—even perhaps severe hardships—is very real. But we are dealing here with far more substantial issues than possible hardships to a child's parents. For the unborn child, the abortion choice is a matter of life and death in virtually every case. A

76 410 U.S. 113, 120

developing human fetus is a living human being, and any decision to allow its destruction should be considered far more carefully than *Roe v. Wade* would indicate.

It must also be acknowledged that the reasons cited for abortion rights, that is, the "detriments" that may be involved, do not end when a child is born alive. Having given birth, the mother may only then discover that child-rearing has indeed brought on psychological harm, affected mental and/or physical health, or caused distress. Parenthood is not an easy task. Even in the case of a planned and wanted pregnancy, the woman may later discover that she is "unable, psychologically or otherwise," to care for her child. A single woman could learn, after giving birth, that it can be very challenging to face the continuing difficulties and stigma of unwed motherhood.

But would anyone dare assert that under such detrimental circumstances the Supreme Court would be justified in declaring an unfettered constitutional right of a woman to take her child's life once these discoveries were made during the months or years after the child was born? The Court could not sanction such action because that would be capital murder. Yet because the unborn child has not yet experienced live birth, the Court found no reason whatsoever to prevent its killing by "the woman and her responsible physician."[77] The Court was unwilling to voice any exceptions to the rule that a mother should have that absolute discretion. Such logic defies all reason in either ethics or justice.

The Balance of Justice

Take special note: *Roe v. Wade,* as decided by the Supreme Court, did not concern itself with a choice between the life or health of the mother and the life or health of her child. Norma McCorvey specifically alleged that her well-being was not threatened by the pregnancy. Rather, the Court in *Roe* chose to weighed the possible inconvenience or "detriment" of motherhood against the

---

77 410 U.S. 113 at 153.

interest of the State of Texas in enforcing its abortion laws, and it determined which of those two interests were more deserving under the Constitution.

The framing of legal issues is a fine art. It has been observed in legal circles that if one can control how the issue in a case is characterized in words, the case has already been substantially decided because the outcome can be made to appear obvious and necessary from the wording of the issue alone—however biased and manipulative the wording of the issue may be. *Roe v. Wade* is a classic example. Here the Supreme Court chose to frame the issue as a balancing of the asserted individual rights of a pregnant woman to an abortion against the rights of a State government to prohibit abortion with it laws. The clear focus was limited to these two claimed rights while any possible interests of the unborn child itself was left in the distant background virtually unnoticeable.

In the opinion itself, however, Justice Blackmun, writing for the majority, was forced to acknowledged the possibility of fetal rights. He said, "If this suggestion of personhood [of the fetus] is established, the appellant's case, of course, collapses, for the fetus' right to life is then guaranteed by the [Fourteenth] Amendment."[78] Not to be deterred from its chosen course, however, the Court summarily dismissed this very important issue by simply stating that "the unborn have never been recognized in the law as persons *in the whole sense*,"[79] a concept the Court chose not to fully explain or define, but in context, appears to mean that the unborn are not entitled to all of the rights afforded those who have been born alive.

To this we must ask: Is a fetus less a person simply because it has not yet seen the light of day outside the womb? Is that the critical difference—that one must be born alive to have value as a "person in the whole sense"? We will explore that question more thoroughly in Chapter 6 where we consider in detail the abortion issue in terms of whether the fetus should have been recognized as a "person" under the Fourteenth Amendment.

---

78 *Roe*, 410 U.S. at 156-57. The Fourteenth Amendment provides that a person may not be deprived of life, liberty or property without "due process of law."

79 *Id*. at 162 (emphasis added)

Having summarily ended any consideration of the right to life for the unborn by declaring the fetus to be less than a whole person, and therefore not a "person" under the Fourteenth Amendment, the Court then had no difficulty in finding the possible detriment to the mother as more worthy than the interest of the State of Texas in the matter. In this limited context, a State that would impose and enforce its anti-abortion laws was portrayed as an insensitive and callous governmental power that would arbitrarily force upon a poor and powerless pregnant woman a life of misery and poverty.

With the issue presented this way, the Court was able to take the position that it had a duty of the highest order to rescue unfortunate women from those tyrannical State governments, quietly ignoring the fact that literally millions of innocent fetal lives would be destroyed in the process. In fact, as quoted above, the Court began its justification in this way: "*The detriment that the State would impose upon the pregnant woman by denying this choice altogether is apparent.*" That declaration forcefully proclaimed the Supreme Court's perceived obligation to protect women from those dreadful and insensitive State governments.

The Bible takes a very different view of this and places on every person a responsibility to protect innocent human life whenever possible. Proverbs 24:11-12 says:

> Rescue those who are being taken away to death;
> hold back those who are stumbling to the slaughter.
> If you say, "Behold, we did not know this,"
> does not he who weighs the heart perceive it?
> Does not he who keeps watch over your soul know it,
> and will he not repay man according to his work?

Instead of rescuing "those being taken away to death," the Supreme Court looked the other way from the procession of "those who are stumbling to the slaughter." Although the Court said, "We need not resolve the difficult question of when life begins," God weighs the hearts of all those who close their eyes to the injustice, and He will ultimately judge.

The Bible also says:

Open your mouth for the mute,
  for the rights of all who are destitute.
Open your mouth, judge righteously,
  defend the rights of the poor and needy. (Prov. 31:8-9)

Who could be less able to speak for themselves than unborn children? Who is poorer or more in need of a champion for their cause than they? We have the obligation by the Word of God to "open our mouths" and speak up. Did the Court rule fairly in allowing the taking of their fragile lives at the whims of their mothers? Has the Court spoken up for the right to life of unborn children so they may grow and develop and experience God's plan for their lives? The fact is that the Court did precisely the opposite, leading the charge against the unborn.

What Is a Fundamental Right?

Regarding the earlier "privacy cases," the Court recognized that "only personal rights that can be deemed 'fundamental' or 'implicit in the concept of ordered liberty'…are included in this guarantee of personal privacy."[80] The term "fundamental right" is a constitutional term that carries with it very serious legal consequences. As noted in *Roe*:

> Where certain "fundamental rights" are involved, the Court has held that regulation limiting these rights may be justified only by a "compelling state interest"…and that legislative enactments must be narrowly drawn to express only the legitimate state interests at stake.[81]

In other words, once the Supreme Court declared that the right to an abortion was "fundamental," any governmental authority that would then attempt to

80 410 U.S. at 152
81 *Id.* at 155 (citations omitted)

regulate in contravention of that right would be required to demonstrate that it had a "compelling interest" in preventing an abortion—some very critical interest of the highest order that would overwhelmingly outweigh a woman's fundamental privacy right to an abortion.

For the State of Texas, that became an extremely difficult legal task once the "fundamental" label was attached because the Supreme Court had obviously established its agenda in support of unfettered abortion rights. The Court made this task particularly difficult since it denied the fetus any constitutional status as a "person," and because God's Word cannot be used to make such a case. To follow biblical teaching would be a violation of another constitutional provision that no laws may be passed that would tend to establish a particular religion or dictate how one must worship.

As Justice Rehnquist noted in his dissenting opinion in *Roe*, without the "fundamental" label attached to a right, the law in question must ordinarily satisfy only what is called the "rational basis" test to be upheld.[82] Under that weaker test, if the Court could find that Texas lawmakers had a "rational basis" for enacting its abortion law, the law would not be stricken.[83] It is only when the law attempts to limit some "fundamental right" that the Court utilizes the "compelling state interest test" that was applied in *Roe*.[84]

But how was it determined that a woman's right to an abortion was *fundamental*? Justice Blackmun's majority opinion offered no explanation at all and provided no controlling precedent on which to base that conclusion. In Justice Rehnquist's dissenting opinion, however, he pointed out that for a right to be deemed "fundamental," it must be shown that the asserted right is "so rooted in the traditions and conscience of our people as to be ranked as fundamental."[85] He then makes the following argument:

> To reach its result, the Court necessarily has had to find within the scope of the Fourteenth Amendment a right that was apparently

---

82 *Id.* at 173

83 Citing *Williamson v. Lee Optical Co.*, 348 U.S. 483, 491 (1955)

84 410 U.S. at 155 (citations omitted)

85 *Id.* at 174

completely unknown to the drafters of the Amendment. As early as 1821, the first state law dealing directly with abortion was enacted by the Connecticut Legislature. Conn.Stat., Tit. 22, §§ 14, 16. By the time of the adoption of the Fourteenth Amendment in 1868, there were at least 36 laws enacted by state or territorial legislatures limiting abortion. [n1] While many States have amended or updated their laws, 21 of the laws on the books in 1868 remain in effect today. [n2] Indeed, the Texas statute struck down today was, as the majority notes, first enacted in 1857, and "has remained substantially unchanged to the present time" (citation omitted). There apparently was no question concerning the validity of this provision or of any of the other state statutes when the Fourteenth Amendment was adopted. The only conclusion possible from this history is that the drafters did not intend to have the Fourteenth Amendment withdraw from the States the power to legislate with respect to this matter.

These facts, as presented by Justice Rehnquist, an eminent scholar who would become Chief Justice of the Supreme Court, would seem to nullify any claim that the right to abortion should be viewed as fundamental, given the historical legal criteria for that determination. It is obvious by their silence on the matter that the majority was at a complete loss to explain why such a right should be "fundamental."

Faced with the label of "fundamental right" to an abortion, however, the State of Texas, whose abortion laws were challenged in *Roe*,[86] urged the Court to accept its argument that Texas had a "compelling interest" in protecting prenatal life.[87] Texas urged that by enactment of its abortion laws in 1857, laws that had stood for 116 years, it had recognized a fetus as a "person" within the meaning of the Fourteenth Amendment.[88] To support this contention, the scientific facts regarding fetal development were presented.[89] Placing these

---

86 *Id*. at 116
87 *Id*. at 155
88 *Id*. at 156
89 *Id*.

facts before the Court, Texas attempted to address the real issue of when life begins—the issue which, as noted above, should have been critical to the Court's decision. This argument was rejected out of hand. Because the Court had decided not to reach that "difficult question,"[90] the plea by the State of Texas simply fell on deaf ears. Protection for the lives of unborn children was not sufficiently compelling, at least during the first 24 weeks of pregnancy, and only after that point if the woman failed to claim some "health" issue related to the pregnancy.

"Potential Life"

The Court was able, however, to conclude that a fetus represented at least "potential life,"[91] another term it did not define. And, because there was this potentiality, the State's interest in fetal protection might become compelling at some point.[92] That point was determined to be at "viability," which the Court reasoned would be reached in the third trimester.[93] Although it understood (without admitting) that human life may indeed be present prior to "viability," the Court held that it had a duty to protect only that which "presumably has the capacity of meaningful life outside the womb."[94]

The Court again failed to explain just what was meant by the term "meaningful life," but in context it seems fair to conclude that it refers to the fetus' ability to live detached from the nourishment and protection of its mother's womb. If the fetus is not presumed capable of surviving apart from such tender care, it is not worthy of constitutional protection. To say it the other way around, the Court presumed that by the third trimester the child was capable of "meaningful life" outside the womb so that a state's interest in protecting that life could, at that point, become so compelling that the state might deny the mother's right to an abortion.

---

90 *Id*. at 159
91 *Id*. at 154, 159, 162, 164
92 *Id*. at 159
93 *Id*. at 163
94 *Id*.

But that did not end the matter. A state's right to regulate abortions, even after "viability," was not assured by the Court's decision. Although the child had developed to the point where it could be born alive, capable of "meaning- ful life" outside the womb, still the mother would have the right to override the state's compelling interest in protecting the child. Under the *Roe* decision, all she had to do was claim some "detriment" to her own health (very broadly defined) and the State would be powerless to stop the abortion. This decision forcefully demonstrates the fact that the Court truly did not care that it would be sacrificing live human beings on its altar of privacy. The child was expend- able in the Court's view, regardless of its prenatal degree of development, and would remain so until the very moment when it was fully expelled from the womb alive.

It is important to understand that the label "potential life" carried with it no admission by the Court of any "actual life,"[95] even in the third trimester after the stage of "viability" had been reached. With any acknowledgment that the child was a living human being, the Court would have found it very difficult to justify its denial of the fetus as a "person" entitled to its Fourteenth Amendment right to life as the State of Texas had argued.[96] Any admission of fetal personhood prior to complete live birth, regardless of the stage of fetal development, would foreclose the woman's right to terminate her child's life by abortion, except perhaps in cases where a choice was necessary between the life of the mother and the life of the child.

But the mere suggestion that the states could lawfully begin to regulate abortions after the point of "viability" was, without any doubt, a thinly veiled confirmation that the *Roe* Court recognized the fetus was rightfully entitled to status as a "person," at least by that late stage of fetal development. The

---

95 The term "actual life," as used here, is a reference to the question of when fetal life begins – a question which the Court was unable (or unwilling) to answer. The term "po- tential life," as used by the Court, is understood to mean that which precedes "actual life." The Court seems to say that "potential life" somehow develops into "actual life" during the normal course of pregnancy.

96 The Fourteenth Amendment prohibits the taking of one's life, liberty or property with- out due process of law.

"difficult question" of whether fetal life was present had been admitted as to a viable fetus. Why else would the Court theorize that the "compelling state interest test" had been satisfied simply on the basis of viability? Answer: It was because a viable fetus was then acknowledged to be a living human being capable of surviving live birth and continuing its "meaningful life" outside the womb in the same manner as a full-term child. For if an unborn human child has become capable of sustained life beyond the womb, how can its person-hood and constitutional rights under the Fourteenth Amendment be properly denied?

Nevertheless, the Court was still loath to curtail a woman's "fundamental right" to an abortion, even once the child was capable of continued life on its own. Instead, the decision was made that, in addition to the typical exception where a mother's life was in serious danger, the woman's "health" concerns, as determined solely by "the woman and her responsible physician," would be a sufficient concern to override the state's compelling interest in protecting fetal life, notwithstanding viability. By that means, the Court virtually nulli-fied any "compelling interest" that might to asserted by the state in order to protect the child's life in the womb.

When we get to Chapter 9 of this book, however, we will see how utterly devoid of substance the Court's argument was, most notably in regard to the requirement for live birth as a condition for fetal personhood. There we dis-cuss a number of cases resulting in convictions for murder or manslaughter where a criminal assailant had forcefully and violently caused the premature birth of a child and the child had later died as a result of its injuries. As a consequence of its live birth, even though birth was prematurely forced by the assault, the child is deemed in such cases to be a "person" and its death then becomes chargeable as murder or manslaughter although the child may have lived only a short time outside the womb.

These children who were murdered were in no way different from the viable fetuses the *Roe* Court refused to recognize as "persons" in the abortion context. Prior to their deaths, both the murdered and the aborted children had existed peacefully in the nurturing sanctum of their mother's wombs and had reached the stage of viability before being violently removed. Yet due to the simple fact of *live birth* occasioned by the criminal assault, the infant victims of such assaults were deemed to be "persons" so their deaths were lawfully held to constitute murder or manslaughter, subjecting their assailants to severe punishment as violent criminals.

By contrast, a child who is aborted has been denied any opportunity for live birth and, therefore, could never be recognized under *Roe v. Wade* as a "person." Although its death may occur at the very same stage of development as the fetal murder victim, and caused by the violent intentional actions of other human beings, there is no crime, even at the point in time when it could have survived outside the womb, and all because it had not yet experienced the live birth necessary to become a "person."

Under *Roe v.* Wade, the abortion itself is the very thing that prevents live birth for a fetus, which, in turn, prevents its recognition as a "person" under the under the Court's interpretation of the Fourteenth Amendment, thereby foreclosing any constitutional rights it might ever have enjoyed. The life of a fetal victim of criminal attack which caused death after premature birth is viewed by the law as having immense value to society so that punishment for its violent loss of life is appropriate. But when a mother chooses an abortion, her child's life is deemed to have no value whatsoever under the law. Such was the wisdom of the Supreme Court in 1973. This disingenuous scheme was devised by the Court in order to legalize abortion and avoid any issue of criminal wrongdoing by those involved. Under the Court's live birth rule, an unborn child was to be afforded no constitutional protection from abortion harm whenever the mother determined that her child's continued life had become a sufficient nuisance.

As noted in Chapter 4, however, no such rationalization and no such scheming was necessary when it came to protecting the eagle, our symbol of American freedom. The Eagle law recognized without question that the "potential life" of the eagle, existing within the eagle's egg, was simply the necessary prelude to "meaningful life" outside the egg that would naturally follow. If the eagle's egg was worthy of protection on those grounds, there can be no reasonable justification to depart from that same logic concerning the unborn human.

In Summary

- Although the Supreme Court stated that it could not determine when life begins, its decision in *Roe v. Wade* declared that a woman has a "fundamental right" to abort her child until at least the 24th week of gestation. But if the mother claimed any detriment to her own health (very broadly defined), she was allowed to abort her child any time prior to live birth.

- The Court used the concept of "privacy" as its basis for the ruling, even though there is no mention of privacy in the Constitution. The decision overturned abortion statutes that existed in many of the states.

- Under *Roe v.* Wade, the decision to abort an unborn child is strictly a matter between the pregnant woman and her doctor; neither the father of the child nor the state government has a right to interfere in that decision.

- The Court justified its decision by citing possible "detriment" to the woman if she was prevented from having an abortion (health and psychological issues, poverty, stigma of unwed mother, etc.).

- Under *Roe v. Wade,* the unborn child was afforded no constitutional right to life because the unborn were not recognized as "persons in the whole sense."

- The Supreme Court refused to acknowledge the fetus as a "person," deeming it to be mere "potential life," even at a point when the fetus could live on its own outside the womb.

Roe v. Wade, A Supreme Folly

'Twas the Highest of Highest, that Court called Supreme,
  Those Matchless of Magistrates in '73.
They pondered, they puzzled, they figured and thunk,
  Nine justices juggling a judgment of junk.
Those silly old thinkers got awf'ly befuddled,
  Their wits all got squizzled, bedrizzled and fuzzled.
They fancied themselves the most smartest of smart,
  By edicts and dictums their wisdoms impart.
Yet no other judgers had ever judged badder,
  They were prone to portray it as a *privacy* matter!
Tiny humans, defenseless, by their genius they doomed,
  Abandoned and scorned them, fair fruit of the womb.
"They're not <u>really</u> people, they can't be, they're small.
  They're just something *fetal*, not people at all,
At least not in the whole sense," they hemmed and they hawed,
  Tried to make it sound legal but their logic was flawed.
"Potential life only," the Court cried with profusion,
  "Not a person 'til they're born under our Constitution."
How silly, intemp'rate, the Court blustered brutish,
  Their wisdom, their prudence, proved nothing but foolish.
Now millions upon millions, yes, millions and more,
  Done under, asunder, great blunders galore.
Little eyes that won't spy one speckle of light,
  Life could have been wonderful, lovely and bright.
God's image, His likeness, He made them so special,
  For smiling and laughter with dimple and freckle.
By wisdom and wonder, wrapped up with God's grace,
  Each child's a gift to the whole human race.

Loren W. Brown

6

Fetal Personhood and the Fourteenth Amendment

IN THE PRECEDING chapter, we outlined the basic tenets of the *Roe v. Wade* decision. We acknowledged there that the Court's ruling was said to be grounded in its interpretation of the Fourteenth Amendment to the Constitution concerning the rights of the pregnant woman, but the Court offered no detailed discussion of fetal rights. In this chapter, we consider carefully the Fourteenth Amendment and whether the fetus should have been recognized as a "person" deserving of constitutional protection from abortion harm.

Do the Unborn Have Legal Rights?

Having avoided close analysis of the privacy issue itself and precisely how that concept requires that a woman must have a *fundamental right* to an abortion under the Fourteenth Amendment, the majority in *Roe* simply stated its decision in conclusory fashion: "This right of privacy…is broad enough to encompass a woman's decision whether or not to terminate her pregnancy."[97] But if the Court had fairly and sincerely considered the privacy issue as it relates to abortion, counterbalanced with a right to life for the fetus, it would

---

97 410 U.S. at 153

have been forced to scrutinize the issue in far greater detail for the benefit of unborn children.

The *Roe v. Wade* case was a jurisprudential minefield for the Supreme Court because neither the Constitution itself, nor any other existing law, supported the Court's chosen course to allow women an unfettered right to an abortion. That supposed fundamental right was not found in the legal precedents of United States law, as pointed out by Justice Rehnquist in his dissent.[98] As we shall see in this chapter, the opposite is true. As a result, it appears the Court allowed itself to "back in" to its decision, meaning that it appears the Court majority first decided how it wanted to rule in the matter and then set about to fashion a way to justify (rationalize) its decision in the final written opinion, notwithstanding the lack of precedential support. This was, of course, decidedly backward from the way it is supposed to work. Courts in the United States, including the Supreme Court, are customarily required by legal principles to follow binding precedents in reaching their decisions, and that means that they start with research to determine what the settled law is and then apply that law to the case at hand to determine its outcome. This practice is known as the doctrine of *stare decisis* which helps to assure both predictability and continuity in the law. This doctrine is also the recognized ethical means to legal decisions.

By its complete lack of scholarly attention to important details in *Roe*, including the "difficult issue" of when life begins, it is obvious that the Court simply sidestepped critical principles that should have been considered when it determined the case. The result has created tremendous inconsistencies in the laws of this nation, as we will see.

This brings to mind the thoughtful and prophetic dissent by Supreme Court Justice Hon. Benjamin Robbins Curtis in the infamous 1857 matter of *Dred Scott v. Sandford*, in which he said:

[W]hen a strict interpretation of the Constitution, according to the fixed rules which govern the interpretation of laws, is abandoned,

---

98 410 U.S. 113, 174

and the theoretical opinions of individuals are allowed to control its meaning, we have no longer a Constitution; we are under the government of individual men who, for the time being, have power to declare what the Constitution is according to their own views of what it ought to mean.[99]

The Supreme Court chose to utilize the concept of privacy in *Roe v. Wade* as grounds for a woman's constitutional right to an abortion. But the precedents cited relating to the privacy issue (discussed in Chapter 5) had nothing whatsoever to do with the rights and concerns related to unborn children. Neither did any of those cases deal with life or death issues as did *Roe*. Each and every precedent that was used to bolster the Court's reliance on privacy as grounds for its decision dealt strictly with established rights of persons who had been born alive and who, therefore, unquestionably enjoyed constitutional status of "personhood" with all of its attendant privileges. In fact, those earlier decisions all dealt with issues affecting adults only and failed to touch in any manner on rights of children, whether born or unborn.

The Court was forced to acknowledge that the privacy precedents it cited were determined under "inherently different" circumstances than the *Roe* case. It said,

> The pregnant woman cannot be isolated in her privacy. She carries an embryo and, later, a fetus, if one accepts the medical definitions of the developing young in the human uterus. See Dorland's Illustrated Medical Dictionary 478-479, 547 (24th ed.1965). The situation therefore is inherently different from marital intimacy, or bedroom possession of obscene material, or marriage, or procreation, or education, with which Eisenstadt and Griswold, Stanley, Loving, Skinner, and Pierce and Meyer were respectively concerned.[100]

---

99 60 U.S. 393 at 621
100 410 U.S. 113 at 159

Despite such acknowledgement, the Court's discussion of those earlier cases was designed to bolster the illusion that the pregnant woman's right to an abortion was consistent with legal precedents and that the right to privacy should attach in the abortion context without the slightest concern for any possible fetal rights.

A proper analysis of the matter would have required the Court to determine, first and foremost, what rights must be afforded the unborn. Then, if appropriate, find a way to balance the rights of the mother against the rights of the child. Only then could it decide whether the laws of Texas that had been challenged were constitutional. But the issue of the unborn child's right to life and whether that right was guaranteed by the Constitution was swept away summarily. This had to be done before the Court could rule as it was apparently predetermined to do.

To decide, as the Court did, that a mother has a right to abort her fetus, the Court could not acknowledge the unborn as living human beings with rights of their own as "persons" under the Constitution, as the State of Texas had argued. To acknowledge such fetal personhood, while supporting abortion rights, would have openly sanctioned murder in violation of the Fourteenth Amendment's due process clause. To rule as it did, therefore, it was vitally necessary for the Court to find a way to diminish any possible rights of the unborn to the point where they could be essentially ignored.

This was largely accomplished by the declaration that "the unborn have never been recognized in the law as persons *in the whole sense*,"[101] and by the declaration that no prior Supreme Court case had specifically determined the unborn to be "persons" under the Fourteenth Amendment[102] (which, as we will see, was not a true statement). With this done, the Court could then label the unborn as mere "potential life," undeserving of constitutional protection. Whatever rights to life the unborn child might claim, such rights would be altogether dismissed and the Court could then focus solely on the rights of the

---

101 410 U.S. at 162.
102 410 U.S. at 157.

pregnant woman vis-a-vis the laws of the State of Texas that were challenged in the case.

Preexisting Law on Rights of the Unborn

Although the *Roe v. Wade* opinion avoided any serious consideration of the unborn child's rights, the common law in the United States—as well as a host of statutory laws—recognized important fetal rights that were largely ignored by the *Roe* Court. As one example, we find in the 1949 case of *Amann v. Faidy* the following:

> [M]edical authority has recognized long since that the child is in existence from the moment of conception, and for many purposes its existence is recognized by the law. The criminal law recognizes it as a separate entity, and the law of property considers it in being for all purposes which are to its benefit, such as taking by will or descent… All writers who have discussed the problem have joined…in maintaining that the unborn child in the path of an automobile is as much a person in the street as the mother.[103]

The common law courts and numerous state statutes have consistently recognized the rights of the unborn to inherit property when a relative has died. As an example, California Probate Code 6407 provides a common theme: "Relatives of the decedent conceived before the decedent's death but born thereafter inherit as if they had been born in the lifetime of the decedent." Minnesota Statutes Annotated 525.171 - 525.173 hold that a posthumous child (a child conceived prior to the death of its parent, but not yet born) "shall be considered as living at the death of its parent." It is, therefore, not uncommon that a woman and her unborn child may both be lawfully entitled to share the estate of the woman's deceased husband, for example.

---

103 *Amann v. Faidy*, 348 Ill. App. 37, 46 (Ill. App. Ct. 1952).

In light of such laws of inheritance, however, and considering also the rule of *Roe v. Wade*, it is now quite possible that a pregnant woman could be held to answer under both civil and criminal laws if she should misappropriate estate funds belonging to her unborn child, yet be completely innocent of any wrongdoing if she simply aborted her child, terminating its life before it could be born, thereby defeating the child's claim to the estate by reason of the child's death. The unlawful taking of the child's inheritance would be a serious crime if done while the child remained alive in the womb, but preventing the child's inheritance would be perfectly legal if the mother simply aborted and ended the child's life.

In 1969, in the matter of *Wagner v. Finch*,[104] the father of an unborn daughter had deceased prior to her birth. A claim for Social Security benefits was filed on her behalf and that application was initially denied on grounds that she was not a "child" of the deceased at the time of his death because she had not yet been born. The Federal Court of Appeals found, however, that, "Medically speaking, Donna was viable from the instant of conception onward." She was, as a result of this ruling, entitled to Social Security benefits after her father's death even though she was unborn at the time of his death. Current rules governing Social Security benefits still allow claims for benefits on behalf of children born after the death of a parent under specified conditions.[105]

In a New Jersey case, doctors of the mother of an unborn child determined that the mother was likely to experience severe hemorrhaging at some time prior to giving birth, but she did not wish to have a blood transfusion because of her religious beliefs. The hospital petitioned the court for the legal authority to administer transfusions against the mother's will if it became necessary to save the life of either mother or child. The court held that "We are satisfied that the unborn child is entitled to the law's protection and that an appropriate order should be made to insure blood transfusions to the mother

---

104 413 F.2d 267at 268 (5th Cir. 1969).

105 See, e.g., SSR 68-22: Sec. 216(h)(3)(C) – Relationship – Status of Illegitimate Posthumous Child

in the event that they are necessary in the opinion of the physician in charge at the time."[106]

Even before the decision in *Roe v. Wade*, there had been numerous challenges to State abortion laws. In one instance, in the 1970 Ohio case of *Steinberg v. Brown*,[107] the Federal Court of Appeals first quoted a dictionary definition of "life" as being:

> that quality or character [that] distinguishes an animal or a plant from inorganic or dead organic bodies and which is especially manifested by metabolism, growth, reproduction and internal powers of adaptation to the environment. Webster's New International Dictionary of the English Language (2nd ed. 1934).[108]

The court then stated categorically that,

> "Biologically, when the spermatozoon penetrates and fertilizes the ovum, the result is the creation of a new organism which conforms to the definition of life just given....Once human life has commenced, the constitutional protections found in the Fifth and Fourteenth Amendments impose upon the state the duty of safeguarding it."[109]

The federal court in *Steinberg* found ample legal authority for the fact that life begins at the moment of conception. At page 747 of the opinion the court quotes the following three legal conclusions that had been reached concerning the unborn and its beginning of life:

---

106 *Raleigh Fitkin-Paul Morgan Memorial Hospital v. Anderson*, 42 N.J. 421, 201 (1964).
107 321 F.Supp. 741 (D.C. Ohio, 1970)
108 *Id. At 746*
109 *Id.* at 746-747

Biologically speaking, the life of a human being begins at the moment of conception in the mother's womb. 42 Am.Jur.2d, Infants § 2 at p. 9 (1968).

From the viewpoint of the civil law and the law of property, a child *en ventre sa mere* is not only regarded as human being, but as such from the moment of conception * * * which it is in fact. Bonbrest v. Kotz, 65 F. Supp. 138, 140 (D.D.C. 1946).

and

medical authority has recognized long since that the child is in existence from the moment of conception * * W. Prosser, The Law of Torts, § 56 at 355 (3rd ed. 1964).

The ruling in *Steinberg* was entirely consistent with an 1885 Supreme Court case called *Wong Wing v. United States*[110] which determined that "*any and every human being within the jurisdiction of the republic,*" is a "person" for constitutional purposes and is entitled to the protections offered by the Fifth and Fourteenth Amendment due process clauses.[111]

What is particularly important about the established law in the cases discussed above is the fact that the Supreme Court was fully aware of them and even cited the *Steinberg* case in *Roe*,[112] but nevertheless made its boldly false statement that "the unborn have never been recognized in the law as persons in the whole sense."[113]

As we will see in Chapter 9 when we consider whether abortion is murder, the laws of a majority of the states, and now federal law as well, call for murder charges for the unlawful killing of an unborn child, but in keeping with the

---

110 163 U.S. 228 (1895)
111 *Id.* at 242
112 410 U.S. 113, 155
113 410 U.S. at 162.

decision in *Roe v. Wade,* such charges may not be brought if the killing was accomplished with the mother's consent.

The laws and legal decisions referenced above and established prior to *Roe v. Wade* are a mere sampling of the many ways in which the unborn had legal rights that were largely ignored by the *Roe* Court. As noted in the above quotation from *Amann v. Faidy,* both civil and criminal laws protecting fetal rights were in place long before the *Roe* Court took up the issue. The Court was certainly aware of such legal authorities on the issue, but chose either not to acknowledge them or to diminish their significance. Certainly, a discussion of that kind would not have aided the Court in its chosen course of action.

Under federal statutory law passed by Congress in 1994 concerning females sentenced to death for crimes committed, 18 U.S. Code §3596 says, "A sentence of death shall not be carried out upon a woman while she is pregnant." This is an obvious and powerful recognition of the separate life of an innocent unborn child in her womb and the government's obligation to preserve and protect that life. By this law, enacted more than 20 years after *Roe v. Wade,* Congress declared that government should not directly involve itself in the injury or killing of an unborn child, even though the mother herself may be deserving of death. The Supreme Court, however, had found no cause to interfere in a woman's decision to destroy her own fetus.

The Question of Personhood under the Fourteenth Amendment

It is difficult, if not impossible, to construct a logical, orderly and coherent legal explanation of the Court's refusal to declare an unborn child to be a human life worthy of constitutional protection under the Fourteenth Amendment, particularly in view of the wealth of information and historical legal precedents that existed at the time of the *Roe* decision. As noted above, the issue of fetal rights was dealt with summarily and simply swept aside by the Court's declaration that the unborn have never been recognized in the law as persons "in the whole sense." By refusing to acknowledge the unborn as "persons," the Court in *Roe* declared that a fetus is not entitled to protection under the Constitution.

Illegal Aliens Are "Persons"

In 1895, as noted above, the Supreme Court announced in the case of *Wong Wing v. United States,*[114] that for constitutional purposes:

> The term "person," as used in the Fifth Amendment, is broad enough to include *any and every human being within the jurisdiction of the republic.*[115]

This was a binding legal precedent established by the Supreme Court itself that was altogether ignored by the 1973 *Roe* Court.

Both the Fifth and Fourteenth Amendments contain very similar language with respect to due process under the law, both requiring that before the government may deprive a "person" of life, liberty or property, he or she must be afforded "due process," meaning, they must be given notice of any charges against them and a right to a fair and impartial hearing. A "person" under either of these amendments means the same thing. The Fifth Amendment was applied to the federal government while the later Fourteenth Amendment applied some of the same concepts to the state and local governments. The purpose of both is to protect "persons" from arbitrary governmental action that would take away their constitutional rights. While *Wong Wing* was decided under the provisions of the Fifth Amendment, other cases decided under the Fourteenth Amendment have rendered identical results.[116] The rule of *Wong Wing* should have applied with full force in *Roe v. Wade.*

The Fifth Amendment provides, in pertinent part, that no person shall be *"deprived of life, liberty, or property, without due process of law.*

---

114 163 U.S. 228 (1895)

115 *Id.* at 242

116 See, e.g., *Yick Wo v. Hopkins,* 118 U. S. 369

In similar fashion, Section 1 of the Fourteenth Amendment states in its entirety:

> All *persons* born or naturalized in the United States, and subject to the jurisdiction thereof, are citizens of the United States and of the State wherein they reside. No state shall make or enforce any law which shall abridge the privileges and immunities of the citizens of the United States; *nor shall any state deprive any person of life, liberty, or property, without due process of law*; nor deny to any *person* within its jurisdiction the equal protection of the laws.[117]

In the *Wong Wing* case, the Court went so far as to rule that a non-citizen Chinese individual, illegally present in the United States, was a "person" entitled to constitutional rights and could not be deprived of life, liberty or property without due process. So strong was the Court's conviction in that regard that it expressed a desire in *Wong Wing* to expand the concept to its maximum reach, stating with strong conviction that,

> The contention that persons within the territorial jurisdiction of this republic might be beyond the protection of the law was heard with pain on the argument at the bar—in face of the great constitutional amendment which declares that no state shall deny to any person within its jurisdiction the equal protection of the laws. Far nobler was the boast of the great French cardinal who exercised power in the public affairs of France for years that never in all his time did he deny justice to any one. "For fifteen years," such were his words, "while in these hands dwelt empire, the humblest craftsman, the obscurest vassal, the very leper shrinking from the sum, though loathed by charity, might ask for justice."

---

117 Fourteenth Amendment, Section 1

If true justice and protection of the law must be available to all, even the humblest craftsman, the obscurest vassal, the most loathed leper, and including the illegal alien like Wong Wing, can we deny the same to the innocent child in a mother's womb? The Court's judgment in *Wong Wing* that "all human beings existing geographically with the United States" should enjoy the rights guaranteed by the due process clause was expressed as broadly as possible, and that description encompasses, without discussion, unborn human beings.

It is not reasonable nor logical that a non-citizen alien, like Wong Wing, a person illegally in the United States, should have greater rights under our Constitution than a child of American citizens based upon the singular ground that such a child is yet in its mother's womb. As we have seen, that same unborn child can be a rightful heir of its relative's estate and can even be entitled to Social Security benefits. It is treated as a "person" for those and other significant purposes and it has every claim to the same consideration when it comes to the right to life. Under U.S. statutory law, even the life of an unborn child in the womb of a woman sentenced to death is protected. Why should the unborn of other women be denied similar rights?

If Wong Wing, as a non-citizen, had not been physically present in the United States, he would have had no lawful claim to constitutional rights in this country. Had he not been physically present, he would not have been a "person" entitled to such rights even though he had been physically born. Yet, by virtue of his mere physical presence within U.S. territory, the Supreme Court found ample cause to acknowledge his Fourteenth Amendment rights, even without citizenship status and even though he had entered this country illegally.

The unborn child of American parents is not only present in the United States, but has a lawful right to be in the United States by virtue of its mother's right to be present. For that reason, its claim to constitutional status as a "person" is by far superior to that of Wong Wing. Furthermore, under the provisions of the Fourteenth Amendment, an unborn child will automatically be recognized as a "citizen" of the United States immediately at birth,[118]

---

118 Fourteenth Amendment, Section 1, Clause 1

while Wong Wing had no such automatic right to citizenship. Despite these incontrovertible truths, the *Roe* Court determined the unborn child is to be afforded no Fourteenth Amendment rights while, under *Wong Wing*, an individual in the U.S. illegally may claim those precious rights. This defies all manner of logic.

The 1973 Supreme Court never considered the precedential effect of the *Wong Wing* case to the abortion issue in *Roe*, at least it did not discuss that precedent in its written opinion. The Court majority in *Roe* avoided using the term "human being," to describe the unborn, perhaps because it was aware of the *Wong Wing* holding. Instead, the court emphasized the word "person" rather than "human being." But the holding in *Wong Wing* declared that both terms meant the very same thing: A person is a human being; a human being is a person. By the criteria set forth in *Wong Wing*, the unborn child is unquestionably a "person" for purposes of the Fourteenth Amendment because of its existence as a human being and its presence within U.S. jurisdiction.

A Corporation Is a "Person"

From another point of reference, we consider the fact that business corporations are likewise declared to enjoy due process and equal protection rights under the Fourteenth Amendment. In 1888, the Supreme Court held in the case of *Pembina Consolidated Silver Mining Co. v. Pennsylvania* that "A private corporation is included under the designation of "person" in the Fourteenth Amendment to the Constitution, section I."[119] Under federal statutory law, corporate constitutional rights are equally applicable to other business entities as well.[120]

We know with assurance that a corporation is not a "person in the whole sense," not even potentially or partially human, yet the Court has determined its mere corporate existence is sufficient for recognition as a "person" entitled to Fourteenth Amendment protection. By contrast, the *Roe* Court held that

---

119 125 U.S. 181 at 181, (1888); see also *Santa Clara County v. Southern Pacific R. Co.,* 118 U.S. at 396 (1886)

120 See, 1 U.S.C. Section 1, which extends such rights to "corporations, companies, associations, firms, partnerships, societies, and joint stock companies."

a human child is not a "person" entitled to similar constitutional protections until it has been born alive, even though it is a real human being in existence in its mother's womb and present within U.S. territory.

Here we are faced with a very peculiar dichotomy. On the one hand, *Roe v. Wade* requires a human being to experience live birth before being deemed a "person" entitled to constitutional rights. But on the other hand, a corporation (a fictitious person), which is not human and has no possible means of live birth, is immediately recognized as a "person" with Fourteenth Amendment rights by the simple act of filing papers and paying appropriate fees. This means that its life, liberty or property as a corporation cannot be deprived without due process, notwithstanding the fact that it is not a "person in the whole sense." Again, by contrast, the unborn human child is denied such rights on the express ground that it is not a "person in the whole sense." This makes no sense whatever.

A "citizen" is not the same thing as a "person," constitutionally speaking. Although a citizen must also be a person, a person is not necessarily a citizen, as was documented in *Wong Wing*. In none of the cases discussed here (concerning an illegal alien, a corporation, or an unborn child) is the citizenship requirement under the Fourteenth Amendment fully satisfied. None of them can claim *citizenship* under the Fourteenth Amendment on the basis of either live birth or naturalization upon which citizenship in the United States depends. But *personhood,* with its due process rights, has been accorded by the Supreme Court to both the illegal alien and to the corporation while denying the same to the unborn human child. No amount of rationalization can explain away these glaring inconsistencies. Non-citizens, illegal aliens, and fictitious non-human corporations are deemed "persons" with superior rights to the unborn who are natural human beings, lawfully present in the United States, and entitled to citizenship automatically upon birth. Even a serial killer or other violent criminal has due process rights superior to those of an innocent unborn child.

Notice again the glaring inconsistency under these laws: By virtue of inheritance laws, unborn children can inherit and become owners of corporate securities in the same way as people who have been born alive. It is possible under *Roe v. Wade*, therefore, that an unborn child who is not recognized as a "person" and is afforded no Fourteenth Amendment rights at all, may inherit corporate stock and become an owner of a non-human corporate entity which is deemed to be a "person" having constitutional rights superior to the unborn human who owns its stock. The inconsistencies in the law created as a result of *Roe v. Wade* appear limitless.

A corporation's legal existence is strictly determined by the *state law* under which it is incorporated. Once established as a corporate entity by filing appropriate papers and paying required fees in accordance with the law of its issuing state, however, corporate rights under the Fourteenth Amendment attach automatically and immediately. It is state law, not federal law, that determines whether or not a corporation exists. But once it does exist, as determined under state law, the U.S. Supreme Court has recognized it to be a "person" with full rights under the due process clause of the Fourteenth Amendment.

In stark contrast to corporate entities, however, when it comes to the rights of unborn children, the Supreme Court has chosen categorically to nullify all state laws that would acknowledge the unborn human beings to be in existence as "persons", thereby denying the unborn any right to be protected under the Fourteenth Amendment. All of this is due to the woman's supposed right of "privacy" that is not stated in the Constitution and which is held to preempt the rights of what the Court would recognize only as "potential life."

As a result of these rulings, state governments are now granted the absolute right to determine whether a corporation validly exists so as to create a fictitious "person" with rights under the Fourteenth Amendment, but a state is not allowed to determine whether a real human person exists within the womb of a pregnant woman so as to assure the unborn similar rights. This is true even though Supreme Court precedents prior to *Roe v. Wade* held that all human beings within U.S. jurisdiction are entitled to such Fourteenth Amendment rights.

A Child Born Prematurely is a "Person"

As we discussed in the preceding chapter, a fetus born prematurely for any reason, including the result of criminal or other forceful actions, is recognized as a "person" even though it would not normally have been born until some later date. It is recognized as a fetus having no constitutional rights until its birth is made necessary by the emergency circumstances. But its acknowledgment as a "person" having full constitutional rights was instant and automatic upon birth. As a result, the one who wrongfully creates the emergency birth circumstances can be convicted for murder or manslaughter if the child then died as a result of its injuries.

When Is a "Person" Really a "Person?"

It goes without saying that the Court majority in *Roe* had never studied the wonderful and insightful literary works of Dr. Seuss, for if they had, they would have learned the truth of the matter concerning personhood. He clears the matter up succinctly in his book, *Horton Hears a Who*, with a single concise phrase, saying, "A person's a person, no matter how small."[121]

Within the Constitution, the word "person" is used many times but without actually defining it, perhaps because the framers felt the word was self-explanatory, like the definition by Dr. Seuss. The *Roe v. Wade* Court relied heavily upon this lack of clear and concise definition. Without a precise delineation within the Constitution itself as to its meaning, the Court majority found themselves free to then characterize "person" any way they chose concerning the unborn.

After reciting various ways in which the word is used in the Constitution, the majority then argued that "*in nearly all these instances*, the use of the word ["person"] is such that it has application only postnatally."[122] The Court then observes that none of these uses "indicates, *with any assurance*, that it has any

---

121 Dr. Seuss, *Horton Hears a Who* (New York NY: Random House, 1954).
122 410 U.S. at 157

possible pre-natal application."[123] By the use of these (italicized) limiting statements, the Court has admitted, although obtusely, that in some instances the word "person" may truly have application prenatally, that is, to the unborn, but did not wish to openly acknowledge it. The Court would have us believe that by the Constitution's lack of precise definition of "person," that it intended to disregard the unborn altogether, providing them no meaningful right to exist unless they are "wanted" and "planned" by their mothers.

In fact, the word "person" is used fifty-one times within the U.S. Constitution and its twenty-seven amendments, as presently constituted. Of these fifty-one, thirty-five deal almost exclusively with issues concerning adult persons. Of the remaining sixteen instances, fourteen apply to any person that has been born, whether adult or child. The remaining two instances are contained in the Fourteenth Amendment due process and equal protection clauses which could, and most assuredly should, apply to all human beings, whether adult or child, born or unborn. With that in mind, it is particularly noteworthy that in describing the usage of the word "person" in Section 1 of the Fourteenth Amendment, the Court in *Roe* observed only that:

> Section 1 of the Fourteenth Amendment contains three references to "person." The first, in defining "citizens," speaks of "persons born or naturalized in the United States." *The word also appears both in the Due Process Clause and in the Equal Protection Clause.*[124] (emphasis added)

This portion of the Court's written opinion makes it a point to explain that the first use of term "person" in Section 1 is for the purpose of defining what constitutes a "citizen," but the Court then goes on in offhand fashion to acknowledge, with respect to the other two instances, only that, "The word *also appears* both in the Due Process Clause and in the Equal Protection

123 *Id.*
124 410 U.S. at 157.

Clause," without explanation. What is important to understand here is that the *Roe* decision was based on the premise that Roe's Fourteenth Amendment due process rights had been violated by the application of Texas abortion laws, yet here, while the Court offers some explanation concerning the use of the word "person" in the citizenship clause, which has no bearing on the *Roe* decision, it offers no insight at all into the use of the term "person" when used with respect to the due process or equal protection clauses which have particular bearing on the *Roe* case.

In both of these latter uses, the context of the word "person" is such that inclusion of the unborn as "persons" would be quite natural. But by ignoring the context of "person" in the due process and equal protection clauses, as it did, the Court majority spared itself the task of explaining why these important rights should not be interpreted to apply with full force to the unborn children of the United States, all the while knowing full well that this distinct and critical issue was begging for discussion and determination in the case.

The term "citizen" is defined in such a way as to require either live birth or naturalization so that the unborn are not themselves "citizens" since they have experienced neither birth nor naturalization. But that does not foreclose the possibility or the likelihood that the unborn are "persons" even though they are not yet "citizens." Unlike the requirements for citizenship, the Fourteenth Amendment does not precondition personhood status upon either live birth or naturalization. As we discovered in *Wong Wing*, a human being can be a "person" entitled to constitutional rights without being a citizen, even if he or she is in this country illegally; and a corporation is also deemed to be a "person," even though it is not a human being at all and has no capability of live birth. By its ruling that an infant must be born alive to inherit status as a "person," the *Roe* Court inferred that the live birth rule applicable to "citizens" within the Fourteenth Amendment was also intended to apply to define a human "person." No such wording is contained in the Fourteenth Amendment, and no such intent was evidenced by its legislative history. This was a flagrant distortion of the intent of the Fourteenth Amendment.

Other Legal Definitions of "Person" from Federal Law

The Unborn Victims of Violence Act of 2004, passed by the U.S. Congress and signed into law by President George W. Bush on April 1, 2004, provides succinct definition by which to understand the unborn to be "persons" contrary to *Roe v. Wade*. It says it plainly:

> "As used in this section, the term "unborn child" means a child in utero, and the term "child in utero" or "child, who is in utero" means *a member of the species homo sapiens, at any stage of development, who is carried in the womb.*[125]

Roe v. Wade and the Unborn Victims of Violence Act are both federal laws, and both refer to the fetus as unborn children.[126] To be consistent within the framework of our government's laws, therefore, the definitions should agree as to the meaning of terms, particularly when they deal with identical subject matter, that is, the injury or death of an unborn child.

The definition drafted by Congress finds the unborn child to be "a member of the species homo sapiens." One cannot be a member of the species homo sapiens and not also be a human being. They are the very same thing. In fact, the definition given by Congress in the Unborn Victims of Violence Act is in complete agreement with the 1895 U.S. Supreme Court definition in *Wong Wing* that declared the term "person" to mean "any and every *human being* within the jurisdiction of the republic." Both descriptions include the unborn.

Under the Unborn Victims of Violence Act, the injury or death of an "unborn child" is punishable in the same way it would be punishable for an injury to or killing of the mother herself, except that the death penalty may not be imposed for the crime.[127] The terms "unborn child," "child in utero,"

---

125 8 U.S. Code § 1841(d)
126 See, e.g., 410 U.S. at 161-162 where the Court discusses some rights of "unborn children."
127 8 U.S. Code § 1841(c)

and "child, who is in utero" are proclaimed to have identical meanings, each of which include an unborn child "at any stage of development."[128] These definitions leave nothing to guesswork: the unborn (child in utero) is a living human being at every stage of gestation, a person distinguishable from other animals and from the mother herself, and "a member of the species homo sapiens." While the Supreme Court had been unable in 1973 to determine when life begins, Congress had no problem at all in answering that "difficult question."

We do not punish a person for the injury or killing of nonhumans in the same manner as humans. It follows that when a child in utero is unlawfully injured or killed, this federal statute will punish the wrongdoer for such crime because the unborn child is a living human being, a "person," the same as the mother is a person.

We will discuss more fully in a later chapter whether abortion is a form of murder, but for now, it is enough to acknowledge that a large majority of the U.S. States have passed statutes similar in function and purpose as the Unborn Victims of Violence Act, some of which were enacted even before *Roe v. Wade*. These statutes vary somewhat from State to the State, particularly with respect to the stage of infant development in the womb, but all acknowledge and criminalize the killing of the unborn as murder. As now required under *Roe v. Wade*, however, an exception is allowed where the killing was accomplished with the mother's consent.

As a federal law having the right of supremacy over contrary state laws,[129] *Roe v. Wade* actually works to prevent the various states from enforcing important constitutional provisions for the protection of the unborn child. We must remember that it was, in fact, the due process clause of the Fourteenth Amendment upon which the Supreme Court relied in reaching its conclusion in *Roe v. Wade*,[130] a decision that relied upon the "liberty" provision of the due process clause in support of a woman's freedom to abort without governmen-

---

128 8 U.S. Code § 1841(d)

129 U.S. Constitution, Art. VI, Clause 2. (the Supremacy Clause)

130 410 U.S. at 164.

tal intrusion, but ignored the "life" provision that would support the unborn child's right to be born alive.

How much clearer could the drafters of the Fourteenth Amendment have made it? *A person's life shall not be deprived without due process of law.* That could have, and most assuredly should have, been acknowledged to mean that an unborn child could not be denied live birth. But that is not what the *Roe* Court wanted to do.

Due process is far more extensive in its reach than the Supreme Court was willing to acknowledge in *Roe,* although other Federal Court decisions had so acknowledged. The Court's written opinion failed to offer serious discussion as to whether the right to "life" might possibly include the right to be born alive, just as the amendment is understood to prevent the taking of life after birth. The text of the Fourteenth Amendment does not qualify the word "life" in any manner that would limit its usage to postnatal life alone, as the *Roe* majority did its best to assert. It refers only to "life," which is certainly broad enough to include the right of every human being to be born without interference from any other person. Indeed, Congress defined an unborn child in the Unborn Victims of Violence Act as "a member of the species homo sapiens, at any stage of development, who is carried in the womb,"[131] and provided for criminal sanctions for violations of that law.

Opposition by the State of Texas

Another important observation with regard to the Fourteenth Amendment is necessary here. For the purpose of undermining the argument by the State of Texas—specifically that Texas laws had recognized the unborn as "persons" for the purpose of the Fourteenth Amendment and that Texas had a "compelling interest" in protecting the life of the fetus—the Supreme Court in *Roe* countered that argument with the observation that Texas abortion laws, as well as abortion laws of many other states, expressly allowed an exception for abortion when the life of the mother was in jeopardy. That fact, the

---

131 As defined in the Unborn Victims of Violence Act, *supra*

Supreme Court argued, proved that the unborn were not considered "persons" under such state abortion laws because any exception to save the mother and allow the unborn child to be aborted would run afoul of the Fourteenth Amendment and its constitutional prohibition against the taking of life without due process.[132]

But that very shallow argument ignores the fact that our laws consistently recognize exceptions under which a person's life may be taken intentionally without due process when it becomes necessary to protect one's own life or the lives of others. Police and other paramilitary personnel, for example, are not, as agents of the government, required to follow due process procedures in emergency situations where peaceful means to protect themselves or others from violent criminal activity would be useless. They are allowed by the rule of law to use necessary means to prevent serious harm by forceful, even deadly means, if the situation demands it. Under such dangerous circumstances, criminals are still deemed to be "persons" for Fourteenth Amendment purposes, yet an exception to their due process rights may be made by virtue of an emergency.

Likewise, when a pregnant woman's life is at stake, a choice of life or death may be deemed necessary and the judgment as to which life should be protected may be unavoidable, again due to the emergency. Even the Catholic Church, which values all life and has been an outspoken opponent of abortion, makes an exception where a mother's life is directly threatened, as in the case of an ectopic pregnancy or other life-threatening malady.[133]

---

132 410 U.S. 113, Footnote 54.

133 In his *Humanae Vitae*, Pope Paul VI wrote that "The Church, on the contrary, does not at all consider illicit the use of those therapeutic means truly necessary to cure diseases of the organism, even if an impediment to procreation, which may be foreseen, should result therefore, provided such impediment is not, for whatever motive, directly willed." Permission granted by © LIBRERIA EDITRICE VATICANA. Retrieved from http://www.papalencyclicals.net/Paul06/p6humana.htm

A Departure from Our National Foundation

The direction taken by the Supreme Court in *Roe* was a complete departure from the venerable words of our Declaration of Independence that made as its foundation the proclamation that:

> We hold these truths to be self-evident, that all men are created equal, that they are endowed by their Creator with certain unalienable Rights, that among these are Life, Liberty and the pursuit of Happiness.

Of first importance is the fact that our nation's founding fathers declared these things to be *truth*. Many of those same founders were intimately involved in the adoption of the federal constitution. Yet by the Court's decision in *Roe v. Wade*, the majority positively declared that the wording of the Preamble to Declaration of Independence was false, ill-conceived, and in error— that, in fact, the Supreme Court is superior, even to the Creator of men, and that it has endowed itself with authority to deny those God-given "unalienable rights" as it alone sees fit. The Court denounced the concept that "all men are created equal" when it declared the unborn to be less than "persons in the whole sense" created by the hand of God, nothing more than "potential life." For what does it mean to be "created equal," if not that every person has a beginning, a time of creation within the womb, and that he or she is equal to other human beings in the sight of their Creator from that very beginning—even before birth?

Under *Roe v. Wade*, the rights of some individuals to "Life, Liberty and the pursuit of Happiness" is now totally dependent (that is, limited and unequal) since those rights are determined in the sole discretion of another person, a mother who may decide they are simply too much trouble. The right to life, in that sense, is not "unalienable," according to the Supreme Court. Such a right is "nonexistent" at the mother's determination.

The Supreme Court's decision in *Roe v. Wade*, more than any other in the history of the United States, was nothing less than an attempt by the Supreme Court to usurp the authority of God Almighty and render Him irrelevant in the lives of mankind and this nation.

In Summary

- An unborn child of American parents is a human being with far greater claim to constitutional rights than illegal aliens. Yet illegal aliens who are present in the country are deemed to be "persons" having constitutional rights which are denied the unborn under *Roe v. Wade*. Unborn children exist, are legally present within the United States, and if allowed to develop in the womb until live birth, would have the right to become "persons" automatically.

- The unborn must have at least equal, if not greater, rights than corporations which enjoy the constitutional status as "persons." Corporations are not human nor are even potentially human, and they exist only by virtue of a document issued by a state. The unborn are human beings, existing physically and not simply by virtue of a paper document.

- *Roe v. Wade* refused to recognize the unborn as "persons" for Fourteenth Amendment purposes. But other laws, both state and federal, have deemed them to be "persons." The Unborn Victims of Violence Act as well as similar state statutes define the unborn such that its personhood cannot be denied.

- The failure of *Roe v. Wade* to recognize the unborn as "persons" has created irreconcilable inconsistencies in the law which defy all logic.

- The common law, both in England and America, recognized rights of the unborn, including rights of inheritance, the right to compensation for injuries or death, and the rights of protection from criminal assault or unlawful death. These rights beg for recognition of the unborn as "persons."

7

Fetal Personhood and the Thirteenth Amendment

S WE HAVE just seen in the preceding chapter, unborn children have been accorded rights as "persons" in many ways and for a very long time. The Supreme Court had no proper basis in law or fact to deny their status as "persons" under the Fourteenth Amendment. The Thirteenth Amendment was not considered in the *Roe v. Wade* decision, although it clearly has application to that question. For that reason, we take a close look at the abortion issue in this chapter as it relates to the Thirteenth Amendment, the law that abolished slavery within United States jurisdiction.

The Thirteenth Amendment

While *Roe v. Wade* focused primarily on issues related to the Fourteenth Amendment, other arguments could have been presented and the Court itself had the right and opportunity to raise other legal precedents either for or against abortion rights. In that regard, and in keeping with this chapter's continued concentration on the issue of personhood, we now consider the Thirteenth Amendment to the Constitution which abolished slavery within the United States following the Civil War. That historic amendment provides:

Section 1.

Neither slavery nor involuntary servitude, except as a punishment for crime whereof the party shall have been duly convicted, shall exist within the United States, or any place subject to their jurisdiction.

Section 2.

Congress shall have the power to enforce this article by appropriate legislation.

Prior to the adoption of the Thirteenth Amendment in 1865, black slaves were deemed by law to be nothing more than the personal property of their owners, like a horse, a mule, or any other thing that could be owned. The full reach of this ante-bellum federal law was made manifest in the 1857 case of *Dred Scott v. Sanford*.[134] That case, handed down by the U.S. Supreme Court, stated positively that:

> The Constitution of the United States recognises slaves as property, and pledges the Federal Government to protect it. And Congress cannot exercise any more authority over property of that description than it may constitutionally exercise over property of any other kind.[135]

Slaves, according to the 1857 Supreme Court, were the white man's property, nothing more and nothing less, and it was the government's solemn responsibility to preserve and protect those ownership rights. Slaves were certainly not recognized as "persons" entitled to the same rights as the white race. Slave rights were nonexistent. As noted in Chapter 4 of this book, the Court in *Dred Scott* declared that negroes are:

> An inferior order, and altogether unfit to associate with the white race, either in social or political relations; and so far inferior, that they had no rights which the white man was bound to respect.[136]

---

134 60 U.S. 393

135 *Id.* at 395

136 Id. at 407

That declaration was hauntingly similar to the decision in *Roe v. Wade*. In both cases, the judgment was made by our nation's highest court that although unquestionably human in nature, the affected lives were unworthy of constitutional rights because they were somehow lacking in the eyes of the Court's esteemed legal scholars who refused to accede to the fact that such lives were "created equal." Both were determined to be "inferior orders" – the slaves by virtue of their skin color and the unborn on grounds that they have not yet experienced the world outside the womb. Both decisions were exceptionally shortsighted and clearly lacking in either wisdom or compassion.

Because of the *Dred Scott* decision (and the provisions of the original Constitution dealing with slavery as interpreted by the Court in *Dred Scott*), slaves had no rights whatsoever, and slave owners were assured unbounded authority and impunity to deal with their slaves in any manner they saw fit. Even the torture or brutal killing of a slave was deemed appropriate and a matter to be determined at the owner's absolute discretion and without interference from government. No rule of law prohibited such extreme and cruel measures. Under the Supreme Court's holding in the *Dred Scott* case, the owner's right to do such things was protected absolutely by the U.S. Constitution.

Those rights of the slave holders were all made possible by the concept of *ownership* under the law, as noted in *Dred Scott*. If a person owned something, no one, not even the government, had the right to dictate to the owner how that property was to be used or treated.

In 1865, following the Civil War, the Thirteenth Amendment finally declared slavery to be abolished and removed the "property" label from former slaves. It took a constitutional amendment to overrule the original constitutional provisions regarding slavery and the Supreme Court's injudicious written opinion in *Dred Scott*. Although slaves were then freed from bondage, questions concerning their citizenship status and rights under the Constitution were left unanswered. The Fourteenth Amendment, adopted in 1868, less than 3 years later, made certain that people of all races and colors, specifically including former black slaves, are "citizens" entitled to the same rights as the white race, provided they are either "born or naturalized in the United States, and subject to the jurisdiction thereof."[137] Under that amendment, blacks were finally recognized as "persons" entitled to due process and equal protection rights. By these two post-Civil War amendments, the Thirteenth and Fourteenth Amendments, blacks were accorded full status under the Constitution and could no longer be lawfully mistreated as though they were mere chattel property. Only the right to vote was left in question. That right was later provided by the ratification of the Fifteenth Amendment in 1870.

The similarities between the plight of pre-Civil War slaves and unborn children today within U.S. jurisdiction are remarkable. When we now consider abortion in light of the Thirteenth and Fourteenth Amendments, it is appropriate that we ask how the concept of privacy could have been a deciding issue at all in the abortion context. Do privacy rights, which are not mentioned in the Constitution and must be inferred in general from its provisions, trump and override the express and concise constitutional provisions found in the Thirteenth and Fourteenth Amendments? Slave owners had been afforded the right to *privately* determine how to treat or mistreat slaves, but that was finally held to be wrong after many years of suffering.

It took eight years, including a devastating civil war that killed over 600,000 men, followed by formal constitutional amendments, to overcome the Supreme Court's fateful decision in the *Dred Scott* matter. It has now been more than forty years in which nearly 60,000,000 innocent fetal lives have been lost as a result of *Roe v. Wade* through abortion, approximately 100 times the number killed during the Civil War, all of which can again be attributed to the Supreme Court's lack of wisdom and integrity.

Interestingly, and very sobering, is the fact that both *Dred Scott v. Sandford* and *Roe v. Wade* were decisions made by the U.S. Supreme Court and both were determined by a 7 to 2 majority. The absurdity of the *Dred Scott* ruling was eventually acknowledged and corrected, although by ratification of a constitutional amendment and not by the Supreme Court itself. It remains to be seen whether the present day Supreme Court will have the rectitude to admit

---

137 Fourteenth Amendment, Section 1.

its own very similar, yet infinitely more costly blunder in terms of suffering and lives lost.

Does A Woman Really Have A Right to an Abortion?

If a mother chose to kill her child after it was born alive, the government would have an absolute obligation under the Constitution to take prompt action to prosecute and punish the offender because children born alive have always been deemed to be persons "in the whole sense" with Fourteenth Amendment protections the same as adults. Why then is the killing of unborn children judged by different criteria? On what grounds can the law justify a woman's right to intentionally kill her child before it has been born but not after birth?

As we discuss in detail later in this book, a fetus is a separate human being from its mother, yet *Roe v. Wade* determined that the mother has the right to harm, even kill her unborn child without governmental interference and despite any governmental attempt to protect it. Does that mean that by virtue of its presence within her body the mother "owns" her unborn child in the same way a slave was owned as mere property, with rights to treat or mistreat the child in any manner she chooses, including the unrestrained right to destroy its life as the Supreme Court determined? Is an unborn child deemed to be a pregnant woman's "property" until he or she has been born alive, thus granting the mother unfettered discretion to do with it as she finds expedient? She does not "own" the child after it is born, so how could she claim ownership of the child before it is born? A mother has no right to injure or kill her child after it has been born, so how does she have the right to injure or kill her child before it is born? Is the child transformed by some mystical means at birth from her personal property with full ownership rights into a "person" who only then finds recognition for its human existence and protection under our laws?

A woman's body may indeed be considered her own "property" to which she has a considerable right to privacy, but to say that her privacy rights encompass the right to injure or kill her unborn child can be explained in only two possible ways, neither of which finds any proper ground in law or fact. The first would be to declare that the fetal life within her is not a human being at all. This was essentially the basis for the *Roe v. Wade* ruling which held that a fetus is not a "person" under our Constitution. But if that is true, it would mean that the killing of a fetus could never be grounds for a murder conviction against anyone—which is not the case since anyone other than the mother of the child can be convicted of murder under the fetal murder statutes. Those statutes provide for a murder conviction only because a fetus is fully recognized as a human being that has been intentionally killed. Somehow the Supreme Court missed that important concept.

The only other possible explanation requires a determination that the unborn child's life *belongs* to the pregnant woman—and not to the child. That, of course, requires a determination that the unborn child is her personal property, like a slave, and that clearly violates the Thirteenth Amendment to the U.S. Constitution which expressly prohibits slavery. Ownership of human beings as "property" was the foundation upon which slavery was built and has been forever outlawed under the Thirteenth Amendment.

No matter how the issue is analyzed, the *Roe* court was totally without proper grounds for its decision. Its holding in *Roe* is contrary to precedents and runs afoul of any reasonable interpretation of the Constitution, particularly the Thirteenth and Fourteenth Amendments.

In terms of its destructive force, if not its lack of moral integrity, *Roe v. Wade* is clearly the very worst Supreme Court decision in U.S. history. In the 40+ years since it was handed down, the equivalent of nearly one-fifth the number of our nation's population has been summarily executed under the Court's banner of "privacy."

The Abolition of Slavery Protects All Americans

The Thirteenth Amendments was, without contradiction, introduced and ratified for the express purpose of making the freedom and constitutional rights of former slaves unassailable for all time throughout the United States. Its provisions, however, say nothing of skin color or race, although its historical setting and immediate purposes were clear. Former slaves were to be freed and no human beings were ever again to be enslaved anywhere in the United States or its territorial possessions.

It is significant that the prohibitions of this amendment were not limited to any particular race, color or other differences that exist among the inhabitants of American territories. The Amendment was to be a lasting declaration for the benefit of all the people of the nation and in every land under its jurisdiction. This was stated unequivocally in *Hodges v. United States*:[138]

> The meaning of this [Thirteenth Amendment] is as clear as language can make it. The things denounced are slavery and involuntary servitude, and Congress is given power to enforce that denunciation.... It is the denunciation of a condition, and not a declaration in favor of a particular people. It reaches every race and every individual, and if in any respect it commits one race to the nation, it commits every race and every individual thereof.[139]

Because of this fact, no one may argue that the provisions of the Thirteenth Amendment may be applied only for the benefit of the black race or other form of human characterization within the U.S. population. We cannot return blacks to slavery, nor can we enslave any other segment of our populace. Human slave ownership and trafficking, whether for labor, sex, or other invidious purpose, was outlawed absolutely and forever—that is, until *Roe v. Wade.*

Some may argue that the Thirteenth Amendment only forbids forced labor.[140] Certainly, forced labor is contained within the term "involuntary servitude." But the Amendment's prohibition is to both "slavery" and "involuntary servitude." By this wording, we may justly conclude that the two terms

---

138 203 U.S. 1

139 *Id.* at 16-17.

140 See, e.g., McAward, J. (2012). Defining Badges and Incidents of Slavery. *Journal of Constitutional Law*, 14(3), 561.

are not to be taken as synonymous. It is not the practice of Congress to be unnecessarily redundant.

Involuntary servitude naturally describes a form of forced labor or forced service and, in any event, envisions actions and services to be done without choice in the matter. But the word "slavery" may be taken for a much fuller meaning than some would ascribe. For example, the issue of ownership of one person by another was inevitably present under slavery whether or not one was forced to work or serve another. The fetus, and later the infant child of a slave woman, was legally the property of the slave owner by virtue of ownership of the mother, as an example. But the infant could not be forced to work or provide other services until he or she had sufficiently matured. In other cases, one could be held in bondage by the owner, but not forced to work or serve.

Other matters were also present in "slavery" that may not have been adequately described under the term "involuntary servitude." The denial of a slave's freedom of movement, the right to go places and do the things of one's own choosing, would be a form of slavery, but not necessarily a form of forced labor or service. Domination, whether physical, psychological or otherwise, was also present and contained in slavery terminology. These are but examples of the many forms of slavery that may or may not have required forced labor. The point to be made here is the fact that the Thirteenth Amendment was intended to denounce and forbid all such forms of total sovereignty, forceful domination and oppression of one person over another, not simply the abolition of coerced labor. Again, it was the concept of *ownership* that made such brutality and total domination possible under the laws of early America. Abortion, wherever it is found, is a modern day equivalent of that terrible practice.

The Thirteenth Amendment Does Not Support Abortion Rights

It may come as no surprise that pro-abortion advocates claim the Thirteenth Amendment as legal grounds for a woman's abortion rights under *Roe v.*

Wade. This argument has been asserted from the standpoint that to force a woman to continue an unwanted pregnancy is tantamount to the coercion of involuntary servitude in violation of the Thirteenth Amendment. Two primary concerns are suggested: the first having to do with slavery practices dealing with forced reproduction by those held in bondage, and the second suggesting that an unwanted pregnancy requires a woman to involuntarily labor for another person, her unborn child. We deal with these suggestions in that order.

The First Argument: Forced Reproduction

The primary appeal of slavery was certainly the promise of inexpensive labor. And because children of slave women were also deemed to be property of the slave owner, the practice of forced reproduction was sure to find popular acceptance – an opportunity to augment the availability of such cheap labor. Furthermore, under the provisions of the Constitution, Article 1, Section 9, the importation of slaves to America was to end not later than the year 1808. For the plantation slave owner, this meant a possible shortage of laborers unless the slaves they already owned produced more offspring. So women slaves may have been given no choice in the matter but to reproduce as demanded by their owners, thereby subjecting them to a heinous form of slavery based upon forced breeding. With these historical facts in mind, some pro-abortion activists would claim that to deny women the right to an abortion is equivalent to a re-enslavement of women in general, in violation of the Thirteenth Amendment, giving women no choice but to reproduce against their will like the former slaves.[141]

But that argument is entirely unavailing. Forced breeding of slaves would have been achieved through complete domination by those who held slave

---

141 See, e.g., Bowie, S. (2016, January 22) The argument for contraception and abortion rights is an argument against reproductive slavery. Retrieved May 6, 2016, from http://www.sevenbowie.com/2013/01/the-argument-for-contraception-and-abortion-rights-is-an-argument-against-reproductive-slavery/

women in bondage. To engage in forced sexual activity for the purpose of reproduction was not a choice freely made by female slaves. Their plight could be most closely compared to the domination by slave traffickers of today who hold women in bondage and sell their female intimacy for profit, or those who would forcibly rape women for their own personal gratification. That is not the story behind the nearly 60 million abortions that have been performed since 1973 in the United States.

To the contrary, women in our modern, post-slavery era have the benefit of enormous choice with respect to their reproductive rights and sexual activities, all of which are jealously guarded by laws that were unavailable to female slaves who had no rights at all. Unless a woman is forcibly raped or otherwise molested against her will in this day and age, which is the case in a very small percentage of pregnancies, her reproduction has not been forced in any manner. In all but a small percentage of pregnancies, women have chosen and given their consent to the sexual activity with full knowledge that pregnancy is a distinct possibility.

By their Thirteenth Amendment arguments, pro-abortion activists have determined to emphasize the fact of the pregnancy itself and completely ignore the circumstances under which the woman has become pregnant. The presence of a woman's consent to sex is quite significant in the matter. As we will find when we consider the statistics concerning abortion in Chapter 10 of this book, women who choose to abort their children do so primarily as a means of "after-the-fact" birth control where their sexual activity has been voluntary and they have been careless about the use of contraceptive measures. This has no relation to the forced breeding of female slaves. Slaves had no choice in the matter and no ready supply of birth control measures to prevent pregnancy. Their children would themselves be slaves, to be oppressed just as their mothers were oppressed.

There is no comparison between the conditions faced by slave women and the women of America in this day and age regarding reproduction. Women of all races, under all the circumstances of life, and regardless of wealth or social position, are infinitely better off than were slaves, all by virtue of laws that protect them from the tyranny of former evil days.

The Second Argument: Involuntary Servitude

The second argument for abortion rights under the Thirteenth Amendment is likewise grounded in its prohibition against involuntary servitude. In support of this argument, Andrew Koppelman, as an example, quotes various definitions of the term "involuntary servitude" from Supreme Court cases dealing with Thirteenth Amendment issues. Those cases variously define "involuntary servitude" as:

1. The control of the labor and services of one man for the benefit of another, and the absence of a legal right to the disposal of his own person, property and services.[142]
2. A condition of forced compulsory service of one to another.[143]

Or,

3. That control by which the personal service of one man is disposed of or coerced for another's benefit which is the essence of involuntary servitude.[144]

Such language, he claims, demands that a woman must not be forced to "serve at the fetus' command" because she would be serving involuntarily for the fetus' benefit which, he asserts, is prohibited by the Thirteenth Amendment. He concludes that "If citizens may not be forced to surrender control of their persons and services, then women's persons may not be invaded and their service may not be coerced for the benefit of fetuses. It is as simple as that."[145]

---

142 *Plessy v. Ferguson*, 163 U.S. 537, 542 (1896)

143 *Hodges v. United States,* 203 U.S. 1,16 (1906)

144 *Bailey v. Alabama*, 219 U.S. 219, 241 (1911)

145 Koppelman, Andrew, "Forced Labor, Revisited: The Thirteenth Amendment and Abortion" (2010). Faculty Working Papers. Paper 32. http://scholarlycommons.law.north-western.edu/facultyworkingpapers/32 Retrieved from http://scholarlycommons.law.north-western.edu/cgi/viewcontent.cgi?article=1031&context=facultyworkingpapers on May 5, 2016.

It truly is not that simple and his argument is without merit. Several important points must be made in response to this argument. First, when the Supreme Court defined involuntary servitude as "labor and services of one man for the benefit of another" or as "forced compulsory service of one to another," it was, by necessity, discussing the circumstances of two distinct persons: one person who is serving and the other who benefits from those services. In the context of the abortion issue, therefore, Mr. Koppelman's theory demands an acknowledgment of fetal personhood. The pregnant woman, by her continued pregnancy, cannot be said to be involuntarily serving another person if her fetus is not a person. By his argument, Mr. Koppelman has, perhaps inadvertently, challenged the *Roe v. Wade* decision which held that a fetus is not a person. If, as Mr. Koppelman asserts, the fetus really is a person, contrary to *Roe v. Wade,* then the fetus has a right to be protected by the Fourteenth Amendment because its right to life may not then be denied without due process.

Secondly, and as noted above, all but very few women who become pregnant have chosen to engage in sexual intercourse with full knowledge that pregnancy is a distinct possibility. They have not been forced; their pregnancies are the result of free choice in the matter. Having become pregnant under those circumstances, they have no right to claim they are or were forced in any manner.

Third, Mr. Koppelman fails to understand that there are many demands under the law that require people to serve other people, even against their will, but which are not deemed to constitute involuntary servitude as that term is used in the Thirteenth Amendment. Such circumstances exist by virtue of a declared *responsibility* of one person to another or to their government. As an example, parents and other adults having custody of children can be prosecuted for failure to provide adequate food, clothing or shelter to a child in their care. A parent can be prosecuted for failure to pay child support that has been ordered by a court. And a former spouse can be prosecuted for failing to pay alimony as ordered by a court. All of these circumstances may include forced service of one person to another against his or her will, but they do not constitute a violation of the Thirteenth Amendment.

In 1916, the Supreme Court heard the matter of *Butler v. Perry*, a case involving a Florida man who challenged, as a Thirteenth Amendment violation, a state law requiring men to work for up to sixty hours toward maintaining public roads. The appellant had been convicted and sentenced to jail time for refusing to comply. The Court held that the term "involuntary servitude" had to do with the forcing of compulsory labor that would "produce undesirable results," and "certainly was not intended to interdict enforcement of those duties which individuals owe to the state, such as services in the army, militia, on the jury, etc."[146]

In the 1918 case of *Arver v. United States*, the selective service system in the United States was also directly challenged as a violation of the Thirteenth Amendment for its mandatory military service requirement. The Supreme Court also rejected that challenge asserting that such military service constitutes a "supreme and noble duty of contributing to the defense of the rights and honor of the nation as the result of a war declared by the great representative body of the people."[147]

Bearing a child is also a "supreme and noble duty" once a woman has become pregnant. A child's parents, both mother and father, have duties and responsibilities of the highest order to preserve and protect a child in their custody and care. These duties are stronger by far as a consequence of their parentage than the duty of others who are not the child's parent. For that reason, laws intended to protect the unborn should apply with even greater force to parents than to others who might choose to harm the child.

Conclusion Regarding "Personhood" of the Fetus

What pro-abortion advocates attempt to accomplish with their Thirteenth Amendment arguments is to simply turn the tables and place women of today in similar dominant and oppressive roles of former slave owners, roles in which the women themselves, and no one else, utterly dominate and control every

---

146 240 U.S. 328, 332-333
147 245 U.S. 366, 390

aspect of reproduction, including complete domination of their unborn child to the point of having final authority over its life or death. The slave owner, in fact, had such rights under laws that recognized their ownership of the slaves.

With the exception of the government's authority to exercise complete domination and control over one who has been duly convicted of a crime, as provided by the Thirteenth Amendment itself, *Roe v. Wade* and its progeny is the only source of law in the United States that would provide such complete authority by one person over another, separate human being. The father of the unborn child has no say in the matter, the unborn child has no say in the matter, and the State government has very limited say in the matter. The women of today have been declared to have rights even to destroy their human "property," and, supposedly, with the full support of our Constitution as boldly, yet wrongly, declared by the Supreme Court—just as was true under the *Dred Scott* decision with respect to slaves.

If a woman considers her career more important than motherhood, then the child may become expendable under current law. If she wants a boy, but learns the fetus is a girl, she can terminate the fetal life and try again for the boy. If she is simply concerned that her pregnancy will leave her with stretch marks, the abortion doctor can prevent that by terminating her pregnancy. If she breaks up with her boyfriend and her child no longer matters to her, abortion is the answer. If she neglects to use one of the many available birth control measures, an abortion will solve her problem. A woman's "health" concerns, no matter how frivolous or contrived, were deemed sufficient under *Roe v. Wade* to allow her the right to dispose of her child's life without a second thought.

Instead of former laws that sanctioned the bondage of slaves, the Thirteenth Amendment was intended to utterly forbid it in all its sordid forms. No one, whether male or female, black or white, rich or poor, privileged or not, should have the unfettered right to deny another human being of his or her life, liberty, or property without due process of law, absent extreme life or death emergency circumstances, and that should apply with full force for the benefit of an unborn human being.

With its decision in *Roe v. Wade*, the Supreme Court ignored and contradicted the Thirteenth Amendment's abolishment of slavery (the ownership and absolute domination of another human being) as well as the Fourteenth Amendment's rights to due process and equal protection. By removing the right of the states to regulate abortions and protect the unborn, the Supreme Court has, in fact, placed women in legal standing as *owners* of their unborn children as if the children's lives belong to the mother and not to the child, just as surely as the law had done prior to the Thirteenth Amendment when slave owners were granted that legal right over black people. Only the unborn in this day and age are subjected to such cruelty and oppression at the hands of those whom the Supreme Court has placed in a position of total dominance over them.

This cannot be allowed to stand. As the law allowed slavery of the past to exist, the law has now, in fact, enslaved unborn children to the domination and oppression of their mothers who may care too little for their child's well-being or their very fragile lives. The unborn are entitled to rights under our Constitution because they are just as human, just as much a person, as any other.

In Summary

- The fetus is a separate and distinct human being and is not a part of the woman's own body. The rights granted to women by the Supreme Court to abort their own fetus, is a blatant violation of the Thirteenth Amendment's prohibition of slavery.
- A woman does not "own" her unborn child any more than she "owns" her child after live birth. Lack of ownership forecloses her right to complete control over her fetus.
- The life of the fetus does not belong to the mother and she should not have a right to control that which is not her own.
- Since the premeditated killing of a fetus is considered murder if committed by one other than the mother, such killing must be also recognized as murder when the mother kills her own child by abortion.

8

The Court's Later Decisions

Almost immediately after the Roe v. Wade decision, various States began devising ways to reduce Roe's very devastating effects. Although the central holding of Roe remained essentially unchanged for many years, the result of subsequent rulings has clarified and, in some cases, undermined and diminished certain aspects of abortion rights to the extent that the Supreme Court has now acknowledged that the original trimester approach of the Roe decision was in error. Nevertheless, abortion is still a woman's fundamental right, although not precisely to the same degree.

The Initial Challenges to Roe v. Wade

Within two years of the *Roe* decision, the Court received its first challenge in *Bigelow v. Virginia*.[148] This 1975 case struck down a Virginia statute that made it a misdemeanor for "any person, by publication, lecture, advertisement, or by the sale or circulation of any publication, or in any other manner, [to encourage or prompt] the procuring of abortion or miscarriage."[149] A director and managing editor of the Virginia Weekly newspaper had been

---

148 421 U.S. 809 (1975)
149 Va. Code Ann. §§ 18.1-63 (1960)

convicted under the statute after the newspaper published an advertisement for an organization whose activities included referring women to facilities that provided abortions. The Court found that the statute violated the newspaper's First Amendment rights and further ruled that the advertisement in question provided important "public interest" information.

Connecticut v. Menillo,[150] decided later in 1975, determined that state law could deny non-physicians the right to perform abortions.

During the following year, 1976, two abortion doctors in Missouri filed an action challenging a state statute that prevented the use of Medicaid funds for abortions, even though some of the abortions were "medically indicated." In this case, entitled *Singleton v. Wulff*,[151] the trial court dismissed the action, finding that the doctors lacked standing—that is, that the doctors had no legal interest in the matter and, therefore, no lawful right to interfere. The Supreme Court, however, considered the matter and held that physicians did have standing and could challenge such statutes on behalf of their patients. As a result of this holding, pro-abortion forces gained considerable legal power. Although few individual women could afford to challenge the laws on their own behalf, especially as far as the Supreme Court, the physicians (who stood to profit from providing abortions) could join forces to promote their collective political and monetary interests.

Spousal Consent Issues

The year 1976 also brought challenges to state statutes which required consent by the woman's husband before an abortion could be obtained. In *Planned Parenthood of Central Missouri v. Danforth*,[152] Missouri law was challenged where it required prior written consent of the woman's spouse during the first 12 weeks of pregnancy unless a licensed physician certified the matter

---

150 423 U.S. 9 (1975)

151 428 U.S. 106 (1976)

152 428 U.S 52 (1976)

as necessary to preserve the mother's life. This spousal consent provision was determined to run afoul of the Constitution and the central holding in *Roe*.

Missouri had argued that the statute was written with the intent to uphold marriage as an honored institution and "that any major change in family status is a decision to be made jointly by the marriage partners."[153]

To further its argument, Missouri called attention to other family matters which generally required consent of both spouses. These included, for example, allowing the adoption of a child that had been born in wedlock, the artificial insemination of a woman to bring about conception, cases where either marriage partner was to be sterilized, and in matters concerning the disposition of real property. The Court, however, rejected this argument and saw the abortion issue as a quite different one. It stated:

> We recognize, of course, that, when a woman, with the approval of her physician but without the approval of her husband, decides to terminate her pregnancy, it could be said that she is acting unilaterally. The obvious fact is that, when the wife and the husband disagree on this decision, the view of only one of the two marriage partners can prevail. Inasmuch as it is the woman who physically bears the child and who is the more directly and immediately affected by the pregnancy, as between the two, the balance weighs in her favor.[154]

The Court then announced its decision that the statute requiring spousal consent was unconstitutional.[155] Note again that the Court centers its attention only on the interests of the woman and her husband. The fetus is of no concern at all. In fact, the *Danforth* decision also overturned a provision in Missouri's law that attempted to ban the use of saline amniocentesis as an abortion procedure, a method which slowly poisons the fetus with salt that

---

153 428 U.S. at 68
154 428 U.S. at 71
155 *Id.*

is injected into the womb,[156] further underscoring the Court's contempt for prenatal life.

Sixteen years later, in 1992, this issue was addressed again in the matter of *Planned Parenthood of Southern Pennsylvania v. Casey*,[157] in which a Pennsylvania law required a woman to indicate in some manner that she had notified her husband of her intention to abort the fetus. Once again, the Court ruled against the husband's interest, saying:

> Section 3209's husband notification provision constitutes an undue burden and is therefore invalid. A significant number of women will likely be prevented from obtaining an abortion just as surely as if Pennsylvania had outlawed the procedure entirely. The fact that § 3209 may affect fewer than one percent of women seeking abortions does not save it from facial invalidity, since the proper focus of constitutional inquiry is the group for whom the law is a restriction, not the group for whom it is irrelevant. Furthermore, *it cannot be claimed that the father's interest in the fetus' welfare is equal to the mother's protected liberty*, since it is an inescapable biological fact that state regulation with respect to the fetus will have a far greater impact on the pregnant woman's bodily integrity than it will on the husband. Section 3209 embodies a view of marriage consonant with the common-law status of married women but repugnant to this Court's present understanding of marriage and of the nature of the rights secured by the Constitution.[158]

Just as *Roe* disregarded any consideration of the fetus' right to life, these cases similarly eliminated any right of the husband concerning the safety and well-being of his child. The husband not only lacks any standing to veto his wife's decision, he has no right even to be informed of her intention to abort. In fact,

---

156 Id. at 79
157 505 U.S. 833 (1992)
158 *Id.* at 837

this decision asserted that the father's interest in the unborn child is "irrele-vant," which answers the question raised in Chapter 5 of this book concerning the *Skinner* case as to whether a woman's "fundament right" to an abortion is a greater right than a man's "basic liberty" to procreate. The italicized por-tion in the quoted language above expressly resolves that issue. Notice also the Court's language dispensing with any consideration of fetal rights, again weighing only the interests of the father versus the interests of the mother.

The Parental Consent/Notification Cases

Turning now to the issue of parental consent for an unmarried woman under age 18, the laws of the state of Missouri that were challenged in *Planned Parenthood of Central Missouri v. Danforth*[159] (discussed above) had also pro-vided that parental consent must be given before an unmarried minor could obtain an abortion during the first 12 weeks of pregnancy. Striking down that provision of Missouri law, the Supreme Court said:

> The State may not constitutionally impose a blanket parental con-sent requirement...as a condition for an unmarried minor's abortion during the first 12 weeks of her pregnancy for substantially the same reasons as in the case of the spousal consent provision, there being no significant state interests, whether to safeguard the family unit and parental authority or other vise, in conditioning an abortion on the consent of a parent with respect to the under-18-year-old pregnant minor. As stressed in Roe, "the abortion decision and its effectuation must be left to the medical judgment of the pregnant woman's attend-ing physician."[160]

Here the Court underscores its intention that the abortion doctor, the one who stands to benefit financially from the minor's decision to abort her fetus,

---

159 428 U.S. 52 (1976)
160 *Id.* at 53-54

who has no familial interest in the young woman's future wellbeing, and who will never be required to deal with adverse consequences of the abortion decision, should and does have rights superior to the girl's own parents. Under this holding, the parents of a pregnant young woman could be kept entirely ignorant of her pregnancy while the abortion doctor substitutes his own judgment for theirs, despite the doctor's obvious conflict of interest. This appears to be in direct conflict with *Pierce v. Society of Sisters* (discussed in Chapter 5 as one of the privacy precedents) which held that parents have an expressed right to "direct the upbringing and education of children under their control."[161]

Bellotti v. Baird,[162] decided the same day as the *Danforth* case in 1976, considered and upheld a Massachusetts law that required parental consent to a minor's abortion, but also provided that "if one or both of the [minor's] parents refuse...consent, consent may be obtained by order of a judge...for good cause shown." This decision was unanimous. The written opinion noted that the Massachusetts law "permits a minor capable of giving informed consent to obtain a court order allowing abortion without parental consultation, and further permits even a minor incapable of giving informed consent to obtain an abortion order without parental consultation where it is shown that abortion would be in her best interests." However, because the law in question had not yet been reviewed by Massachusetts' highest court, the U.S. Supreme Court determined to wait until the State had interpreted its own statute before ruling on other controversial provisions of the law.

The issue was revisited in 1979 in another U.S. Supreme Court case by the same name,[163] referred to as *Bellotti v. Baird II.* By this time, the Massachusetts highest court had determined that parental consent was required for every nonemergency abortion so long as a parent was available, and, further, that a parent must be notified of any judicial proceedings if the minor attempted to bypass the parental consent requirement and obtain a judge's consent to an abortion. It had also been ruled that a court could refuse consent if it found

---

161 268 U.S. 510 at 534-535

162 428 U.S. 132 (1976)

163 443 U.S. 622 (1979)

that either a parent's decision or that of the court's was a better decision than that of the minor concerning the abortion.

On the basis of these determinations, the U.S. Supreme Court determined that the statute, as interpreted by Massachusetts, was unconstitutional for two reasons. First, it found that even though a minor might be capable of making her own decision independently, judicial consent could be withheld. And, second, the law required parental notification in every case. Even if the minor attempted to bypass the parental consent requirement and obtain the court's authorization, the parents had to be notified of such court proceeding. These provisions rendered the law unconstitutional because they unduly burdened the minor's right to seek an abortion.[164] The case did, however, indicate that some requirement for parental involvement could be constitutional. The court stated:

> If a State decides to require a pregnant minor to obtain one or both parents' consent to an abortion, it also must provide an alternative procedure whereby authorization for the abortion can be obtained. A pregnant minor is entitled in such a proceeding to show either that she is mature enough and well enough informed to make her abortion decision, in consultation with her physician, independently of her parents' wishes, or that, even if she is not able to make this decision independently, the desired abortion would be in her best interests. Such a procedure must ensure that the provision requiring parental consent does not, in fact, amount to an impermissible "absolute, and possibly arbitrary, veto."[165]

In 1981, the Supreme Court heard and decided the case of *H.L. v. Matheson*,[166] concerning a Utah statute that required a physician to "notify, if possible" a dependent, unmarried minor's parents or guardians that the minor intended

---

164 *Id.* at 623
165 *Id.*
166 450 U.S. 398 (1981)

to obtain an abortion. The Court first noted that the U.S. District Court for Utah had already ruled that the statute did not apply to emancipated minors, and was, therefore, not unconstitutional as applied.[167] Whether it would be unconstitutional as applied to a demonstrably mature minor was not before the Court at that time and the Court had no reason to comment on that issue.[168] So the only issue to be decided in the case was whether the statute requiring a doctor's notification to the parents "if possible" was constitutional. The Court first cited the 1976 *Danforth* case for the proposition that a state cannot constitutionally veto the decision of a doctor and the pregnant woman concerning an abortion.[169] But the Court was then reminded that it had emphasized in *Danforth* that "that our holding…does not suggest that every minor, regardless of age or maturity, may give effective consent for termination of her pregnancy."[170] With that in mind, the Court upheld the Utah law, finding that the statute served the important considerations of family integrity and the protection of adolescents. As applied to "immature and dependent minors," the law served a…

…significant state interest by providing an opportunity for parents to supply essential medical and other information to a physician. The medical, emotional, and psychological consequences of an abortion are serious and can be lasting; this is particularly so when the patient is immature. An adequate medical and psychological case history is important to the physician. Parents can provide medical and psychological data, refer the physician to other sources of medical history, such as family physicians, and authorize family physicians to give relevant data.[171]

---

167 *Id*. at 406
168 *Id*.
169 *Id*. at 406
170 *Id*. at 408, citing 428 U.S. at 75
171 *Id*. at 411

It must be observed, parenthetically, that the Court's view of parental consent and/or notification had, in fact, changed since its 1976 decision in *Danforth.* In *Danforth,* the Court had determined that there existed "no significant state interests, whether to safeguard the family unit and parental authority or other vise, in conditioning an abortion on the consent of a parent with respect to the under-18-year-old pregnant minor."[172] Yet by 1981, in *H.L. v. Matheson,* the Court was willing to acknowledge a "significant state interest," as noted immediately above, due to the serious "medical, emotional and psychological consequences of abortion." Now, in this later decision, the Court recognized the State's interest in "providing an opportunity for parents to supply essential medical and other information to a physician." The holding falls short, however, of providing parents with any form of veto power over the wishes of the minor and her abortion doctor.

Two years later, however, the Court again invalidated a provision in an ordinance adopted by the City of Akron[173] in which minors under the age of 15 years were, without exception, deemed too immature to decide for themselves whether or not to abort, and further, that it was improper for the law to assume that it was never in a minor's best interest to obtain an abortion without parental consent.[174]

The 1990 *Hodgson v. Minnesota*[175] case revisited the issue of parental notification. The Minnesota law required notice to be given to both parents of a minor seeking an abortion. The Court observed that the statute in question failed to consider the fact that half of Minnesota children lived without both of their biological parents. However, the law provided that the parental notification requirement could be avoided if the pregnant minor signed a declaration that she was a victim of abuse or neglect by her parents. That declaration would then be delivered to the state authorities. The court could then authorize the abortion to proceed without the required parental notice, provided the minor was able to prove she was "mature and capable of giving informed

---

172   428 U.S. at 53

173   City of Akron v. Akron Center for Reproductive Health, 462 U.S. 416 (1983)

174   *Id.* at 439-440

175   497 U.S. 417 (1990)

consent" or that the abortion would be in her best interest without the two-parent notice. The U.S. Supreme Court determined that without the judicial bypass provision the statute would be unconstitutional, but that the bypass saved it. The Court then upheld the statute in its entirety, stating:

> Minnesota has done nothing other than attempt to fit its legislation into the framework that we have supplied in our previous cases. The simple fact is that our decision in *Bellotti II* stands for the proposition that a two-parent consent law is constitutional if it provides for a sufficient judicial bypass alternative, and it requires us to sustain the statute before us here.[176]

In a companion case decided at the same time as *Hodgson,* the Court upheld an Ohio statute in *Ohio v. Akron Center for Reproductive Health*[177] that required minors either to notify one parent or seek the approval of a court. The question here was whether too many burdens were placed in the way of the minor who sought an abortion. The Ohio law made it a crime for any person to perform an abortion on an unmarried, unemancipated minor unless he or she first provided timely notice to one of the minor's parents or an order by the juvenile court was issued authorizing the minor to consent. To bypass the parental notification, the minor was required to present clear and convincing proof to the court that she was sufficiently mature and could make the decision on her own...based on sufficient information and that a parent had abused her physically, emotionally or sexually, or that notice to her parents was not in her best interests.[178]

As a result of these cases, the current standard for determining whether parental notification is required is centered on whether there is a reasonable alternative available, meaning an alternative that does not unduly burden the young woman's availability to an abortion. This available "bypass" procedure

---

176 *Id.* at 497-498
177 497 U.S. 502 (1990)
178 *Id.* at 502

is critical to the issue. Without it, the state's restrictions will certainly be stricken upon Supreme Court review.

"Waiting Period" Requirements

The issue of whether a mandatory waiting period for an abortion would be allowed was first addressed in the 1983 case of *City of Akron v. Akron Center for Reproductive Health.*[179] There, a city ordinance required a woman seeking an abortion to wait 24 hours after the first visit to an abortion clinic before the procedure could be performed. In striking down this ordinance, the Supreme Court stated:

> We find that Akron has failed to demonstrate that any legitimate state interest is furthered by an arbitrary and inflexible waiting period. There is no evidence suggesting that the abortion procedure will be performed more safely. Nor are we convinced that the State's legitimate concern that the woman's decision be informed is reasonably served by requiring a 24-hour delay as a matter of course. The decision whether to proceed with an abortion is one as to which it is important to "affor[d] the physician adequate discretion in the exercise of his medical judgment." *Colautti v. Franklin,* 439 U.S. at 439 U. S. 387. In accordance with the ethical standards of the profession, a physician will advise the patient to defer the abortion when he thinks this will be beneficial to her (footnote omitted). But if a woman, after appropriate counseling, is prepared to give her written informed consent and proceed with the abortion, a State may not demand that she delay the effectuation of that decision.[180]

Given the obvious conflict of interest the abortion doctor has in such a situation, it is certainly not clear that the doctor "will advise the patient to defer the

---

179 462 U.S. 416 (1983)
180 462 U.S. 450-451

abortion when he thinks this will be beneficial to her," particularly when the opportunity to make money is present. The doctor's "medical judgment" may very likely be influenced to his or her own personal benefit. The Court once again failed to comment on this very obvious issue and presumed, without discussion, that the abortion practitioner would act in accordance with "ethical standards of the profession." The Court ignored completely the fact that many physicians view abortions as patently unethical and a violation of the Hippocratic Oath,[181] and, by extension, that abortion doctors may be considered unethical by definition.

In 1990, just seven years later, in *Hodgson v. Minnesota*,[182] the Court considered and upheld a 48-hour waiting period for minors after the minor's parents had been notified. This time the Court found that:

> To the extent that [the state statute] requires that a minor wait 48 hours after notifying a single parent of her intention to obtain an abortion, it reasonably furthers the legitimate state interest in ensuring that the minor's decision is knowing and intelligent. The State may properly enact laws designed to aid a parent who has assumed "primary responsibility" for a minor's wellbeing in discharging that responsibility, and the 48-hour delay provides the parent the opportunity to consult with his or her spouse and a family physician, to inquire into the competency of the abortion doctor, and to discuss the decision's religious and moral implications with the minor and provide needed guidance and counsel as to how the decision will affect her future. The delay imposes only a minimal burden on the minor's rights. The statute does not impose any period of delay if the parents

---

181 The Court acknowledged that the Hippocratic Oath, attributed to Hippocrates the Greek physician, "has stood so long as the ethical guide of the medical profession" and provides that "I will give no deadly medicine to anyone if asked, nor suggest any such counsel; and in like manner I will not give to a woman a pessary to produce abortion," or, alternatively, "I will neither give a deadly drug to anybody if asked for it, nor will I make a suggestion to this effect. Similarly, I will not give to a woman an abortive remedy." 410 U.S. at 131.
182　497 U.S. 417 (1990)

or a court, acting *in loco parentis,* provide consent to the procedure. Moreover, the record reveals that the waiting period may run concurrently with the time necessary to make an appointment for the abortion.[183]

Note that, in the quotation above, the Court states plainly that the question of an abortion doctor's competency is a valid concern. Until this point, the Court had uniformly assumed that abortion doctors are both competent and unquestionably ethical. It is further noteworthy that the Court here recognizes that there are "religious and moral implications" to the abortion decision. Having now determined that a waiting period was both reasonable and beneficial for minors, the Court was forced to reconsider and overrule its own 1983 holding in the *Akron* case.[184]

In *Planned Parenthood of Southern Pennsylvania v. Casey,*[185] decided in 1992, a challenged provision of Pennsylvania law requiring a 24-hour waiting period for adult women was upheld. That statute required that a woman considering an abortion must be first offered truthful information about the abortion decision and that the abortion procedure be delayed for 24 hours except in cases of emergency. Upon reflection, the Court determined that a waiting period of 24 hours did not present an undue burden on the woman's right to an abortion. The Court said:

> Our analysis of Pennsylvania's 24-hour waiting period between the provision of the information deemed necessary to informed consent and the performance of an abortion under the undue burden standard requires us to reconsider the premise behind the decision in Akron I invalidating a parallel requirement. In Akron I we said: "Nor are we convinced that the State's legitimate concern that the woman's decision be informed is reasonably served by requiring a 24-hour delay as

---

183 *Id.* at 419-420
184 462 U.S. 416 (1983)
185 505 U.S. 833 (1992)

a matter of course." 462 U. S., at 450. *We consider that conclusion to be wrong.* The idea that important decisions will be more informed and deliberate if they follow some period of reflection does not strike us as unreasonable, particularly where the statute directs that important information become part of the background of the decision. The statute, as construed by the Court of Appeals, permits avoidance of the waiting period in the event of a medical emergency and the record evidence shows that in the vast majority of cases, a 24-hour delay does not create any appreciable health risk. In theory, at least, the waiting period is a reasonable measure to implement the State's interest in *protecting the life of the unborn*, a measure that does not amount to an undue burden.[186] (emphasis added)

Here the Court acknowledged the very serious nature of the abortion decision and the importance of careful consideration the waiting period affords, regardless of the woman's age. Even more importantly, the Court acknowledged the State has a legitimate interest "in protecting the *life* of the unborn," a consideration it had sidestepped completely in *Roe* by referring to the fetus as mere "potential life." Having acknowledged that a fetus is a living being, however, the Court was still unwilling to grant it personhood status, so the fetus was still lacking any Fourteenth Amendment rights to "life."

Informed Consent

In *Planned Parenthood v. Danforth*,[187] decided in 1976, the challenged Missouri statute had included a provision requiring that:

A woman, prior to submitting to an abortion during the first 12 weeks of pregnancy, must certify in writing her consent to the procedure

---

186 505 U.S. at 885
187 428 U.S. 52 (1976)

and "that her consent is informed and freely given, and is not the result of coercion."[188]

Planned Parenthood argued that the statute violated a woman's rights "by imposing an extra layer and burden of regulation on the abortion decision" and because "the provision is overbroad and vague."[189] The Court, however, saw no reason to invalidate the statute. Instead, they found adequate cause to uphold it, saying:

> The decision to abort, indeed, is an important and often a stressful one, and it is desirable and imperative that it be made with full knowledge of its nature and consequences. The woman is the one primarily concerned, and her awareness of the decision and its significance may be assured, constitutionally, by the State to the extent of requiring her prior written consent. ¶We could not say that a requirement imposed by the State that a prior written consent for any surgery would be unconstitutional.[190]

It should be noted, again, that the "woman is the one primarily concerned" and that neither the life of the unborn child nor the interest of the father need be considered.

In 1983, the Court took a backward step in *City of Akron v. Akron Center for Reproductive Health.*[191] In that case, a statute required that prior to an abortion the attending physician must…

> …inform his patient of the status of her pregnancy, the development of her fetus, the date of possible viability, the physical and emotional complications that may result from an abortion, and the availability of agencies to provide her with assistance and information with

---

188 428 U.S. at 65
189 *Id.* at 66
190 428 U.S. at 67
191 462 U.S. 416 (1983)

respect to birth control, adoption, and childbirth...and also inform her of the particular risks associated with her pregnancy and the abortion technique to be employed.[192]

Although this statute, like the Missouri statute in *Danforth*, required written consent of the woman, the Court believed the statute went too far. The Court invalidated the law, apparently convinced that the provisions of the statute were designed to influence a woman in favor of maintaining her pregnancy. It said:

> The validity of an informed consent requirement thus rests on the State's interest in protecting the health of the pregnant woman. The decision to have an abortion has "implications far broader than those associated with most other kinds of medical treatment," *Bellotti II,* 443 U.S. at 443 U. S. 649 (plurality opinion), and thus the State legitimately may seek to ensure that it has been made "in the light of all attendant circumstances – psychological and emotional as well as physical – that might be relevant to the wellbeing of the patient." Colautti v. Franklin, 439 U.S. at 439 U. S. 394. This does not mean, however, that a State has unreviewable authority to decide what information a woman must be given before she chooses to have an abortion. *It remains primarily the responsibility of the physician to ensure that appropriate information is conveyed to his patient, depending on her particular circumstances. Danforth's* recognition of the State's interest in ensuring that this information be given will not justify abortion regulations designed to influence the woman's informed choice between abortion or childbirth (emphasis added).

Once again, the Court has voiced its opinion in favor of the abortion doctor, assuming, without question, that the doctor will always act in the best interests of his or her patient.

---

192 *Id.* at 416

The next case, just three years later, dealing with the informed consent issue was *Thornburgh v. American College of Obstetricians and Gynecologists*.[193] As part of its informed consent provisions, the law in question required that a woman considering abortion be provided with all of the following:

- The name of the physician who will perform the abortion.
- The "particular medical risks" of the abortion procedure to be used and of carrying her child to term.
- That there may be "detrimental physical and psychological effects" of the abortion.
- Medical assistance benefits may be available for prenatal care, childbirth, and neonatal care.
- The father is liable to assist in the child's support.
- And printed materials are available from the State that describe the fetus and list agencies offering alternatives to abortion.

Following the precedent established in *Akron,* the Court struck the statute saying, "The requirements of [the statute] that the woman be advised that medical assistance benefits may be available, and that the father is responsible for financial assistance in the support of the child, similarly are poorly disguised elements of discouragement for the abortion decision....Under the guise of informed consent, the Act requires the dissemination of information that is not relevant to such consent, and, thus, it advances no legitimate state interest."

As a result of these cases, the Supreme Court chose again to rely upon the integrity and competence of the abortion doctor. However, in 1992, just six years later, the Court substantially altered its position in the case of *Planned Parenthood of Southeastern Pennsylvania v. Casey*.[194] The challenged law in this case was very similar to that in *Thornburgh,* but with a very different

---

193 476 U.S. 747 (1986)
194 505 U.S 833 (1992)

result. The Pennsylvania law required a woman's informed consent 24 hours in advance of the procedure in the following particulars:

- The nature of the proposed procedure or treatment.
- The risks and alternatives to the procedure or treatment;
- The probable gestational age of the unborn child at the time the abortion is to be performed.
- The medical risks associated with carrying her child to term.
- The department's published printed materials which describe the unborn child and list agencies which offer alternatives to abortion and that she has a right to review the printed materials and that a copy will be provided to her free of charge if she chooses to review it.
- That Medical assistance benefits may be available for prenatal care, childbirth and neonatal care, and that more detailed information on the availability of such assistance is contained in the printed materials published by the department.
- That the father of the unborn child is liable to assist in the support of her child, even in instances where he has offered to pay for the abortion (in the case of rape, this information may be omitted).
- And that a copy of the printed materials has been provided to the woman if she chooses to view these materials.

The law also provided that any physician who violated the law would be guilty of "unprofessional conduct" and his license for the practice of medicine and surgery shall be subject to suspension or revocation.

Despite the very close resemblance of this law to that which was overturned in *Thornburgh*, this time the Court found no violation of the Constitution. Here the Court stated:

To the extent *Akron I* and *Thornburgh* find a constitutional violation when the government requires, as it does here, the giving of truthful, nonmisleading information about the nature of the procedure, the attendant health risks and those of childbirth, and the "probable gestational age" of the fetus, those cases go too far, are inconsistent with *Roe's* acknowledgment of an important interest in potential life, and are overruled. This is clear even on the very terms of *Akron I* and *Thornburgh*. Those decisions, along with *Danforth*, recognize a substantial government interest justifying a requirement that a woman be apprised of the health risks of abortion and childbirth. E.g., *Danforth, supra*, at 66-67. It cannot be questioned that psychological well-being is a facet of health. Nor can it be doubted that most women considering an abortion would deem the impact on the fetus relevant, if not dispositive, to the decision. In attempting to ensure that a woman apprehend the full consequences of her decision, the State furthers the legitimate purpose of reducing the risk that a woman may elect an abortion, only to discover later, with devastating psychological consequences, that her decision was not fully informed. If the information the State requires to be made available to the woman is truthful and not misleading, the requirement may be permissible.[195]

Finally, the Court has recognized the possible "devastating psychological consequences" of the abortion decision and that informed consent is simply not possible without the pertinent information.

It should be noted, however, that although the Supreme Court has finally recognized the psychological harm that an abortion can cause, there is nothing in the Court's ruling that mandates disclosure of any specific information. The State legislatures are the determinative factors in whether or not such disclosures are required. Though some States have followed the Pennsylvania example and required very specific information to be provided, many others have not.

Viability Issues

As noted in Chapter 5 of this book, the *Roe* decision provided a trimester regulation scenario whereby there could be no state regulation of abortion

---

195 *Id.* at 882

during the first trimester, and only limited regulation during the second trimester (e.g., regulations concerning the licensing of physicians and abortion facilities). It was only during the third trimester that a state "may go so far as to proscribe abortion during that period, except when it is necessary to preserve the life or health of the mother."[196] Quite naturally, then, various States have attempted to regulate abortions beginning with the third trimester (at approximately 24 weeks), the point at which *Roe* determined it likely that the fetus would be "viable."

The first case to deal with this issue, only three years after *Roe*, was *Colautti v. Franklin*[197] in which a Pennsylvania statute was challenged as constitutionally vague. The challenged statute is described as follows:

Section 5(a) of the Pennsylvania Abortion Control Act requires every person who performs an abortion to make a determination, "based on his experience, judgment or professional competence," that the fetus is not viable. If such person determines that the fetus "is viable," or "if there is sufficient reason to believe that the fetus may be viable," then he must exercise the same care to preserve the fetus' life and health as would be required in the case of a fetus intended to be born alive, and must use the abortion technique providing the best opportunity for the fetus to be aborted alive, so long as a different technique is not necessary to preserve the mother's life or health.[198]

The Court determined the statute was vague, particularly in its use of the terms "is viable" and "may be viable." Here the person performing the abortion was required to determine the status of the fetus "based on his experience, judgment or professional competence," and failure to meet these standards gave rise to punitive sanctions. How in each case was the physician to make this determination? Although *Roe* suggested that a fetus would become viable

---

196 410 U.S. 113 at 163-64
197 439 U.S. 379 (1979)
198 *Id.*

at approximately 24 weeks, that standard alone was insufficient because not all fetuses become viable at the same point. Some may be viable at 20 weeks, while others may not become viable until much later. Some babies born alive are so sickly that they may not be viable even following a full-term birth. For these and other reasons, the Court rejected the statute.

Four years later, in *Akron v. Akron Center for Reproductive Health*,[199] the court considered and rejected a requirement of an Akron, Ohio ordinance that all abortions after the first trimester be performed in a hospital. The Court determined this to be an unreasonable restriction because it found that in…

> …preventing the performance of dilatation-and-evacuation abortions in an appropriate nonhospital setting, Akron has imposed a heavy and unnecessary burden on women's access to a relatively inexpensive, otherwise accessible, and safe abortion procedure. Section 1870.03 has the effect of inhibiting the vast majority of abortions after the first trimester, and therefore unreasonably infringes upon a woman's constitutional right to obtain an abortion.

Planned Parenthood Association v. Ashcroft,[200] decided in 1983 and the same day as *Akron*, dealt with similar issues. There, a Missouri law required all abortions after 12 weeks to be performed in a hospital, a pathology report for each abortion, and the presence of a second physician for abortions performed after the fetus was viable. The provision requiring that abortions be performed in a hospital was rejected for the same reasons stated in *Akron*.[201] However, the other two provisions were held to be constitutional.

With respect to the requirement that two physicians be present during the abortion of a viable fetus, the Court was now willing to acknowledge that the State has a "compelling interest in the life of a *viable fetus*." The Court reiterated its holding in *Roe* that during the third trimester a "State in promoting

---

199 462 U.S. 416 (1983)
200 462 U.S. 476 (1983)
201 *Id*. at 481-82

its interest in the potentiality of human life may, if it chooses, regulate, and even proscribe, abortion except where it is necessary, in appropriate medical judgment, for the preservation of the life or health of the mother."[202] Noting that the second doctor was required by the law to "take all reasonable steps in keeping with good medical practice…to preserve the life and health of the viable unborn child; provided that it does not pose an increased risk to the life or health of the woman" and to "take control of and provide immediate medical care for a child born as a result of the abortion,"[203] the Court found nothing in these requirements that violated the woman's right to an abortion. The first doctor's immediate responsibility would be to care for the mother and the second doctor would tend to the needs of the aborted child. Given the dire circumstances surrounding the abortion of the child, the Court determined the second doctor's presence was a reasonable requirement.[204] It must be noted, however, that the term "health of the mother" is still defined very broadly so as to prevent few abortions where the mother is determined to abort.

Looking next to the requirement that a pathology report be made, the Court also found this requirement reasonable. Just as Missouri law required pathology reports for other surgical procedures, and there were ample reasons for such reports, the Court was convinced that the same procedures following an abortion were not unduly restrictive because the reports are useful and not cost prohibitive.[205]

In the 1986 *Thornburgh* case,[206] the Pennsylvania law in question required physicians who performed abortions after the first trimester to report the basis for their determination that a fetus was not viable. If they could not make such a determination, it became incumbent upon them to take two primary actions: (1) employ the level of care necessary to preserve the child's life and health using the abortion procedure that would give the child the best opportunity to be born alive and well (unless it would present a significantly greater

---

202 *Id.* at 482
203 *Id.* at 483
204 *Id.* at 485
205 *Id.* at 486-89
206 476 U.S. 747 (1986)

medical risk to the pregnant woman's life or health) and (2) require that a second physician be present during the abortion procedure whenever viability was possible, who would then be charged with the responsibility for taking all reasonable steps to preserve the child's life and health.[207] The Supreme Court agreed with the holding by the Court of Appeals that the first provision was unconstitutional because:

> It required a "trade-off" between the woman's health and fetal survival, and failed to require that maternal health be the physician's paramount consideration.[208]

The second requirement, that a second doctor be present to provide care for the aborted child, was likewise held unconstitutional because it failed to provide an express exception for the contingency of the mother's health being endangered by a delay in the second physician's arrival.

The case of *Webster v. Reproductive Health Services*,[209] decided in 1989, brought about substantial change concerning this issue of viability and the State's rights with respect to protecting a viable fetus. The Missouri law in question, as described in the opinion, required that all Missouri laws be interpreted so as to provide unborn children with all rights as "persons," subject to the Federal Constitution and the Supreme Court's precedents; it also specified that before a physician could perform an abortion on a woman believed to be 20 or more weeks pregnant, he or she would have to determine whether the fetus was "viable" by conducting "such medical examinations and tests as are necessary to make a finding of gestational age, weight, and lung maturity."[210] As to the first part dealing with the unborn child's rights as "persons," the Court noted that the language of the statute did nothing more than accurately state the true status of the law. Personhood of unborn children, as determined by the state, is limited as determined by the Supreme Court's decisions.

---

207 *Id.* at 768
208 *Id.* at 768-69
209 492 U.S. 490 (1989)
210 *Id.* at 490

The second part of the law, requiring certain tests to determine viability if there was reason to believe the fetus had reached 20 weeks or more of development, was found to be constitutional and…

> …reasonably designed to ensure that abortions are not performed where the fetus is viable. The section's tests are intended to determine viability, the State having chosen viability as the point at which its interest in potential human life must be safeguarded. The section creates what is essentially a presumption of viability at 20 weeks, which the physician, prior to performing an abortion, must rebut with tests – including, if feasible, those for gestational age, fetal weight, and lung capacity – indicating that the fetus is not viable. While the District Court found that uncontradicted medical evidence established that a 20-week fetus is *not* viable, and that 23 1/2 to 24 weeks' gestation is the earliest point at which a reasonable possibility of viability exists, it also found that there may be a 4-week error in estimating gestational age, which supports testing at 20 weeks.

The truly remarkable part of the decision came as a partial overturning of the *Roe v. Wade* decision with respect to the trimester approach that had been mandated. *Roe* allowed no state regulation of abortion during the first trimester. The state could only regulate during the second trimester in ways reasonably related to assuring the mother's health. Here, the Missouri law was attempting to regulate beginning with the 20th week, which is still at least four weeks in advance of the third trimester when the state could proscribe abortion except where the mother's life or health was endangered. In this sense, *Webster* was acknowledged as having run afoul of *Roe*.[211] However, the Court then announced that:

> *Roe's* rigid trimester analysis has proved to be unsound in principle and unworkable in practice…There is also no reason why the State's compelling interest in protecting potential human life should not

---

211 *Id.* at 493

extend throughout pregnancy, rather than coming into existence only at the point of viability. *Thus, the Roe trimester framework should be abandoned.*[212] (emphasis added)

The elimination of the trimester approach that was established in *Roe* has opened the door to increased state regulation much earlier than had been possible since *Roe* was decided in 1973. In its acknowledgment of this possibility, the Court then said:

> Although this decision will undoubtedly allow more governmental regulation of abortion than was permissible before, the goal of constitutional adjudication is not to remove inexorably "politically divisive" issues from the ambit of the legislative process, but is, rather, to hold true the balance between that which the Constitution puts beyond the reach of the democratic process and that which it does not.[213]

Recall that, in the original *Roe v. Wade* decision, the Court forcefully rejected the argument by the State of Texas that it had a "compelling interest" in the protection of the unborn and that its abortion laws had been enacted in recognition of the fetus as a person. Here, sixteen years later in the *Webster* case, the Court acknowledges that "There is also no reason why the State's *compelling interest in protecting potential human life* should not extend throughout pregnancy, rather than coming into existence only at the point of viability."[214] Thus, it would appear that the legal basis upon which *Roe* was decided in 1973 has been seriously undermined and there no longer exists any proper basis for continued recognition of a woman's fundamental right to an abortion designed to destroy fetal life after the 20th week of gestation. As of the writing of this book, however, the Court has not seen fit to go that far and state legislatures are not required to enact statutes designed to protect fetal life.

---

212 *Id.* at 494
213 *Id.*
214 *Id.*

Partial Birth Abortions

Twice, once in 1995 and again in 1997, Congress passed laws banning an abortion procedure that had come to be known as "Partial Birth Abortion." Both of these laws were vetoed by President Bill Clinton. In June, 2000, in a case named *Stenberg v. Carhart,*[215] the Supreme Court overturned a Nebraska law that outlawed the procedure and provided for revocation of the doctor's license for violation of the statute. The Court determined that the statute was unconstitutionally vague and in violation of *Roe* for lack of an exception to preserve the health of the pregnant woman.

In 2003, however, Congress enacted the Partial Birth Abortion Ban Act,[216] dubbed the "PBA Ban," which was signed into law by President George Bush. This act defines "Partial Birth Abortion" as follows:

An abortion in which the person performing the abortion, deliberately and intentionally vaginally delivers a living fetus until, in the case of a head-first presentation, the entire fetal head is outside the body of the mother, or, in the case of breech presentation, any part of the fetal trunk past the navel is outside the body of the mother, for the purpose of performing an overt act that the person knows will kill the partially delivered living fetus; and performs the overt act, other than completion of delivery, that kills the partially delivered living fetus.

Additionally, as part of the statute, Congress made the following findings of fact:

(1) A moral, medical, and ethical consensus exists that the practice of performing a partial-birth abortion... is a gruesome and inhumane procedure that is never medically necessary and should be prohibited. (2) Rather than being an abortion procedure that is embraced by the medical community, particularly among physicians who routinely

215 530 U.S. 914 (2000)
216 18 U.S.C. §1531

perform other abortion procedures, partial-birth abortion remains a disfavored procedure that is not only unnecessary to preserve the health of the mother, but in fact poses serious risks to the long-term health of women and in some circumstances, their lives. As a result, at least 27 States banned the procedure as did the United States Congress which voted to ban the procedure during the 104th, 105th, and 106th Congresses.[217]

As a result of these findings, Congress determined there was no need for an exception to preserve the health of the pregnant woman. The law does allow a doctor charged with violation to seek a determination by the State Medical Board that such an abortion was necessary due to a "physical disorder, physical illness, or physical injury, including a life-endangering physical condition caused by or arising from the pregnancy itself."

Finally, after nearly 35 years since *Roe*, Congress acknowledged in the PBA Ban that abortion doctors have, in fact, made decisions and taken actions that are patently unethical, even "gruesome and inhumane," at least with respect to the practice of partial birth abortions. Congress stopped short, however, of labeling all abortions as such. Since it was, in fact, the Supreme Court's decision in *Roe* that made partial birth abortions legal, the passage of the PBA Ban therefore constitutes a direct censure of the Court's involvement in that gruesome and inhumane abortion practice.

The PBA Ban was itself challenged in the case of *Gonzales v. Carhart*,[218] but was finally upheld in 2007 by the Supreme Court, which noted that the Act departed "in material ways" from the provisions of the Nebraska law that was held unconstitutional in the *Stenberg* case six years earlier (discussed above). Following the *Gonzales v. Carhart* case, several States have enacted more restrictive abortion laws in which doctors may be required to perform an ultrasound prior to the abortion procedure, and some have even outlawed abortions after 20 weeks of gestation. Some of these enactments have been based

---

217 *Id.*
218 550 U.S. 124 (2006)

on the acknowledgment that a fetus at that stage of development experiences "fetal pain," a claim that has now been litigated in a Federal Court of Appeals case entitled *Isaacson v. Horne,*[219] that had been filed in 2012 and challenged an Arizona statute that relied on the theory that a 20-week fetus is capable of sensing pain. The Court of Appeals issued its opinion in 2013, declaring that the statute was unconstitutional because it proscribed abortions prior to the point of viability, notwithstanding the Supreme Court's decision in *Webster,* discussed above, that acknowledged the possibility of viability as early as 20 weeks. In 2014, the Supreme Court refused to hear the matter, thereby allowing the decision of the Court of Appeals to stand.

Other Important Decisions

As mentioned above, it was determined in *Connecticut v. Menillo* (1975)[220] that state law could prohibit non-physicians from performing abortions. This, however, did not end the controversy. In 1977, the Supreme Court heard and decided the matter of *Poelker v. Doe,*[221] a case that challenged a policy of the City of St. Louis that prohibited nontherapeutic abortions from being performed in the hospitals operated by the city. Asked whether this policy violated the Equal Protection Clause of the Fourteenth Amendment, the Court ruled that it did not, even though the same hospital regularly provided childbirth services. The Court noted that the City was not in violation of the Constitution because it was not denying or interfering with the abortion rights guaranteed by *Roe v. Wade.* Rather, the city was simply encouraging an alternative activity for the hospitals by choosing to assist in childbirths rather than abortions. There were other facilities available for the obtaining of abortion services.

In 1979, in *Williams v. Zbaraz,*[222] the Court was asked to determine whether a State must provide funding for medically necessary abortions

---

219 716 F.3d 1213 (2013)
220 423 U.S. 9 (1975)
221 432 U.S. 519 (1977)
222 442 U.S. 1309 (1979)

performed prior to fetal viability. It was alleged that pregnant women were denied reimbursement for abortions in violation of the Social Security Acts and the Fourteenth Amendment. The Court held, however, that under the provisions of the Hyde Amendment (which restricted the use of federal funds for abortions except under certain conditions) a State was not obligated to fund abortions that were not funded by the federal government, although it could opt to do so.

On June 27, 2016, the Supreme Court announced its decision in the matter of *Whole Woman's Health v. Hellerstedt*[223] in which the laws of the State of Texas were again challenged. The law in question, enacted in 2013 as House Bill 2 (H.B. 2) contained the two provisions in question. The first was referred to as the "admitting-privileges requirement" and required that a "physician performing or inducing an abortion . . . must, on the date [of service], have active admitting privileges at a hospital . . . located not further than 30 miles from the" abortion facility." The other challenged provision was called the "surgical-center requirement" which mandated that abortion facilities in the State of Texas must meet the same minimum standards established for "ambulatory surgical centers" within the state. It was stipulated in the case that the number of abortion clinics within Texas had diminished from approximately 40 to approximately 20 facilities after the law was enacted. The Supreme Court determined, in a 5-3 vote, that together the challenged provisions "place a substantial obstacle in the path of women seeking a previability abortion, constitute an undue burden on abortion access, and thus violate the Constitution."

So, after all these legal issues have been challenged and decided by the Supreme Court, where does the matter now stand? As we attempt to summarize the resulting parameters of the law, bear in mind that the right to abortion remains secure and is still recognized as a fundamental constitutional right even though the Court has admitted (in *Webster v. Reproductive Health Services*) that States have a legitimate compelling interest in safeguarding the

---

223 136 S.Ct. 2292 (2016), recorded as No. 15-274. As of the copyright date for publication of this book, the Court's written opinion had not been formally published in the official United States Reports.

life of a fetus throughout pregnancy. The Supreme Court decisions, discussed above, place limits on the extent to which state laws are allowed to regulate or interfere with that fundamental right and there is no requirement that the individual States must regulate abortions in any particular way. Some States strive by their laws to restrict abortions while others do not.

In Summary
Is the unborn child deemed to be a "person" under the Fourteenth Amendment?

No. Despite major changes in the law, including the admission that the unborn child is a "life," the Supreme Court has ruled that it is not a "person."

Who can perform abortions?

State laws may require abortionists to be licensed physicians.

Spousal Consent to Abortion

Fathers of unborn children have no legal right to interfere in in any manner in the abortion decision. The abortion decision is the exclusive domain of the pregnant woman and her "responsible physician." The father has no right to veto the abortion decision and no right even to be informed of the mother's decision to abort their child. The father's rights in the abortion context are constitutionally "irrelevant," contrary to the earlier Supreme Court rulings in the *Skinner* and *Eisenstadt* cases.

Parental Consent and/or Notification

States may not require the consent of a pregnant minor's parents to the abortion decision. Further, States may not unconditionally require that the parents of a non-emancipated pregnant minor be notified of an intended abortion. Unless the minor is, in fact, deemed to be emancipated and mature enough to make her own decision in the matter, there must be some means by which parental involvement may be bypassed, which, in most cases decided thus far, has meant that the judgment of a court of law may be substituted for that of the minor's parents. The Court has ruled, however, that a requirement that parents be notified "if possible" is constitutional based on the notion that parents can provide substantial guidance to an immature and dependent minor.

Waiting Periods

Although waiting periods were initially ruled unconstitutional, two Supreme Court decisions have now held that state law may provide that a woman seeking an abortion be required to wait a short time (24 to 48 hours) following the first visit to an abortion clinic before the abortion may be performed.

Informed Consent

Early post-Roe decisions struck down laws requiring dissemination of childbirth information. Recognizing that the abortion decision can bring about "devastating psychological consequences," state laws may now require that a woman seeking an abortion be provided with non-misleading information concerning the nature of the abortion procedure, the health risks involved, the probable gestational age of the fetus, and other information important to the abortion decision.

Viability of the Fetus

The "viability" requirement set forth in *Roe v. Wade* under which a State could proscribe abortion beginning with the third trimester of pregnancy (except where the woman's health could be adversely affected) has been abandoned. The Court has now determined that a fetus may become "viable" much earlier, perhaps as early as the 20th week of gestation. State laws may now require that a determination be made by the abortion doctor whether the fetus has reached the approximate age of viability, and if so, steps to protect the life of the fetus may be required by law.

Partial Birth Abortions

Partial birth abortions (performed in the very late stages of pregnancy) are now outlawed by federal law except when necessary due to a "physical disorder, physical illness, or physical injury, including a life-endangering physical condition caused by or arising from the pregnancy itself."

As a result of these decisions, the fundamental right to an abortion first announced in *Roe v. Wade* has been diminished, at least to some degree. Importantly, the Supreme Court has recently stated that "There is also no reason why the State's compelling interest in protecting potential human life should not extend throughout pregnancy, rather than coming into existence only at the point of viability," perhaps opening the door to further abortion regulation in the future.

9

Is Abortion Murder?

ABORTION RIGHTS ADVOCATES have gone to great lengths to distinguish abortion from any hint of murder. Any acknowledgement that abortion is truly murder would seriously undermine their efforts and their agenda. Public opinion, upon which their power depends, could be altered significantly. In this chapter, we will look behind all the rhetoric and public relations slogans and search for the truth of the matter.

What Is Murder?

Whenever a human life is taken at the hands of another person we call it "homicide." This is a general classification that refers to all forms of human killings by other humans and includes murder, voluntary manslaughter, involuntary manslaughter, or negligent homicide. Some jurisdictions refer to different types of human killings as "first degree murder," "second degree murder," and so forth. Whatever they are called, these classifications are made on the basis of perceived severity of the crime. "Murder" or "first degree murder" is generally defined as an intentional killing of a human being with malice aforethought or premeditation. Intent to commit a murder is any act designed to bring about great bodily harm or death of another human being. Lesser forms of homicide result in lesser penalties because of mitigating circumstances such as a lack of malice aforethought or because the killing was accidental.

Delineation of this sort among the forms of homicide has been followed throughout civilized history. In Exodus 20:13 we find the direct command by God that "You shall not murder." This, again, speaks of an intentional act of killing a fellow man. In Chapter 21 of Exodus, we find further clarifications of the meaning of that commandment. For example:

> Whoever strikes a man so that he dies shall be put to death. But if he did not lie in wait for him, but God let him fall into his hand, then I will appoint for you a place to which he may flee. But if a man willfully attacks another to kill him by cunning, you shall take him from my altar, that he may die. (Ex. 21:12-14)

Accidental killing is not murder. But where one "willfully attacks another to kill him by cunning" (another way of saying "malice aforethought"), it is considered murder and, by Old Testament standards, was punishable by death as the prescribed penalty.

Cain and Abel

The very first biblical record of murder was the killing of Abel by his brother Cain, both sons of Adam and Eve. This account, found in Genesis 4 following the initial sin of the first man and woman, is a classic case and deserves our attention. In the first two verses of Genesis 4, we learn that Cain was Eve's first-born son and Abel was his younger brother. Abel was a shepherd while Cain was a farmer. "In the course of time" both Cain and Abel brought offerings to the Lord and the Lord was pleased with Abel's offering, but not with Cain's.[224]

As a result of God's displeasure, Cain became jealous of his brother and his jealousy soon turned to anger and his anger to hatred. No doubt he reasoned that he had done the same act as Abel. After all, both brothers had

---

224 Gen. 4:3-5

brought offerings – the fruits of their toils – and God's rejection was, therefore, unfair. Cain may have reasoned that Abel was receiving special treatment, special favor.

In verse 7, God specifically warned Cain not to allow his anger to lead him astray, saying, "Sin is crouching at the door. Its desire is for you, but you must rule over it."

Despite God's severe warning, verse 8 reveals that Cain lured his brother out to a field, and "while they were in the field, Cain attacked Abel and killed him." This was cold-blooded murder. The fact that he lured Abel away from his home and into the field to kill him shows clearly the requisite intent and premeditation. He was guilty of killing with "malice aforethought."

There were apparently no human eyewitnesses to the crime. As is common with many sinful acts, the murder of Abel was done in secret because Cain knew it was utterly wrong. He was forewarned by God of its sinfulness. Yet he lured Abel to the field, away from other possible witnesses, so the killing could be accomplished in "privacy." The judgment in *Roe* is of like character, allowing the abortion decision to be made secretly, that is, in privacy. Jesus taught in John 3:19-21 that:

> And this is the judgment: the light has come into the world, and people loved the darkness rather than the light because their works were evil. For everyone who does wicked things hates the light and does not come to the light, lest his works should be exposed. But whoever does what is true comes to the light, so that it may be clearly seen that his works have been carried out in God."

Try as he might, Cain could not hide the truth from God. In verse 9, God confronts Cain and asks, "Where is Abel your brother?" Cain replies, "I do not know," and then adds, "Am I my brother's keeper?" God then exposes the evil deed.

> And the LORD said, "What have you done? The voice of your brother's blood is crying to me from the ground. And now you are cursed

from the ground, which has opened its mouth to receive your brother's blood from your hand. When you work the ground, it shall no longer yield to you its strength. You shall be a fugitive and a wanderer on the earth." (Gen. 4:10-12)

The blood of those who are murdered cries out to God who sees all things, whether they are done openly or in privacy. When this passage in Chapter 4 says, "The voice of your brother's blood is crying to me from the ground," it is very possible that God allowed Cain to literally hear Abel's shed blood crying out. It may have been an audible voice or perhaps Cain was simply forced to recall Abel's frantic calls for help. Regardless of how it was accomplished, Cain was directly confronted with the awful truth of what he had done. Even then, Cain remained unrepentant. Instead of falling to his knees and pleading, "Lord forgive me," Cain resorted to self-pity. Hearing his sentence, he cries out, "My punishment is greater than I can bear" (Gen. 4:13). It is as though he still blames God and he complains of the unfairness of it all. He reasons that if only God had accepted his offering, he would never have been motivated to kill Abel. It was all God's fault.

Those who would demand abortion rights may have fallen into the same trap. Refusing to repent, to acknowledge their self-centered motivations, and renouncing their responsibility to rule over sin, the easier choice is to blame God for their predicament. It is unfair, they may reason, that a woman should be required to bear a greater burden than a man in the reproduction process. The right to abort an unwanted child simply helps to even the score. And because God claims to have created us, one could be tempted to see it all as His fault for giving such preferential treatment to the male of the species. If there is any doubt as to whether God should be blamed, the book of James answers it directly:

Let no one say when he is tempted, "I am being tempted by God," for God cannot be tempted with evil, and he himself tempts no one. But each person is tempted when he is lured and enticed by his own desire. Then desire when it has conceived gives birth to sin, and sin when it is fully grown brings forth death. (James 1:13-15)

God does not tempt anyone to evil. Rather, it is God who lovingly provides a way to avoid temptation if we will only trust Him:

> No temptation has overtaken you that is not common to man. God is faithful, and he will not let you be tempted beyond your ability, but with the temptation he will also provide the way of escape, that you may be able to endure it. (1 Cor. 10:13)

And even after we have sinned, He still provides a means of forgiveness:

> If we confess our sins, he is faithful and just to forgive us our sins and to cleanse us from all unrighteousness. (1 John 1:9)

Unfortunately, many allow their pride to stand in the way of such forgiveness so freely offered. Forgiveness and cleansing from sin was available to Cain, even after he chose not to heed God's warning, but Cain could not humble himself to ask for it.

Because of the sin of Cain's father, Adam, as recorded in Genesis 3, God had cursed the ground so that it would produce thorns and thistles. Because of Abel's murder, as reported in Chapter 4 of Genesis, Adam's son, Cain, is now cursed and driven from the ground upon which the blood of Abel had been spilled. Cain would be a "fugitive and a wanderer on the earth," a punishment understood by Cain to carry with it banishment from God. Cain says in verse 14, "Behold, you have driven me today away from the ground, and from your face I shall be hidden." For Cain's great and unrepentant sin, especially after he was forewarned, God drove him away to live without His blessings and guidance. The Apostle Paul could have been speaking specifically of Cain when he wrote in the book of Romans:

> And since they did not see fit to acknowledge God, God gave them up to a debased mind to do what ought not to be done. They were filled with all manner of unrighteousness, evil, covetousness, malice. They are full of envy, murder, strife, deceit, maliciousness. They

are gossips, slanderers, haters of God, insolent, haughty, boastful, inventors of evil, disobedient to parents, foolish, faithless, heartless, ruthless. Though they know God's righteous decree that those who practice such things deserve to die, they not only do them but give approval to those who practice them. (Rom. 1:28-32)

From the account of Abel's murder and from many other biblical passages, it is clear that God abhors murder and will deal severely with those who commit it. Following the great flood that is said to have destroyed all mankind except Noah's family, we find God's decree that:

Whoever sheds the blood of man,
    by man shall his blood be shed,
for God made man in his own image. (Gen. 9:6)

Murder is an act that shows great contempt, not only for the one murdered, but for God Himself, "for God made man in his own image." Murder is the intentional destruction of God's wonderful creative work which He deemed "very good." And, what is more, each human being is considered to be part of God's breath or spirit as we have discussed. The death of each human being is, in that way, the death of part of God Himself or the cessation of His breathing or outpouring of His Spirit in that person.

The Value of Fetal Life

As we have seen from our analysis of the *Roe v. Wade* case, the Supreme Court found no reason to protect the unborn fetus if the mother was determined to obtain an abortion. But, as we will see, Scripture shows plainly the true value of unborn life. In Exodus 21:22-25, we find this instruction:

When men strive together and hit a pregnant woman, so that her children come out, but there is no harm, the one who hit her shall surely be fined, as the woman's husband shall impose on him, and he shall pay as the judges determine. But if there is harm, then you shall pay life for life, eye for eye, tooth for tooth, hand for hand, foot for foot, burn for burn, wound for wound, stripe for stripe.

It must be noted initially that this does not involve an intentional act of either abortion or murder. But it is instructive on the issue of the value of life, including unborn life, and the seriousness of the taking of life, even if unintentional. It also deals with the inducement of a premature birth (or a miscarriage), and punishment is imposed. For these reasons, it is useful in our quest to understand God's will about the taking of fetal life or causing any injury to it.

Admittedly, this passage is not a model of clarity, at least in the English translation. We have to ask ourselves who has been injured when it speaks of "harm." It seems clear enough that it does not refer to injury of the men who are fighting as it is one of them "who hit her" and the fine is given to "the woman's husband." But is the passage concerned with injury to the woman, to her fetus, or to both the woman and her fetus? Furthermore, what is the serious injury about which this verse speaks?

One possible interpretation is that the serious injury concerns only the woman and that the fetus itself is not to be considered in the imposition of punishment; recompense is to be made only for injury to woman. But this would ignore the fact that the passage is dealing with an induced premature birth or miscarriage and that harm to the baby represents a loss to both the woman and her husband if their baby is injured, dies, or is somehow crippled.

Another possibility is that a fine is to be imposed for the loss of a stillborn child, but that if the woman is killed or seriously injured, the punishment is to correspond directly to her injuries, that is: "life for life, eye for eye," and so forth. If this interpretation is accepted, then at least we can establish that the fetus has some value because a fine has been imposed. But if a fine is imposed for an accidental killing of the fetus, it would follow that an intentional act to cause its death would bring about greater retribution, requiring greater recompense and/or greater punishment.

Third, it could be argued that the passage deals only with serious injury to the fetus and assumes that the woman will fully recover. Under this interpretation, a fine would be imposed if the prematurely delivered infant is uninjured and lives, but that serious injury or death of the fetus would be punished by taking "life for life, eye for eye," and so on. This interpretation is credible because it requires recompense (the fine) for the obvious trauma to the woman in causing her to deliver prematurely, even if her child is not injured, while more serious injuries to the child would be dealt with by more severe punishment. The problem is that such an interpretation would disregard the possibility that the woman herself might be seriously injured or killed.

The most logical interpretation is that the passage concerns itself with serious injury to either the mother or the fetus, or both, because that is the only explanation that encompasses the full extent of the injuries that are likely to occur under the circumstances. Certainly, the fetus has value to the parents, for there is no indication that either of them intended the child to be aborted or to be born prematurely, so its death or injury should be acknowledged in some serious manner. It is also certain that punishment should be imposed for the woman's injuries. Furthermore, because the passage speaks of a situation in which there could be injuries or death of either the mother or fetus without specifically identifying which serious injury is to be punished, it would follow that injury to either mother or child is encompassed by this law. This, again, is the only interpretation that would fully address the harm that may have been caused.

Whether the injury or death is to the mother or her child, such a wrong requires an appropriate remedy. Notice that the text refers to the unborn as "her children" whether they are viable or not and whether they survive or not, just as Job referred to the ostrich's eggs as "her young." As no distinction is made as to the stage of the pregnancy, it follows from this passage that the unborn are again considered to be her children, real human lives, regardless of their gestational maturity.

Also, the ambiguity of the passage is likely intentional so that it would have the broadest application. "No harm," in this context, likely implies that the woman and her children survive without serious injury, so the fine is for the pain, inconvenience and potential risks associated with the incident. Any resulting "harm" would then refer to either the child or the mother, and the retaliation prescribed by the passage would be equivalent to the harm done. And even though an accidental injury is encompassed by these circumstances, the prescribed remedies are very severe for any serious injury, calling for payment of "life for life, eye for eye, tooth for tooth, hand for hand, foot for foot, burn for burn, wound for wound, stripe for stripe."

Other biblical passages concerning unborn children also support this conclusion. In the earlier chapters dealing with the beginning of life, we have noted that God values all life, even before birth. We saw, for example, that He knits the fetus together in the mother's womb[225]; He knows all the days of our lives before any of them have come to pass[226]; and He chastises the foolish ostrich for dealing harshly with her unborn young.[227] To be consistent in light of such other instructions, the interpretation of Exodus 21:22-25 must include a proscription of harm to the fetus as well as its mother.

But Is Abortion Murder?

There remains yet the issue of whether abortion is a form of murder. The law has coined other terms for the killing of a fetus: we call it "feticide" or "fetal murder." These terms are not specifically used in the Bible. But as we have seen from the preceding discussion, Scripture has shown us how valuable fetal life truly is to the One who is at work in the womb.

Having considered the biblical perspective on fetal harm, let us now compare God's law to our own manmade laws. How do our laws differ from biblical teachings?

In 1970, three years prior to *Roe v. Wade*, the definition of "murder" in California was substantially modified as a result of a case entitled *Keeler v. Superior Court*.[228] Before that case, California Penal Code section 187(a) provided a very conventional definition of murder:

---

225 Ps. 139:13
226 Ps. 139:16
227 Job 39:13-18
228 Keeler v. Superior Court (1970) 2 Cal.3d 619

"Murder is the unlawful killing of a human being, with malice aforethought."

Before looking at how that statute was changed, it will be helpful to know something about the *Keeler* case. It has been summarized as follows:

The material facts of *Keeler* (citation omitted) were essentially undisputed. When Robert and Teresa Keeler were granted an interlocutory decree of divorce on September 27, 1968, Teresa was already pregnant by one Ernest Vogt. She began living with Vogt in a different city and concealed the fact from Robert. Under the decree of divorce Robert had custody of their two daughters, but Teresa had the right to take the girls on alternate weekends. Five months later, on February 23, 1969, Robert encountered Teresa driving on a rural road after delivering the girls to their home. He said to her, "I hear you're pregnant. If you are you had better stay away from the girls and from here." When Teresa got out of her car Robert looked at her abdomen and became "extremely upset." Saying, "You sure are. I'm going to stomp it out of you," he struck her in the face and pushed his knee into her abdomen. When doctors subsequently performed a Caesarean section of Teresa the fetus was delivered stillborn. The pathologist was of the opinion that the fetus's fatal injury – a skull fracture – could have been caused by a blow to Teresa's abdomen.

At the time of delivery, the fetus weighed five pounds and was eighteen inches in length. In light of these facts Teresa's obstetrician estimated the fetus was 35 weeks old. An attending pediatrician likewise estimated the age of the fetus as between 34-1/2 and 36 weeks. The expert testimony thus concluded "with reasonable medical certainty" that the fetus had developed to the stage of viability, i.e., that in the event of premature birth on the date in question it would have had a 75 percent to 96 percent chance of survival (citations omitted).[229]

---

229 *Id.* at 624

It bears mentioning here that the unborn child in the *Keeler* matter would have been "viable" under the *Roe v. Wade* criteria. It was virtually full-term and would likely have been delivered within the following month. If the child had been born prematurely on the same day of the attack by Mr. Keeler, it would have had very strong chance of "meaningful life" outside the womb as the court made note.

Murder charges were brought against Robert for the death of the baby as well as assault and battery charges for his injuries to Teresa. Before any trial could be held, however, Robert petitioned for a writ of prohibition to eliminate the murder charge. The California Supreme Court granted his request and the murder charge was dropped. The Court traced the history of laws concerning the killing of a fetus, including the enactment of Penal Code section 187, and stated:

> We hold that in adopting the definition of murder in Penal Code section 187 the Legislature intended to exclude from its reach the act of killing an unborn fetus.[230]

The decision in *Keeler* brought a quick reaction by the California Legislature. The malicious killing of a fetus, as in the *Keeler* case, constitutes a serious infringement of parental rights, as well as depriving the child of its life, and must not go without legal remedy. Later that same year, Penal Code 187(a) was amended to provide that,

> Murder is the unlawful killing of a human being, *or a fetus*, with malice aforethought.

It should be noted, however, that this California statute expressly does not apply to abortions under the Therapeutic Abortion Act, those performed by a doctor to save the mother's life, or (in keeping with *Roe v.* Wade) whenever the mother has consented to abort her fetus.[231]

---

230 2 Cal.3d at 631
231 California Penal Code section 187(b)

Roe v. Wade, decided three years later, held that in the context of a woman's right to an abortion, a State had no legitimate interest in protecting a fetus at least until the point of "viability," that is, until it was "capable of meaningful life outside the mother's womb."[232]

In 1976, in a California case entitled *People v. Smith*,[233] an appellate court interpreted the term "fetus" in the amended Penal Code section 187(a) to mean a "viable fetus" as that term was used in *Roe v. Wade*.[234] In this later case, a woman 12 to 15 weeks pregnant was beaten by her husband resulting in a miscarriage. During the beating, the husband told his wife that he did not want the baby to live. But because the fetus was not "viable" (as defined in *Roe v.* Wade) at the time of the miscarriage, and therefore not considered a "person" under *Roe v. Wade*, the trial court dismissed the murder charge reasoning that "one cannot destroy independent human life prior to the time it has come into existence."[235]

Subsequent cases tended to follow the reasoning in the *Smith* case, requiring that the fetus must be found viable before a fetal murder conviction would be allowed to stand. In 1990, for example, in a case entitled *People v. Henderson*,[236] a Court of Appeals allowed a conviction of second degree murder of a 30-week-old viable fetus to stand. In that case, the defendant was also found guilty of first degree murder of the mother and it was determined that the fetus was viable and had died as a result of the mother's death.

In May, 1994, the California Supreme Court rendered its decision in the case of *People v. Davis*,[237] a case that dramatically changed interpretation of the fetal murder law in California. Davis had been convicted of the murder of a fetus during an armed robbery. The mother, Maria Flores, had just cashed a $378 welfare check at a check-cashing store when Davis attempted to rob her at gunpoint. He shot her in the chest when she refused to hand over her purse.

---

232 Roe v. Wade, 410 U.S. at 163

233 59 Cal.App.3d 751

234 59 Cal.App.3d at 757

235 59 Cal.App.3d at 756

236 225 Cal.App.3d 1129

237 7 Cal.4th 797

Maria's life was saved, but the fetus, which was between 23 and 25 weeks old, was stillborn the next day "as a direct result of its mother's blood loss, low blood pressure and state of shock."[238]

Davis appealed his conviction on the basis of the viability requirement. The evidence at trial showed that the fetus had less than a 50% chance of survival outside the womb at the time of the shooting.[239] The jury was instructed, however, that "A fetus is viable when it has achieved the capability for independent existence; that is, when it is *possible* for it to survive the trauma of birth, although with artificial medical aid."[240] Attorneys for Davis contended that the viability definition should have been given in terms of "probabilities, not possibilities" and that the instruction was, therefore, prejudicial error by the trial court.[241] As the California Supreme Court described it, "Essentially, defendant claims that because the fetus could have been legally aborted under *Roe v. Wade* (citation omitted) at the time it was killed, it did not attain the protection of section 187, subdivision (a)."[242] The Court considered and rejected that argument.

In its decision, the California Supreme Court quoted various commentators who had observed that *Roe v. Wade* had been decided in the very narrow context of the mother's right to privacy in determining whether or not to abort her child; as such, *Roe* simply does not apply in cases where the fetus has been killed by someone other than the mother and without the mother's consent.[243] Support for this position was found in similar laws of Illinois and Minnesota, both of which held that the killing of an "unborn child" at any stage of development is murder.[244] The *Davis* Court then quoted a Minnesota Supreme Court case that had considered challenges to its fetal homicide statute and which stated:

---

238 *Id.* at 800
239 *Id.* at 801
240 *Id.*
241 *Id.*
242 *Id.* at 806
243 *Id.* at 806-07
244 *Id.* at 807-08

In our case, the fetal homicide statutes seek to protect the 'potentiality of human life,' and they do so without impinging directly or indirectly on a pregnant woman's privacy rights. [¶] The state's interest in protecting the 'potentiality of human life' includes protection of the unborn child, whether an embryo or a nonviable or viable fetus, and it protects, too, the woman's interest in her unborn child and her right to decide whether it shall be carried *in utero*. The interest of a criminal assailant in terminating a woman's pregnancy does not outweigh the woman's right to continue the pregnancy. In the context, the viability of the fetus is 'simply immaterial' to an equal protection challenge to the feticide statute.[245]

On the basis of this and other authorities—and after noting that the fetus stage is reached at approximately seven to eight weeks—the California Supreme Court then stated its decision in the *Davis* appeal:

We conclude that viability is not an element of fetal homicide under section 187, subdivision (a). The third-party killing of a fetus with malice aforethought is murder under section 187, subdivision (a), as long as the state can show that the fetus has progressed beyond the embryonic state of seven to eight weeks.[246]

The *Davis* case and other similar cases raised several new issues relevant to the abortion question. For example, it is clear by the use of the phrase "killing of a fetus" that a fetus is acknowledged to have life, for otherwise it could not be killed. This is in marked contrast to the Supreme Court's prevaricating statement in *Roe v. Wade* that a fetus represents only *potential life*. The *Roe* Court never referred to the killing of a fetus, and only used the word "life" where it referred to "potentiality of human life."[247] In *Davis*, the California Supreme

---

245 *Id*. at 809
246 *Id*. at 814-15
247 410 U.S. at 66.

Court further determined that the fetus has life at least as early as seven to eight weeks and that killing the fetus at any time beyond that stage is murder. Under *Roe v. Wade* and its progeny, however, the mother was given an absolute right to abort her fetus up to the end of the second trimester, or approximately 24 weeks, and even later if she claimed any form of detriment to her "health." As we discussed in Chapter 8, the trimester approached announced in *Roe*, has since been overturned and state regulation of abortion practices are now possible at least as early as the 20th week of gestation.

If the reasoning of the *Davis* Court in California is followed to its natural conclusion, simple logic dictates that when a fetus is aborted after approximately the first seven to eight weeks, a killing has occurred—a human life has been destroyed—and the killing would be murder if done by anyone other than the mother without her consent. Under the fetal murder laws of other States, a killing at any stage of development (literally, at any point following conception) would render the same result. Simply stated, these laws demand acknowledgment that pregnant women have been given a fundamental right under *Roe v. Wade* to do that which would otherwise be chargeable as murder. The only real difference is that we change the label and call it abortion.

Fetal Murder In States Which Have No Such Statute

In addition to those cases where fetal murder statutes have been enacted, there have been numerous criminal convictions for murder even in states which have no such fetal murder statutes. If a fetus has been injured in the womb by someone other than the mother without her consent and those injuries have led to death after the child was expelled from the mother's womb, a murder conviction often results, even in the absence of a fetal murder statute, because once born alive the child is deemed to be a person, even under *Roe v. Wade*, with full rights under the Fourteenth Amendment. In the 1988 case of *United States v. Spencer*,[248] for example, the defendant was convicted of fetal murder where it was determined that he had kicked and stabbed a pregnant woman in

---

248 839 F.2d 1341 (9th Cir.)

the abdomen and those injuries necessitated an emergency Caesarean section. The child was born alive and lived for only ten minutes, yet the assailant was convicted of murder.

In like manner, in the 1989 Maryland case of *Williams v. State*,[249] a defendant was convicted of two counts of manslaughter where he shot an arrow that struck a pregnant woman. The woman died from the wound approximately one hour later and her baby lived for only seventeen hours following emergency birth.

In the New York case of *People v. Hall*,[250] the defendant was convicted of criminal homicide of a child after shooting a gun into a crowd and injuring a pregnant woman, striking her once in the arm and once in the abdomen. The wound in the abdomen severed the placenta which caused a lack of oxygen to the fetus, requiring immediate delivery. The baby lived thirty-six hours before dying as a result of maladies brought on by the gun shot.

In each of these cases, the fetus was less than full term and would not have been born prematurely except for the injuries caused by the defendants. These cases, and others like them, demonstrate plainly how very arbitrary the live birth rule can be concerning whether a fetus is a "person" deserving of constitutional protection. Although these children would not otherwise have been born alive for perhaps several weeks or months, their killing constitutes homicide properly punishable as murder, even in those states where no fetal murder statute exists, because they died after being expelled alive from the womb. Yet their mothers would have been allowed to end their fetal lives through abortion at the very same stage of gestation and with complete impunity. *Roe v. Wade* held that the killing by abortion is a woman's fundamental right so long as it is accomplished prior to complete live birth at which time the fetus would then be considered a "person" in the eyes of the law.

The Center for Disease Control reports that during the year 2011 nearly two thirds (63.9%) of all abortions in the United States were performed after seven to eight weeks, 26.9% were performed at 9 to 13 weeks, 3.5% at 14 to

---

249 561 A.2d 216
250 557 N.Y.S.2nd 879 (N.Y. App. Div. 1990)

15 weeks, 1.9% at 16 to 17 weeks, 1.9% at 18 to 19 weeks, and 1.4% after 21 weeks.[251] Nearly two-thirds of all U.S. abortions, therefore, are being performed at or after the same stage at which they would be punishable as murder in California if they were killed without the mother's consent. Of course, Minnesota and Illinois and many other state statutes criminalize the killing of an unborn child at any stage of development, literally any time after conception, if done without the mother's consent.

What is the difference between a mother choosing to end the life of her fetus by abortion and the murder of that same fetus by someone else? When Robert Keeler attacked his pregnant former wife saying, "I'm going to stomp it out of you," the California Legislature acted quickly to amend its statute to qualify such an act as "murder" because it was an intentional killing of a human being. When a pregnant woman asks for and obtains the destruction of her own fetus, however, the very same intent is present: that is, the intent to destroy the life of her child. An intentional killing has occurred in either case.

If a State has an interest in protecting human life at all, and if that interest includes the right to protect a fetus by means of fetal murder statutes, why then should that interest not apply to protect all fetuses from all intentional killings regardless of who has committed or sanctioned their killing? Can any of these intentional killings be justified simply because the decision to kill was a private consensual matter? The *Roe* Court purported to find that privacy right in the Constitution, although it could not say exactly where in the Constitution that right was to be found. It avoided the murder issue by defining the fetus as only "potential life." But if it is only "potential life" in the sense that "real life" is not yet present, how can its killing by someone other than the mother be punishable as murder?

Fetal murder statutes now exist in at least thirty-eight of the fifty States,[252] and now under federal law as well (discussed below). There is every reason

---

251 Abortion Surveillance — United States, 2011. (2014, November 28). Retrieved from http://www.cdc.gov/mmwr/preview/mmwrhtml/ss6311a1.htm#Tab7

252 According to the National Conference of State Legislatures, at least 38 States now have fetal murder statutes, including Alabama, Alaska, Arizona, Arkansas, California, Colorado, Florida, Georgia, Idaho, Illinois, Indiana, Iowa, Kansas, Kentucky, Louisiana, Maine,

to believe that this trend will continue and that more States will pass similar laws. The basis for these laws is sound. Life of an unborn child is recognized to exist at every stage of development, contrary to the evasive written opinion in *Roe v. Wade*. That life is *real life*, not merely "potential life," and the government has a legitimate interest in its protection, regardless of the stage of fetal development.

Federal Fetal Murder Law

Fetal murder statutes are no longer limited to state law. As of 2004, and despite the Supreme Court's ruling in *Roe v. Wade,* the U.S. Congress embraced the very same fetal murder concepts by the passage of the Unborn Victims of Violence Act of 2004,[253] signed into law by President George W. Bush on April 1, 2004. This federal statute was purportedly enacted in response to the horrific murder in California of Laci Peterson and her unborn child in 2002 at the hands of her husband, Scott Peterson.[254]

What is particularly unique, and at the same time conflicting about this law, is that it recognizes the humanity and "real life" of the unborn child in contrast to the characterization in *Roe v. Wade* as mere "potential life." Under this federal statute, a "child in utero" is defined as "a member of the species Homo sapiens, *at any stage of development*, who is carried in the womb," and its injury or death is punishable as provided by federal law in the same way it would be punishable for an injury or killing of the mother herself, except that

---

Maryland, Massachusetts, Michigan, Minnesota, Mississippi, Nebraska, Nevada, North Carolina, North Dakota, Ohio, Oklahoma, Pennsylvania, Rhode Island, South Carolina, South Dakota, Tennessee, Texas, Utah, Virginia, Washington, West Virginia and Wisconsin. At least 23 states have fetal homicide laws that apply to the earliest stages of pregnancy ("any state of gestation," "conception," "fertilization" or "post-fertilization"). See http://www.ncsl.org/research/health/fetal-homicide-state-laws.aspx, accessed on 2/12/2016.

253 18 USC 1841; see also, Uniform Code of Military Justice §919a

254 After Laci Peterson had been reported missing, her body and that of her unborn son, Connor, were discovered on the shore of San Francisco Bay. It was learned during the case that Scott had been having an affair with one Amber Frey prior to Laci's disappearance. Scott was found guilty of the murders of both Laci and Connor.

the death penalty may not be imposed for the crime. In keeping with *Roe v. Wade,* however, the statute necessarily exempts from its reach any act to abort an unborn child with the consent of its mother.

Recall from the earlier analysis that Justice Blackmun stated clearly in the *Roe* opinion that "If this suggestion of personhood [of the fetus] is established, the appellant's case, of course, collapses, for the fetus' right to life is then guaranteed by the [Fourteenth] Amendment."[255] So we are, again, left with conflicting laws that cannot be reconciled, both of which are laws of the same federal government, and both of which deal with the very critical issue of a child's right to life.

There can be no justification for labeling fetal life as *real life*, recognizing it as a "person" for purposes of the fetal murder statutes of 38 states and a federal statute while deeming it only *potential life*, with no acknowledgment of personhood, when it is killed with the mother's consent. A mother's attitude toward her fetus does not determine whether or not the fetus is a living human being. The presence of human life is a fact, regardless of the Supreme Court's claimed ignorance, and the intentional killing of an unborn child cannot be justified simply because it may create personal hardships or inconveniences.

The fetal murder statutes present a very difficult problem for those who support a woman's right to choose an abortion. On the one hand, they dare not oppose such laws because the laws are designed to protect a woman's right to carry her child to term and give birth without violent interference from anyone else. Any opposition by abortion supporters to such a necessary and desirable protection under the law would totally undermine their standing among the citizenry. Yet if they support such laws, they are forced to admit that a fetus is a valuable real life, the intentional killing of which is properly punishable as murder. A mother's consent in the abortion decision does not change the fact that an intentional killing has been committed. By her consent, the child's mother has taken an active and intentional role (premeditation), no less culpable than any other person who would destroy fetal life.

---

255 *Roe,* 410 U.S. at 156-57. The Fourteenth Amendment provides that a person may not be deprived of life, liberty or property without "due process of law."

As discussed above, the fetal murder statutes of many States and the federal Unborn Victims of Violence Act make it clear that the unborn are properly "persons" entitled to protection under our Constitution. *Roe v. Wade* runs contrary to all such laws. Its decision was wrong in 1973 and it is wrong today.

Abortion is murder.

Early Christian Teaching

We end this discussion with an historical perspective. Early Christian leaders were very familiar with the abortion practices of their day, and they were also very vocal about it. The ancient writings of Christianity soundly opposed abortion practices. The *Didache*, for example (also referred to as *The Teaching of the Twelve Apostles*), taught the following even during the first century and while some of the apostles yet lived:

> Thou shalt not kill; thou shalt not commit adultery; thou shalt not corrupt youth; thou shalt not commit fornication; thou shalt not steal; thou shalt not use soothsaying; thou shalt not practise sorcery; *thou shalt not kill a child by abortion, neither shalt thou slay it when born.*[256]

The theologian, Tertullian, wrote during the second century:

> For us murder is once for all forbidden; so even the child in the womb, while yet the mother's blood is still being drawn on to form the human being, it is not lawful for us to destroy. To forbid birth is only quicker murder. It makes no difference whether one take away the life once born or destroy it as it comes to birth. He is a man who is to be a man; the fruit is always present in the seed.[257]

---

256 Hoole, C. (1894). The Didache. Retrieved from http://www.sacred-texts.com/chr/did/did03.htm

257 Tertullian, *Apology* 9:6. Cf. *Bioethics*, p. 129, and *Patrology*, Vol. II.; See text of Apology also at http://www.tertullian.org/works/apologeticum.htm Accessed on 3/23/2016.

We see, therefore, that the issue is not a new one at all. Although the status of the unborn and the value of prenatal life has been hotly debated for many centuries, biblical teaching, both from the Old and New Testaments, agree that the unborn are merely young children deserving of nurture and loving care. The early Christian church was steadfast in its opposition to abortion from the first century onward and even described the practice as "only quicker murder."

In Summary

- Murder is the premeditated killing of a human being by a human being. It is an act that shows great contempt, not only for the one murdered, but for God Himself, "for God made man in his own image."
- The law has coined a special term for the killing of a fetus: we call it "feticide" or "fetal murder," and at least 38 of the 50 states have passed such laws forbidding it. These laws apply where the unborn is killed by a person other than the mother and without her consent. The laws acknowledge the personhood of the fetus. As a "person," the unborn deserves protection under the Fourteenth Amendment.
- The Unborn Victims of Violence Act is a federal law that also recognizes the unborn as "persons" and provides for murder conviction for the killing by one other than the mother without her consent.
- The Unborn Victims of Violence Act and *Roe v. Wade* are completely contrary, and these two federal laws cannot be reconciled.
- A mother's consent to the killing of the unborn changes nothing: the life of a human being has been destroyed whether or not she consents.
- The early Christian church leaders soundly denounced abortion.
- Abortion is merely "quicker murder."

10

The Scientific Facts

OUR DISCUSSION OF abortion has thus far centered on aspects of the law and biblical teachings. But the issue cuts across so many different disciplines, and a look at some of those other areas can be extremely helpful to our complete understanding. In this chapter, we will consider scientific data concerning the unborn to see what can be learned from biology and the medical sciences. This will be followed in the next chapter by the statistics relating to abortions.

Is It Really <u>Her</u> Body?

Pro-abortion activists are often heard to say, "It's a woman's body, and she has a right to control her own body." This concept truly represents at least a portion of the theory behind the *Roe v. Wade* decision that posits the right to privacy as grounds for a woman's abortion rights. But, there are at least two bodies involved in every pregnancy: the pregnant woman herself *and* the unborn child (or children where there are twins or more). This fact cannot be disputed. There are two sets of brain waves. There are two heartbeats, one from the mother and one from the child. It is also common for the mother to have a blood type different from her child. From medical science, we know that one human body cannot have more than one blood type. And what can be said of the woman who carries a male child? Can the woman be both male and female at the same time? Similarly, there are four legs, four arms, four ears, four eyes, two noses and two mouths. That is not one person alone.

If a child dies in utero and a miscarriage results, the woman's life can continue because her life is separate and distinct from the life of her unborn child. In the same way, there have even been numerous cases where a pregnant woman has died and her child has been born alive following the mother's death, as we have seen in the previous chapter. This, again, is proof positive that the mother's life and the infant's life are completely separate.

In view of these facts, it is simply irrational to speak of abortion as a right of a woman to control her own body. The child inside her womb is not her own body. The right of "control" she demands is the right to determine life or death issues for another separate and distinct person: her child.

From the instant the sperm penetrates the ovum, a human being is created. How can we be sure of this? We only have to consider the fertilized egg itself (called a zygote) that is now comprised of forty-six chromosomes, the full complement required to make a complete human being. Twenty-three of these chromosomes are provided by the egg and twenty-three by the sperm.

As we noted in Chapter 2, we know the sperm is a living thing because it can move and work its way inside the egg, but it cannot reproduce by itself. In fact, the sperm cannot even make another sperm, let alone a complete human being. The sperm contains only half of the chromosomes needed to create a new human. The other half must be provided by the ovum, it being impossible also for the egg to reproduce absent the presence of the sperm and its chromosomal makeup. But having united together to form the zygote, *nothing* is lacking. The entire genetic makeup of the new individual is present and will, in the normal course of events, become the child to be born alive unless its progress is halted either by natural or by artificial means.

Scientific Facts Presented to the Roe Court

In 1972, prior to and in anticipation of the decision in *Roe v. Wade*, a group of more than 200 medical doctors filed a Friend of the Court Brief with the

Supreme Court in which they urged the Court to consider the fetus a "person" based on these same medical and scientific facts.[258] The argument presented in their Amicus Curiae is summarized with the following quoted excerpts:

- From conception the child is a complex, dynamic, rapidly growing organism.
- At fertilization a new and unique being is created which, although receiving one half of its chromosomes from each parent, is really unlike either.
- About seven to nine days after conception, when there are already several hundred cells of the new individual formed, contact with the uterus is made and implantation begins.
- Blood cells begin at 17 days and a heart as early as 18 days. This embryonic heart which begins as a simple tube starts irregular pulsations at 24 days, which, in about one week, smooth into a rhythmic contraction and expansion.
- Commencing at 18 days the developmental emphasis is on the nervous system even though other vital organs, such as the heart, are commencing development at the same time. By the end of the 20th day the foundation of the child's brain, spinal cord and entire nervous system will have been established.
- The baby's eyes begin to form at 19 days. By the end of the first month the foundation of the brain, spinal cord, nerves and sense organs is completely formed.
- By 28 days the embryo has the building blocks for 40 pairs of muscles situated from the base of its skull to the lower end of its spinal column. By the end of the first month the child has completed the period of relatively greatest size increase and the greatest physical change of a lifetime. He or she is ten thousand times larger than the fertilized egg

---

258 *Amicus Curiae*, pp. 8-25. See also Schwarz, S. (1990). *The Moral Question of Abortion* (pp. 2-6). Chicago, Illinois: Loyola University Press.

and will increase its weight six billion times by birth, having in only the first month gone from one cell to millions of cells.

- By the beginning of the second month the unborn child, small as it is, looks distinctly human. Yet by this time the child's mother is not even aware that she is pregnant.

- At the end of the first month the child is about 1/4 of an inch in length.

- At 30 days the primary brain is present and the eyes, ears and nasal organs have started to form. Although the heart is still incomplete, it is beating regularly and pumping blood cells through a closed vascular system. The child and mother do not exchange blood, the child having from a very early point in its development its own and complete vascular system.

- Earliest reflexes begin as early as the 42nd day. The child is almost ½ inch long and cartilage has begun to develop.

- Even at 5 ½ weeks the fetal heartbeat is essentially similar to that of an adult in general configuration.

- By the end of the seventh week we see a well-proportioned small scale baby. In the seventh week, it bears the familiar external features and all the internal organs of an adult, even though it is less than an inch long and weighs only 1/30th of an ounce. The body has become nicely rounded, padded with muscles and covered by a thin skin. The arms are as long as printed exclamation marks, and have hands with fingers and thumbs. The slower growing legs have recognizable knees, ankles and toes.

- The new body not only exists, it also functions. The brain in configuration is already like the adult brain and sends out impulses that coordinate the function of the other organs. The brain waves have been noted at 43 days. The heart beats sturdily. The stomach produces digestive juices. The liver manufactures blood cells and the kidneys begin to function by extracting uric acid from the child's blood. The muscles of the arms and body can already be set in motion.

- *After the eighth week no further primordia will form; everything is already present that will be found in the full term baby* (emphasis added). *From this point until adulthood, when full growth is achieved somewhere between 25 and 27 years, the changes in the body will be mainly in dimension and gradual refinement of the working parts* (emphasis added).

Let us stop for a moment and consider more carefully the information given covering the first eight weeks. As already stated in Chapter 9, the Center for Disease Control in Atlanta, Georgia, reports that the earliest abortions take place prior to six weeks of gestation and nearly two-thirds of all abortions are performed at approximately 7 to 8 weeks of gestation.[259] This occurs even though the child is now fully formed, including a distinct heartbeat and functioning nervous system, constituting a complete working organism comparable to that of an adult, only smaller. We have approximately four weeks to go before the end of the first trimester (12 weeks gestation), the gestational stage during which the *Roe v. Wade* Court declared that no regulation of abortion would be allowed. But an abortion at this point literally destroys a complete, though tiny, human child.

In view of the facts presented so far, it is unequivocal that a fetus is far more than "potential life," the term used by the Supreme Court, and the Court was fully aware of that fact by the amicus brief that had been presented. The fertilized egg begins its continuous rapid growth in human form even from the very moment of conception. It is at all times and in every way human and its final form is fully determined from the very beginning. If the developing child reaches even the eighth week, it is a complete functioning person as these doctors have testified. Given their description of the child's formation process, it is no wonder that the Bible says:

For you formed my inward parts;
  you knitted me together in my mother's womb.

---

259 Abortion Surveillance — United States, 2011. (2014, November 28). Retrieved from http://www.cdc.gov/mmwr/preview/mmwrhtml/ss6311a1.htm#Tab7 Accessed on 3/23/2016.

I praise you, for I am fearfully and wonderfully made.
Wonderful are your works;
    my soul knows it very well.
My frame was not hidden from you,
when I was being made in secret,
    intricately woven in the depths of the earth.
Your eyes saw my unformed substance;
in your book were written, every one of them,
    the days that were formed for me,
    when as yet there was none of them. (Ps. 139:13-16)

In Chapter 2 of her book, *The First Nine Months of Life*, Geraldine Lux Flanagan observes that the first bone cells are found at this stage of development and marks the end of the embryonic period. She also notes that the timing of development is so consistent that an embryologist can determine its exact age during the first forty-eight days of gestation.[260] These are common facts known by doctors everywhere.

When one stops to consider just how intricate and consistent the formation of a new human being is, developing in only about nine months from the very smallest of beginnings to a complete infant child, it becomes obvious that the process is far beyond our comprehension. From approximately the 8th week until the time of its birth, the only significant change is mere size and refinement as the child grows inside the womb until it is born alive and allowed to continue its growth outside the womb.

If we were to consider the development of only a single part of the human body, like the eye or the ear, for example, the process of formation of that one part alone would exceed our most sophisticated imaginings. If we then attempted to comprehend how all of the various parts can be formed from a single set of forty-six infinitely small chromosomes into a complete, functioning individual that can see and hear, breathe, smell, think, move, talk, eat and digest, feel both physical sensations and emotions—and a host of other

---

260 G. Flanagan, The First Nine Months of Life (1962)

necessary functions too numerous to list—we begin to appreciate just how limited we are in our knowledge of this most incredible process. God alone knows how it all works. Only He is able to "knit" us together in the womb in this marvelous and miraculous way.

We continue now with excerpts from the doctors' medical brief to the *Roe* Supreme Court:

- In the ninth and tenth weeks, the child's activity leaps ahead. Now if the forehead is touched, he may turn his head away and pucker up his brow and frown. He now has full use of his arms and can bend the elbow and wrist independently. In the same week, the entire body becomes sensitive to touch.

- Further refinements are noted in the third month. The fingernails appear. The child's face becomes much prettier. His eyes, previously far apart, move now closer together. The eyelids close over the eyes. Sexual differentiation is apparent in both internal and external sex organs, and primitive eggs and sperm are formed. The vocal cords are completed...the taste buds and salivary glands develop in this month, as do the digestive glands in the stomach...the child starts to urinate.

We are now in the second trimester, during which time *Roe vs. Wade* allowed only such regulation as the licensing of abortion clinics and the people who operate them. Even at this point, *Roe v. Wade* granted the mother an unrestricted, fundamental right to abort her child.

- From the twelfth to the sixteenth week, the child grows very rapidly. His weight increases six times, and he grows to eight to ten inches in height. For this incredible growth spurt, the child needs oxygen and food. This he receives from the mother through the placental attachment—much like he receives food from her after he is born. His dependence does not end with the expulsion into the external environment. We now know that the placenta belongs to the baby, not the mother, as was long thought.

- In the fifth month, the baby gains two inches in height and ten ounces in weight. By the end of the month, he will be about one-foot-tall and will weigh one pound...The baby's muscles become much stronger, and as the child becomes larger, his mother finally perceives his many activities. The child's mother comes to recognize the movement and can feel the baby's head, arms, and legs. She may even perceive a rhythmic jolting movement—fifteen to thirty per minute. This is due to the child hiccoughing...The doctor can already hear the heartbeat with his stethoscope.
- The baby sleeps and wakes just as it will after birth...A loud concert or the vibrations of a washing machine may also stir him into activity. The child hears...his mother's voice before birth.
- In the sixth month, the baby will grow about two more inches, to become fourteen inches tall...This month the permanent teeth buds come in high in the gums behind the milk teeth.
- In the sixth month, the child develops a strong muscular grip with his hands. He also starts to breathe regularly and can maintain respiratory response for twenty-four hours if born prematurely. He may even have a slim chance of surviving in an incubator. The youngest children known to survive were between twenty to twenty-five weeks old.

The excerpts presented above from the brief filed by trained and licensed physicians state plainly that from the moment of fertilization of the ovum, a new and very distinct human being apart from its mother has been created. It has an entirely different and unique genetic code due to a combination of chromosomes, half from the mother and half from the father. It is not part of the mother's own body like a kidney or liver. And the fact that it grows and develops very quickly and in a manner so complicated that we cannot comprehend it, shows unequivocally that it is a live being. Its heart begins rhythmic expansions and contractions even during the third week following conception, again separate and apart from the heart activity of the mother.

The embryo, and later a fetus, is a very small, completely defenseless person. And the fact of its extremely small size, by comparison to individuals born alive, is a characteristic which works to its great disadvantage when its fate is to be determined by the ignorance of mankind. Being so small and hidden from our sight, it can easily be dismissed as a nothing, a non-entity, an intrusive small thing that is easily disregarded. People naturally tend to equate larger size with increased humanity, that is, the greater the size of the child, the more "human" it has become. But such thinking is not based upon either science or logic. As we have seen from the scientific and medical facts, the unquestionable humanity of the developing child is readily observed even from its very early beginnings. Recall the lesson of the ostrich where we were told plainly that the fertilized egg is truly her "young," her offspring even from conception, and proper treatment of it requires wisdom and understanding.

In ages past, it might have been possible to argue, even convincingly perhaps, against fetal personhood. But science has developed so dramatically as to effectively eliminate any such argument. At the current level of scientific knowledge, described in considerable detail in the quoted excerpts above, we can no longer avoid admitting the true status of the fetus as a person. The case can be made even without biblical guidance. Scientific facts alone make a complete *prima facie* case for fetal personhood, yet the Supreme Court chose to reject all of the clear and convincing evidence. For more than 40 years the Court has stubbornly ignored these incredible facts of life. And because our society attributes to these men and women such exalted status, believing them to be wise and unerring, their rulings on abortion have convinced many that abortion is perfectly acceptable. It is not. As we have seen in the preceding chapter, abortion is just one of the many forms of murder.

It bears mentioning at this point that pro-abortion forces have worked very hard to prevent the scientific and biological information from becoming common knowledge. Their agenda is to keep the public ignorant of the true facts. In the 1990s, for example, Planned Parenthood challenged a Pennsylvania statute which required, among other things, that a woman considering abortion be properly informed so as to enable her to give informed consent to the abortion procedure.[261] The case was finally heard by the U.S. Supreme Court

---

261 505 U.S. 833

and decided in 1992. The court determined, however, that the "informed consent" rule did not unreasonably restrict a woman's access to an abortion.[262]

Nevertheless, although abortion clinics typically perform a sonogram or ultrasound procedure prior to the abortion (now required by law in some states) so that an image of the fetus can be viewed first hand, the pregnant woman may not be allowed to view the computer screen! The clinic's reason for this is obvious: If a mother is allowed to see her unborn child, watch its movements, and see for herself that it is truly a tiny human being, she might change her mind. She might come to realize that the pro-abortion message is false—that what shows on the screen is far more than a "blob of protoplasm" or "uterine contents" that must be swept away like the removal of a burst appendix. Moreover, a decision by the mother to forego an abortion means the clinic would not receive its handsome fee for its services. This is truly a conspiracy of silence, and one which actively works to conceal the true facts. Our legal system has knowingly allowed this sedition to continue. As a result, many women who have obtained an abortion now find themselves regretful and angry because they were ill-informed and no one shared critical information that might have changed their minds and avoided their later anguish.

As we will see in the next chapter, the vast majority of women electing abortions are under the age of 25 and approximately eighty percent are unmarried. It is clear from the statistics that these are young women, possibly inexperienced and impressionable in many ways, who may view their situation as a crisis, and are perhaps easily convinced by those who stand to profit from their circumstance. They are, in that sense, victims of not only their own ignorance, but of the pro-abortion activists and their agenda, principal of which is the Supreme Court itself.

The Opposite End of the Life Spectrum

So far our study has centered on the beginning of life. Let us now consider for a moment the other end of the life spectrum: the scientific and medical facts

---

262 *Id.* at 882

about the point of death. Certainly, there are comparisons and contrasts that can be made between the beginning of life and the ending of life. We know, for example, that when a person dies, bodily functions cease. Breathing stops unless artificially stimulated. The heart stops and the brain ceases to function. But how do we know for certain a person is truly dead?

In 1980, the Uniform Law Commissioners ("ULC") completed their drafting of what has come to be known as the Uniform Determination of Death Act ("UDDA") which has now been adopted by a majority of States without modification and provides that:

> An individual who has sustained either (1) irreversible cessation of circulatory and respiratory functions, or (2) irreversible cessation of all functions of the entire brain, including the brain stem, is dead. A determination of death must be made in accordance with accepted medical standards.[263]

At this date, at least forty U.S. States, the District of Columbia, and two U.S. territories have adopted this statute.

The concept of brain death as a means of conclusively determining death gained popular acceptance beginning in the 1960s. By that time, doctors and medical science had developed effective mechanical and artificial methods to keep vital bodily functions operating, including the other primary indicators of life. Before these medical advances, death had been determined most often by the lack of respiration and heartbeat. However, such indicators of life became less reliable once doctors were able to artificially stimulate those functions. The cessation of brain activity then promised a more accurate and reliable indicator of the existence of life. Even if the heart and respiratory functions are still operating, albeit through mechanical or artificial means, the lack of measurable brain activity will nonetheless indicate death.

---

263 California Health and Safety Code section 7180.

An Example of the Importance of the UDDA

The determination of life or death is extremely important in many situations, particularly with respect to the prosecution of crimes. As an example, consider the matter of *Dority v. Superior Court*,[264] a California case that was finally decided on July 21, 1983. In that case, a 19-day-old infant had been admitted to a hospital after experiencing serious trauma. Although placed on life support, the child's condition deteriorated to the point that it was unable to respond to any stimulation. Tests conducted by the doctors to determine brain activity showed "electrocerebral silence," indicating a lack of electrical brain function. The doctors determined the child was brain dead and recommended he be removed from the life support device. The parents refused to consent to the removal of the device and the matter proceeded to court for determination.

The written opinion of the court included the following statement:

> Investigations revealed the parents in this case may have been responsible for the child's injuries. The parents had been held to answer on charges of child neglect and child abuse.[265]

It appears, therefore, that one of the reasons the parents would not consent to the removal of life support was the fear that their small son would, in legal terms, expire as a result of his injuries and the parents might then be charged with homicide in addition to the charges of neglect and abuse. The doctors and hospital were reluctant to remove life supports for fear of potential liability if they should remove the life supports in direct opposition to the parent's wishes.

The child was appointed a temporary guardian who sought court guidance.[266] The court accepted the testimony of the doctors and determined that the child was legally dead in accordance with the UDDA statute which had

---

264 145 Cal.App.3d 273 (1983)

265 *Id.* at 278.

266 *Id.*

been adopted in California. The court then ordered the life support device be removed.[267]

For the purposes of our study, *Dority* and other similar cases, together with the UDDA statutes now existing in approximately four-fifths of U.S. jurisdictions, offer powerful evidence that the personhood of the fetus should be acknowledged under our U.S. Constitution. For if the absence of life is determined by the lack of circulatory and respiratory functions, or by the absence of brain activity as was true in the *Dority* case, the reverse must also be true: the presence of these functions is proof positive of the presence of life. It is simply impossible for inanimate things, or things which represent only "potential life," to have any form of brain activity. Neither do inanimate things display vascular or respiratory functions.

Constitutionally speaking, an individual's status as a "person" ends at death. Once a person dies, his or her constitutional rights are terminated. If, therefore, personhood ceases upon death, determined conclusively by the lack of brain activity and/or the cessation of circulatory and respiratory functions, then personhood must likewise begin at least as early as when the presence of life is indicated by such life activity. Recall that the doctors' argument to the Supreme Court, as excerpted above, stated plainly that vital bodily functions, including heart, nervous system, and brain activity in a fetus are present by the fourth week of gestation. In their own words, by the end of the seventh week:

> The brain in configuration is already like the adult brain and sends out impulses that coordinate the function of the other organs. The brain waves have been noted at 43 days.

Since the absence of these functions conclusively determines death, and all of these same functions are present and observable in the developing fetus without any form of artificial stimuli, it cannot be denied that the fetus is alive and the life it possesses is "actual and present life," as opposed to the

---

267 *Id.* at 280

concept of "potential life" employed by the *Roe v. Wade* Court. Personhood of the fetus is thereby fully established by means of these scientific facts. The "difficult question" of when life begins, which was avoided by the Court, has been positively answered.

The reader should take note that the Supreme Court has taken what appears to be a very small step toward possibly recognizing the personhood of the fetus. As discussed in Chapter 8, an important feature of the *Roe v. Wade* decision was overturned in the 1989 case of *Webster v. Reproductive Health Services*,[268] where the Court eliminated the trimester approach which had prevented state regulation of abortions prior to the third trimester, the point at which the fetus had been considered "viable." In so doing, the Court recognized that use of viability, as a measure of fetal value, is extremely arbitrary, ambiguous, and completely indefensible, when it said:

> There is also no reason why the State's compelling interest in protecting potential human life should not extend *throughout pregnancy*, rather than coming into existence only at the point of viability. Thus, the *Roe* trimester framework should be abandoned.[269] (emphasis added)

This statement, while maintaining the *Roe* Court's position that the fetus represents only "potential life," falls short of restricting a woman's right under *Roe* to obtain an abortion if the continued pregnancy would have any kind of adverse effect on her "health." But it does open the way to possible increased state regulation prior to viability in recognition of the "State's compelling interest" in protecting the fetal life. This is one small step toward recognizing the undeniable personhood of the unborn and its unalienable right to life.

Can anyone argue convincingly and with authority that once a human fetus has developed to a stage that brain, circulatory and respiratory functions are present, it is not a person capable of claiming the "inalienable right to

---

268 492 U.S. 490
269 *Id.* at 494

Life"? Thankfully, as a result of *Webster v. Reproductive Health Serivces*[270] and *Gonzales v. Carhart*,[271] discussed in Chapter 8 above, several States have now enacted laws to protect the unborn who have reached at least the 20th week of gestation. But if life ends with the cessation of brain waves, allowing such a person to be declared legally dead, the opposite must also be true. At least by the stage when brain waves are present in the unborn child at approximately 7 weeks, it must be recognized as a living human being and accorded personhood with all attendant constitutional rights as a person "in the whole sense." To allow state law to regulate abortions once brain waves are detectable would not be the complete answer, of course, for as we have seen, life begins immediately with conception, but it would certainly be a logical, albeit partial, step in the right direction.

In view of all of the available evidence, it is clear that *Roe v. Wade* and its progeny were wrongly decided, should be overruled, and the fundamental right to an abortion ended once and for all. Because an unborn child is a living human being from conception onward, a proper interpretation of the Fourteenth Amendment requires the practice of abortion to be outlawed regardless of the stage of fetal development.

In Summary

- A fetus is not part of the mother's body; it is a separate being:
  - There are two sets of brain waves, two heartbeats, one from the mother and one from the child.
  - It is common for the mother to have a blood type different from her child. An individual cannot have more than one blood type.
  - A woman can be pregnant with a male child, but she is still female.

---

270 492 U.S. 490 (1989)
271 550 U.S. 124 (2006)

- o If the child dies and a miscarriage results, the woman's life can continue because her life is separate and distinct from the life of her unborn child.
- o A pregnant woman may die, yet her child still live because they are two separate and distinct human beings.
- After the eighth week of gestation, everything is already present in the fetus that will be found in the full term baby, yet the vast majority of abortions are performed after that stage of development.
- Human life continuously develops from the moment of conception until death.
- Death is determined by a lack of heartbeat and brainwaves. A fetus has both of these very early in its development and must be acknowledged as a living being.

11

What Statistics Tell Us About Abortions

D EPENDING ON WHICH statistics are considered, somewhere between 700,000 and 1.6 million women in the United States have chosen to abort their unborn children each year – nearly 60 million abortions – since the 1973 *Roe v. Wade* decision. Questions must be asked: Why? Who are these women? How many abortions are performed because the woman's life or health is seriously threatened? How many are the victims of rape or incest? Are there any lasting effects on women who choose an abortion? How do fathers of aborted children feel about it? In this chapter, we look to statistics for answers to these and other important questions concerning the abortion issue.

Why Are Women Choosing Abortions?

On March 19, 1989, sixteen years after *Roe v. Wade*, two major California newspapers ran lengthy articles concerning abortion as the U.S. Supreme Court was again ready to consider the issue in a Missouri case entitled *Webster v. Reproductive Health Services.*[272] The Orange County Register cited

---

272 492 U.S. 490

an extensive study conducted by the Alan Guttmacher Institute.[273] The Los Angeles Times conducted its own survey. The Times article was entitled "Most Americans Think Abortion Is Immoral,"[274] and it stated that a clear majority of Americans believe abortion is immoral – in fact, "murder." But despite that finding, the Times also discovered that 74 percent of the American public felt that each woman should have the right to choose whether to abort her child.[275]

These results are astounding. Even though a solid majority said abortion is immoral and even acknowledged that it was murder (57% according to the Times article), nearly three-quarters of the respondents agreed that the abortion decision should be made by the woman for herself. In other words, if this survey is to be taken literally, a clear majority of Americans believed that a woman should have the right to murder her child!

To complicate the issue further, the survey found that abortion was strongly opposed where the procedure was used as a mere alternative method of birth control while almost all of the responders felt that abortion was justified in those circumstances where the mother's life was endangered or the pregnancy had resulted from either incest or rape. Most felt that abortion could be justified when the child was likely to have some form of serious birth defect.

What is it about the abortion issue that raises such obviously contradictory emotions and beliefs in people? Emotions must play a very important part in arriving at these beliefs, for it is clear that results like these are not based upon logic. At least a part of the answer must lie in the fact that a great many people believe that abortions are chosen for reasons that, to them, are justifiable – that there are extenuating circumstances that render abortion a permissible evil.

It is not difficult to understand one's sincere sympathy for women who are victims of very harsh and trying circumstances, especially where the woman's life is at stake. If *Roe v. Wade* had decided that women under those very

---

273 The Orange County Register, Mar. 19, 1989, at 1, col. 1
274 Los Angeles Times, Mar. 19, 1989, at 1, col. 2
275 *Id.*

limited circumstances could not be denied the right to an abortion, there would surely be far less controversy. But the truth is that Norma McCorvey (the real name of Jane Roe) specifically did not claim she was a victim of any such circumstances, and the Court's decision was not so limited. *Roe v. Wade* made abortion legal for any woman under any circumstances during the first 24 weeks of pregnancy and at any stage of pregnancy if the woman's "health" was somehow deemed compromised. That ruling has since been modified, but the essential part of that decision remains intact.

A later report by the Guttmacher Institute dated July, 2014,[276] shows that nearly 53 million abortions were performed in the United States from 1973 until 2011, an average of approximately 1.4 million abortions per year. This indicates an average of approximately 159 abortions per hour, 24 hours per day, in the United States alone. The report states that 21% of all pregnancies (excluding miscarriages) end in abortion.[277] It is a very big and very lucrative business for the abortionists. At an average of approximately $500 per abortion,[278] this translates to $600,000,000 per year in the United States. As is usually true, the truth of a matter can be found by following the money.

How many of those abortions are performed for the reasons which found high public approval? The Alan Guttmacher Institute published its findings in an article entitled *Reasons U.S. Women Have Abortions: Quantitative and Qualitative Perspectives*[279] and reported that 1% said they were victims of rape and less than half a percent claimed to be victims of incest. In summary, the article concluded that although a small percentage of abortions were performed due to the woman's health concerns or possible fetal anomalies, most women chose an abortion simply because the pregnancy was unintended.[280]

---

276 Alan Guttmacher Institute (July 2014). Induced Abortion in the United States. Retrieved from https://www.guttmacher.org/pubs/fb_induced_abortion.html

277 *Id.*

278 *Id.*

279 Finer LB, Frohwirth LF, Dauphinee LA, Singh S and Moore AM, Reasons U.S. Women Have Abortions: Quantitative and Qualitative Perspectives, Perspectives on Sexual and Reproductive Health, 2005, Vol 37, No. 3, online at www.guttmacher.org/pubs/journals/3711005.html

280 *Id.*

If we accept the truth of these facts, it becomes immediately clear that very few abortions are actually performed for the reasons found compelling by a majority of Americans. The following additional results were published from the 1989 Los Angeles Times Poll:

- 49% opposed abortions where the reason given was that the family could not afford more children, 41% approved.
- 51% opposed abortions when the woman has determined not to marry the child's father, 40% approved.
- 54% opposed abortions for married women who simply do not want more children, 36% approved.
- 57% opposed abortion no matter what the reason given, 34% approved.
- 80% opposed abortion as a birth control method, while only 13% approved.

Another 2005 article from the Alan Guttmacher Institute[281] showed that a vast majority of abortions were being performed for the very same reasons most Americans oppose abortion:

- 74% said that it would dramatically change the mother's life to have a child.
- 73% cited financial difficulties associated with having a child.
- 48% claimed problematic relationships or just a wish to avoid being a single parent.
- 38% said they did not want more children.
- 32% said they were not ready for another child.
- 25% were distressed to have people know she had sex or had become pregnant.

---

281 *Id.*

In light of these additional findings, it is difficult to avoid the conclusion that abortion is being used simply as a form of birth control in the vast majority of cases. The Times Poll reported that approximately half admitted not using a contraceptive at the time they became pregnant. A recent Guttmacher Institute study reported 51% used a contraceptive during the month they became pregnant, 49% used no contraceptive.[282] Eight percent have never used a contraceptive method. Given that virtually all commercially available contraception methods are much more than 50% effective, it is obvious that many more than half failed to use a contraceptive at the time they became pregnant.

With 80% of the public opposing abortion on that basis, it is again difficult to understand the report of strong public support for on-demand abortion rights. The answer must lie either in the fact that there is widespread misunderstanding about the reasons women have abortions, or that the general public feels strong sympathy for the woman who does not want to be pregnant, notwithstanding their belief that abortion is immoral, even murder.

Who Chooses to Abort Their Children?

According to the 1989 Orange County Register article, which relied upon a Guttmacher study, 62% of women having abortions were under 25 years of age; 27% were teenagers; 81% were unmarried; 26% had a previous abortion while 61% said they had never had an abortion before. Two of three abortions are among women who have never married. More than 60% have had one or more children. A more recent report shows that females under age 20 account for approximately 35% of all abortions and women 20 to 29 years of age account for nearly half.[283] These two age groups account for approximately 85% of all abortions in the United States.

---

282 Alan Guttmacher Institute (July 2014). Induced Abortion in the United States. Retrieved from https://www.guttmacher.org/pubs/fb_induced_abortion.html

283 Alan Guttmacher Institute (July 2014). Induced Abortion in the United States. Retrieved from https://www.guttmacher.org/pubs/fb_induced_abortion.html

The statistics are not particularly startling. Clearly the vast majority of these women are quite young, and more than 80% are single. The Times article stated that when asked why they had an abortion, the principle reason cited was that "I was too young." The sexual revolution has had its effect on our nation's youth. Rather than encouraging our young people to abstain from sexual activities until marriage, the prevailing view of society has been to encourage whatever feels good. We have been led to believe that there are no lasting consequences to an unwanted pregnancy that cannot be cured by an abortion. It is quick, simple, and cost efficient – no more complex than having a tooth filled. But is this the real truth?

The Los Angeles Times article reported that an abortion can lead to feelings of guilt and regret. One-fifth of the women who responded admitted that they had not shared their abortion experience with anyone prior to their response to the Times interview. A clear majority experienced guilt feelings related to the abortion and more than a quarter said they "mostly regret" their abortion decision. Of the 1,050 men surveyed, seven percent acknowledged being the father of an aborted child, to which nearly two-thirds felt guilty and more than one-third admitted regret.

The result of these studies show that the choice to have an abortion does not necessarily end the matter. The studies indicate that feelings of guilt and regret may last a long time, perhaps a lifetime. Some of those who denied feeling guilt or regret may someday change their minds. It will, of course, be too late to undo what has been done. And though God offers complete forgiveness through confession and true repentance, it is often more difficult to forgive oneself.

A Living Example

The Orange County Register in its coverage of the abortion issue carried a related article entitled, "Huntington Woman Has Change of Heart."[284] The subtitle read, "After 3 abortions, activist counsels against practice." It was the story of Christine Heacox who was only 20 years old when *Roe v. Wade* was

---

284 The Orange County Register, Mar. 19, 1989, at A16, col. 1

decided. Because her story is based on real-life experiences, and because it deals sensitively, yet straight-forwardly, with the issues of guilt and regret, a substantial portion of it will be quoted here. Her story begins soon after *Roe v. Wade* was decided:

"I was kind of liberal," the Huntington Beach woman recalled, "very supportive of the women's movement and all that it encompassed."

Two years later, when she found herself pregnant and unmarried, she felt no qualms about scanning a list she got at the free clinic in Venice and picking the name of a doctor who performed abortions.

"I called and he said, 'We do our procedures on Saturday, be there with x number of dollars – cash, we don't accept checks,'" Heacox said.

That day, "They did another pregnancy test, and, as I recall, they took me aside to do some counseling, which amounted to, 'Well, what kind of birth control are you going to use after this?' Then they gave me a Valium and used a suction machine and aborted the baby I was carrying at about seven weeks, eight weeks, something like that."

"And, hey, big deal – it didn't hurt much. The people there (at the clinic) were really warm and caring, and I felt like they were really concerned about me."

That made the decision easier for Heacox – who said she was careless about practicing contraception – when she became pregnant again twice in the next two years. [¶] . . . "All I knew was that I was pregnant and didn't want to be, and this was the way."

Years passed. Heacox married, settled down and decided to start going to church again. She became pregnant once more.

This time, she studied with fascination a book on fetal development.

"I kept looking at these pictures and showing them to my husband and saying, 'Look, honey, this is what our baby looks like right now,'" she recalled.

But her new found wonder had another, more disturbing effect: "The more I looked and the more I studied, I was aghast that I had done this thing three times, without knowing what I was doing." . . . [¶] "I don't even have the words to describe all the emotions I felt," she said. "I grieved. And I still do for those babies that died, and because I was selfish and stupid. I was angry. Gosh, I was angry – at myself, my (then) boyfriend, at the doctor. At just anybody who was there and could have said, 'Wait, wait a minute, let me tell you what's going on.'"

"All of those feelings still churn around inside of me. The anger, it comes up once in a while. But it was my decision. I can't blame anybody else."

The article ends next to a picture of Heacox with her 5-year-old daughter and states:

. . . Heacox, drawing from her own experience, seems firm on one point: When a woman has an abortion, "At some point in the future the chance is real good that she'll regret what she's done."

The purpose in discussing here the guilt and regret felt by both women and men after an abortion is not to condemn anyone. God has provided a way to receive complete absolution, and we are certainly not in a position to condemn. The issue is presented in an effort to bring truth to light and to sound a warning. Perhaps it may save some from making a very tragic mistake. The choice to abort a child can have enormous consequences. It is a choice that brings death to an average of more than a million American children each year and long-lasting, traumatic feelings of guilt and regret for the women and men alike who make that choice. Many who make the abortion choice are perhaps like Christine Heacox – at the time they simply do not understand the enormity of their choice, and nobody has bothered, or dared, to tell them.

A pregnancy cannot be undone as though it never happened; it can only be terminated in some manner or allowed to continue until live birth. As we discovered in the earlier chapters, the Bible instructs that it is God who has allowed the pregnancy. He is the one at work in the womb and His work is marvelous. An abortion is a deliberate attempt to thwart God's purposes, and it cannot be accomplished without consequences. Even where the decision was made in ignorance, research shows that repercussions will be felt.

It is unfortunate that those who promote the right to an abortion are, to a very great extent, responsible for the ignorance. Their misinformation and deliberate falsehoods about the issue have lead many down a wrong path from which there is no return for the innocent small lives that are lost and for the women and men who are left to discover their terrible mistake. Christ prayed, "Father, forgive them, for they know not what they do" (Luke 23:34). This must be our prayer today for those who abort their children in ignorance.

The 2014 study by the Guttmacher Institute (cited above) discovered that the number of abortions in the United States had declined by 13% between 2008 and 2011. Hopefully, that trend will continue as more people become better informed.

In Summary

- Nearly 60 Million abortions have been performed in the United States since *Roe v. Wade* was decided in 1973. This is approximately 1/5 of the population of the United States.
- A solid majority of Americans believe abortion is murder, yet the majority also voices a belief that a woman should have the right to choose an abortion.
- Nearly three-fourths of abortions performed in the U.S. are elected either because a baby would change the mother's life too much or because having a baby would be too costly.
- At least half of the women who choose abortion failed to use a contraceptive during the month of pregnancy.
- More than 80% of women electing abortion are single and the vast majority of them are under age 30.
- A sense of guilt concerning abortion is felt by more than half of the women and two-thirds of the men involved.

12

"Freedom of Choice" – A War of Words

I N EPHESIANS 5:6, the Apostle Paul warns us, "Let no one deceive you with empty words, for because of such things God's wrath comes on those who are disobedient." In this chapter, we will examine the message preached by Pro-Choice advocates. Is it a message of truth and love or simply empty words designed to deceive? Are we to be tolerant and accepting of their message? What does God expect from us concerning the plight of the unborn?

The Gospel of Tolerance

Freedom is a cherished American ideal, a precious commodity that has been enjoyed more in the United States than almost anywhere else on earth. And what could be more American than the freedom to choose the way we live our lives—the careers we choose, the friends we choose, the clothes we wear, the way we comb our hair, where we live, what we believe and what we say? These are the freedoms that have drawn people in vast numbers to America in search of personal liberties unavailable in many places but guaranteed by our Constitution.

Unlimited liberty, however, ceases to be true liberty. Complete freedom to do anything we want was never the intent of the framers of our Constitution.

If we were free to do whatever we wish, then our freedom would eventually invade the freedom of others. A person is not free, for example, to simply take what belongs to another just because he wants it; for when he does, he has trampled on the other person's right to keep what is rightfully his own.

Our Constitution has survived the tests of time because it has, for the most part, struck a delicate balance of the rights of government with the rights of its people, while at the same time balancing the rights of individuals with the rights of all other individuals. It is only through this critical balancing that freedom can be maximized for all of us. In the Sermon on the Mount, Jesus taught a similar concept in what has come to be known as "The Golden Rule."

> "So whatever you wish that others would do to you, do also to them,
> for this is the Law and the Prophets." (Matt. 7:12; Luke 6:31)

The fact that people are drawn to America from virtually every corner of the world and that America has been willing to accept them has earned our country a description as a "melting pot" where diverse races, cultures and belief systems are allowed to peacefully coexist. It is by necessity that tolerance has become a foundational requirement for our nation's continuity and success. Without tolerance for the tremendous diversity among its citizens, the United States would be in a constant state of agitation. It is only through tolerance that peace and individual freedoms in America are attainable.

But just as our freedom must have limits, tolerance must also have boundaries. The diversity within this country, in terms of age, race, religion, ethnicity, social status, and the like, is viewed by many as a primary strength, but diversity can also be a two-edged sword. Tolerance of ungodly ideas and practices leads a people to sin and degrades their society.

The Bible records the history of the Jews, descendants of the patriarch Abraham through his son Isaac and his grandson Jacob. The Israelites were to be a people set apart for God, undefiled by the sinful practices of other nations. The covenant of circumcision established by God with Abraham in Genesis 17 was to be an everlasting covenant and an outward sign that Israel was God's chosen and holy people. God promised to give the entire land of Canaan to Abraham and his descendants, an everlasting possession, on the one condition of their continued faithfulness. So long as His people remained dedicated to Him and kept His commands, they would be blessed. God Himself would be their strength and their redeemer forever. He alone was to be their God, a jealous God that would not share His people's allegiance with any other god.

The book of Exodus records that when the Israelites were set free from the Egyptians after four centuries of bondage, God led them toward the Promised Land. Before He allowed them to enter, however, He gave them strong warning that they were not to forget their heritage and the covenant made with Abraham. They were to remain a people undefiled by the traditions and cultures of those nations that they would drive out of the land. The Ten Commandments given to Moses begins this way:

> I am the LORD your God, who brought you out of the land of Egypt, out of the house of slavery.
> You shall have no other gods before me.
> You shall not make for yourself a carved image, or any likeness of anything that is in heaven above, or that is in the earth beneath, or that is in the water under the earth. You shall not bow down to them or serve them, for I the LORD your God am a jealous God, visiting the iniquity of the fathers on the children to the third and the fourth generation of those who hate me, but showing steadfast love to thousands of those who love me and keep my commandments. (Ex.20:2-6)

To make certain that this law was kept, Moses warned his people that they were to make no treaty with those living in the land nor intermarry with them,

> For they would turn away your sons from following me, to serve other gods. Then the anger of the LORD would be kindled against you, and he would destroy you quickly. (Deut. 7:4)

As Christians, we also are a people set apart to serve the Lord God. By faith, Christians have become Abraham's heirs, the new "Israel of God." Notice what St. Paul wrote to the Galatians:

> Know then that it is those of faith who are the sons of Abraham... Now the promises were made to Abraham and to his offspring. It does not say, 'And to offsprings,' referring to many, but referring to one, 'And to your offspring,' who is Christ... For as many of you as were baptized into Christ have put on Christ. There is neither Jew nor Greek, there is neither slave nor free, there is no male and female, for you are all one in Christ Jesus. And if you are Christ's, then you are Abraham's offspring, heirs according to promise. (Gal. 3:7, 16, 27-39)

Christians, like the ancient Israelites, are not to be tolerant of sin in any form within Christian ranks. When ungodliness becomes apparent in the Christian community, we are to take action to denounce and overcome it. In his first epistle to the Corinthians, the Apostle Paul proclaimed these precepts to the church. Regarding known sexual sin in their community, he writes:

> It is actually reported that there is sexual immorality among you, and of a kind that is not tolerated even among pagans, for a man has his father's wife. And you are arrogant! Ought you not rather to mourn? Let him who has done this be removed from among you.
>
> For though absent in body, I am present in spirit; and as if present, I have already pronounced judgment on the one who did such a thing. When you are assembled in the name of the Lord Jesus and my spirit is present, with the power of our Lord Jesus, you are to deliver this man to Satan for the destruction of the flesh, so that his spirit may be saved in the day of the Lord.
>
> Your boasting is not good. Do you not know that a little leaven leavens the whole lump? Cleanse out the old leaven that you may be a new lump, as you really are unleavened. For Christ, our Passover lamb, has been sacrificed. Let us therefore celebrate the festival, not

with the old leaven, the leaven of malice and evil, but with the unleavened bread of sincerity and truth. (1 Cor. 5:1-8)

Sin is the yeast that works through the whole batch of dough like the rotten apple that spoils the barrel. And tolerance is what allows it to spread unchecked. The Bible warns us not to simply accept sinful practices as a normal part of our society. We are to take action to rid ourselves of it, to stand up for the things of God. We are to be the salt of the earth and a light to the sinful world around us.

The Marketing of Abortion

Within our complex society are many competing interests. Businesses compete for profits, athletes and sports teams rival to win, religious groups vie for converts, politicians campaign for public office, and a host of special interest groups fight to gain an advantage. Each of these groups is constantly working to devise more effective ways to win and receive their coveted prize. The means they choose to accomplish their goals can vary widely. But whenever the need to persuade others plays a part in reaching a goal, the outcome of the battle is largely determined by the words used to convey the message. Huge investments are made in research to discover the most effective combination of words that will win over the greatest number within the intended audience.

The use of catchy phrases and jingles in marketing is not limited to the advertisement of ordinary goods and services. Where an organization's purpose is met with negative or questionable public perceptions, the method of presentation and choice of words becomes even more critical. The homosexual community, for example, has expended vast resources to gain public support by sponsoring "Gay Pride" rallies and presenting homosexuality as a mere "alternative lifestyle," a term that begs for tolerance and understanding. These labels have proven very effective in gaining acceptance because they present homosexuality to the straight community in the most favorable light through the clever use of words.

Those who preach the gospel of "choice" concerning abortion have likewise devised and implemented marketing plans that rely heavily upon the use of a carefully developed vocabulary. This is the language of euphemism—deceptive words and terms that disguise the truth and present unpleasant matters in ways less likely to offend. It is literally a conspiracy of misinformation. Their goal is unchecked tolerance for their agenda.

The term "abortion," for example, is most often referred to as "termination of pregnancy," an abstract phrase designed to camouflage the real essence of the abortion process and to numb our senses to what really happens. Through the use of such words, abortion is marketed as nothing more than the surgical correction of an unwanted medical "condition," the removal of an unwelcome bodily intrusion. Avoided at all costs is the extremely ugly truth that a living, yet unborn child may be intentionally destroyed by poisoning, shredding, mutilation or dismemberment and then forcibly sucked through a tube from the sanctum of its mother's womb.

Abortion is also presented as a "safe" procedure, despite the fact that the life of the fetus is violently taken in the process. Legalized abortion is portrayed as a necessary alternative to the illegal back-alley "coat hanger" procedures of the past, as though there are no other alternatives, like adoption, available. Pregnant women are portrayed as victims for whom the only feasible choice is an abortion. It is a conspiracy designed to elicit sympathy and tolerance in the face of certain death for literally millions of children. The Supreme Court is perhaps the most successful proponent of these tactics, using terms like "potential life" to describe the unborn and asserting that the unborn are not "persons in the whole sense."

The gospel of abortion tolerance is most apparent in the often-quoted phrase, "I might not choose to have an abortion, but I respect the right of every woman to make that decision for herself." It was no different in the period before the Civil War when many expressed the view that they would never choose to own slaves, but they respected the rights of others to own them. How many of us today would dare take such a stand? Who of us would be heard to say, "I would never condemn Jewish people to die in gas chambers, but I respect the rights of Hitler's forces to do that?" Yet these things happened.

Slavery of black Americans and the killing of Jews in Nazi Germany are facts of human history, largely because so many people who knew better failed to take a stand.

Early Christians were also persecuted and forced to live underground for fear of being burned at the stake, torn in half, or devoured by wild animals. Can any of these actions be justified by a "tolerance" that says, "I wouldn't choose to do it myself, but I respect the rights of others to make that choice?" Atrocities like these against humanity are now recognized as depraved acts, unthinkable in this age. But through effective marketing, the abortion activists have convinced a majority of Americans to look the other way as more than a million babies lose their lives each year in the United States alone—far more worldwide—all in the euphemistic name of "Freedom of Choice." The Supreme Court used the same strategy of deception when it pronounced in *Roe* that abortion is a fundamental right within the concept of "privacy," a term used to camouflage the true essence of the Court's decision and obfuscate the killing of innocent fetal lives.

What Does an Abortion Abort?

The terms and phrases used by Pro-Choice advocates to describe the fetus are especially creative. They would never admit that a *baby* or a *child* is being destroyed. Instead, every means possible is used to depersonalize the fetus with innocuous terms like "blob of tissue," "tissue mass," "fetal tissue," "fetal matter," "uterine contents," "product of conception," or "birth matter," all of which avoid any hint that human life is at stake.

Unborn children are, however, just as "human" and are just as alive as those who have been given birth. God's example of the ostrich has made that clear. The terms "embryo" and "fetus" are but terms used to describe their stage of gestation and relative maturity prior to birth in the same manner as the terms "baby," "infant," "toddler," "child," "adolescent," and "adult" are used to describe the relative maturity of humans following birth. The humanity of every person from Creation to the present has followed precisely the same path. Our physical lives here on earth are merely a segment of the life continuum that began in the Garden of Eden and finds its new start with each generation at the moment of conception, continuing to the moment of death. None of us can claim uniqueness apart from that pattern.

To declare an unborn child to be less than a human being or less than a person, one must first accept the argument that personhood is dependent upon the degree of development or the completeness of its eventual being. This is precisely what was done by the Supreme Court in *Roe v. Wade* when it labelled the unborn as nothing more than *potential life*. But that argument was flawed from beginning to end. The Court used such terms in order to "sell" the concept of abortion rights to the public and in an attempt to rationalize its own deceptive agenda.

Consider, for instance, a person who has been born alive and, therefore, has attained the status of personhood under the U.S. Constitution. If that person should lose his or her limbs, by accident or as a result of war, for example, is he or she thereafter denied status as a person due to the lack of those missing body members? If one loses the ability to reproduce, does that make the person less a person? If a person loses consciousness, perhaps in a coma, so that the mind ceases to function normally, does that strip away the status of a person? A comatose person or one kept alive by a machine, for example, is much like the fetus, requiring constant care and nourishment from others. If that person is unable to care for himself or herself, does it mean they are less a person? In each of these cases, personhood is present despite the lack of some body member or function. Similarly, when a person comes from the womb lacking some part of the normal body, we do not consider them less than human or less a person. One born without an arm is still a person.

It is the essence of humanity, the humanness, that makes a person a person, and the unborn possesses that same essence of humanity—only smaller in physical scale than those born alive. This begs the question further: If one is a small person, an adult by age but small by comparison to others, would we deny his or her personhood on the basis of size? The result is the same in every case. One's size, stage of development, completeness of body members or ability to fully function does not define their personhood. Rather, it is their humanity, their innate existence as a human being that determines their personhood.

We have already seen that the Bible clearly recognizes the life of the unborn and its personhood. In Chapter 1 of this book, we saw that God considered the unborn twins in Rebekah's womb to be "two nations" and "two peoples." In Chapter 3, it was discovered that the Hebrew word interpreted as "child" or "son" and is used to describe both the born and the unborn child—and even future generations not yet conceived. They are simply the offspring of their parents from the moment of conception, just as the ostrich egg was deemed to be the young of its parents.

Another example of the humanity of the unborn is found in Chapter 1 of the Gospel of Luke. Elizabeth, the mother of John the Baptist, became pregnant in her old age after her husband was visited by an angel while he was serving as priest in the temple. During the sixth month of Elizabeth's pregnancy, Mary, the mother of Jesus, came to visit. Upon her entering the house, Luke recounts:

> And when Elizabeth heard the greeting of Mary, the baby leaped in her womb. And Elizabeth was filled with the Holy Spirit, and she exclaimed with a loud cry, "Blessed are you among women, and blessed is the fruit of your womb! And why is this granted to me that the mother of my Lord should come to me? For behold, when the sound of your greeting came to my ears, the baby in my womb leaped for joy. And blessed is she who believed that there would be a fulfillment of what was spoken to her from the Lord." (Luke 1:41-45)

Inanimate "blobs of tissue" or "birth matter" do not leap for joy. This was the joyful leap of a *baby*. Being filled with the Holy Spirit, Elizabeth prophesied and described her "uterine contents" as "the *baby* in my womb." This word translated "baby" is the Greek word *brephos,* which literally means an "infant," "babe," or "child." It is the same word used by Luke the physician in Luke 18:15, where we find:

Now they were bringing even infants (*brephos*) to him that he might touch them. And when the disciples saw it, they rebuked them. (Luke 18:15)

These *brephos* discussed by Dr. Luke were brought for Jesus to *touch*. These babies had been born. Yet the same term is used to describe them as was used by Elizabeth under the power of the Holy Spirit to describe her unborn child. To the Lord, it is again clear that the fact of birth changes nothing. A child is a living human being whether it has been born or is yet in the womb, a tiny child created in the image of God Himself and worthy of love and care from the moment of conception. Its destruction is truly the shedding of innocent blood.

Notice also from the biblical description of the meeting of the pregnant Elizabeth and Mary in Luke 1:41-45 above, that Mary is referred to as "the mother of my Lord." Elizabeth was describing the unborn baby Jesus as "my Lord." Is it possible that Mary's "uterine contents" could be so worthy of admiration to be called "my Lord"? The truth is that Jesus was a person, fully human and fully God even in the womb, even prior to His live birth.

The argument over abortion was summed up well by President Ronald Reagan during a presidential debate on September 21, 1980, when he said, "I think all of us should have a respect for innocent life. With regard to the freedom of the individual for choice with regard to abortion, there's one individual who's not being considered at all. That's the one who is being aborted. And I've noticed that everybody that is for abortion has already been born."[285]

A Right to Control Her Own Body

One of the most often heard sayings of the Pro-Choice movement is: "All women have a right to control their own body." This is a very persuasive

285 Presidential Candidates Debates: "Presidential Debate in Baltimore (Reagan-Anderson)," September 21, 1980. Online by Gerhard Peters and John T. Woolley, The American Presidency Project. http://www.presidency.ucsb.edu/ws/?pid=29407.

slogan that finds immediate appeal for many. Virtually everyone has a desire to be in control of their own destiny. We want to be our own person and make our own choices. We strongly assert our First Amendment right of free speech. We vigorously protect against any hint of government sponsored religion. We cherish the right to associate ourselves with others of our own choosing. These, and many other rights are guaranteed by our Constitution and we will not let anyone take them from us. These are rights worth fighting for. In short, we want no one arbitrarily telling us what to do.

To the Christian, however, our bodies are far more than a personal possession, a thing over which we are to have complete control. The control we are to have is limited to that which glorifies God. Our bodies are His possession and our duty is to use our bodies in service to Him.

> Or do you not know that your body is a temple of the Holy Spirit within you, whom you have from God? You are not your own, for you were bought with a price. So glorify God in your body. (1 Cor. 6:19-20)

We have already determined that it is God who is at work in the womb of a pregnant woman. From Psalm 139 we saw that He is the one who "knits" us together, and even before we are conceived, He knows everything about us. We are literally His handiwork and are made for the express purpose to bring glory to Him. When Paul says in the passage above that "you were bought with a price," it was the very life of Jesus Christ that was given to ransom us from the hold of sin. Because of the great price that was paid, we have an obligation to dedicate all that we are and all we do to Him. Just as Christ was sacrificed for us, we are to be living sacrifices to God.

> I appeal to you therefore, brothers, by the mercies of God, to *present your bodies as a living sacrifice, holy and acceptable to God*, which is your spiritual worship. Do not be conformed to this world, but be transformed by the renewal of your mind, that by testing you may discern what is the will of God, what is good and acceptable and perfect. (Rom. 12:1-2)

When a woman becomes pregnant, she honors God by submitting herself to the creative work He will accomplish within her body. She is to be like Mary who, upon learning from the angel Gabriel that she would be pregnant, replied, "Behold, I am the servant of the Lord; let it be to me according to your word" (Luke 1:38). There was no foolish talk of the right to control her body. It was because God knew Mary would obey and submit to His will that Gabriel was able to announce to her, "Greetings, O favored one, the Lord is with you!" (Luke 1:28).

Just as we began this chapter acknowledging that unlimited liberty would cease to be liberty, a woman's right must have boundaries that end at the point of harming another separate human being, no matter how small or defenseless. One who justifies abortion by claiming the right to control her own body has, first of all, determined not to offer her body as a "living sacrifice, holy and pleasing to God." Indeed, she has missed the truth entirely. The "control" she seeks is not merely the control of her own body. If it were that simple, there would be far less controversy. There are, in fact, two bodies involved: the pregnant woman *and* the unborn child. This fact cannot be disputed. The woman has one body and her child has another, and both lives are precious to the One who made them.

The Easy Solution

As discussed above, Pro-Choice activists present the abortion choice as a quick and easy solution to the issues surrounding an unwanted or unplanned pregnancy. The procedure is promised to be relatively inexpensive and readily available at the pregnant woman's convenience. It is advertised as a simple surgical procedure and with minimal discomfort. That's all there is to it, they say, and your problems are easily solved. Unfortunately, this is a vast distortion of the truth. It is not that simple. There can be, and often are, serious consequences to the abortion choice.

Numerous studies have been conducted, and are ongoing, concerning the aftereffects of the abortion decision. The results of these studies indicate a myriad of possible serious complications, some of which are lifelong and include both physical and mental effects on the patient.[286] According to these studies, physical complications may include damage to reproductive organs with increased risk of difficulties in later pregnancies, including ectopic pregnancies, increased risk of breast cancer, sexual difficulties involving pain or frigidity, and even sterility. Psychological complications may include what is known as Post-Abortion Syndrome, in which women experience a wide variety of mental challenges that can result in depression, grief, remorse, guilt, and loss of sleep, all of which can bring about self-destructive tendencies and the need for psychiatric treatment. Not surprising, some of these studies also find a greatly increased risk of suicide among women who have chosen to abort their children.

The list of potential problems and difficulties that follow the abortion procedure is far more extensive than those listed here. The studies find, however, that many women suffer long term effects that can greatly diminish the quality of their lives. In the final analysis, the quick and easy solution promised by Pro-Abortion activists can be very evasive while the adverse effects may continue indefinitely, sometimes for the rest of a woman's life.

In Summary

- Pro-Choice advocates rely heavily on distortions of the truth to market their philosophy, using euphemistic terms that hide the true essence of the abortion choice.
- The fetus is depersonalized with innocuous terms like "blob of tissue," "tissue mass," "fetal tissue," "fetal matter," "uterine contents,"

---

286 See, e.g., the following online reports: *The After Effects of Abortion* which can be viewed at http://www.abortionfacts.com/reardon/the-after-effects-of-abortion Accessed on 3/23/2016; *Abortion Complications* at http://www.teenbreaks.com/abortion/complications-girls.cfm Accessed on 3/23/2016. *Abortion Risks | Abortion Complications | Abortion Dangers | Abortion Side Effects* at http://afterabortion.org/2012/abortion-risks-abortion-complications-abortion-dangers-abortion-side-effects/ Accessed on 3/23/2016. There many others. These are simply examples that are readily available by searching "after effects of abortion" online.

"product of conception," or "birth matter," all of which avoid any hint that human life is at stake.

- Abortion advocates claim the right of the woman to "control her own body," meaning they should have the right to choose to abort their fetus. But the unborn is not part of the mother's body. To abort the unborn is to control and destroy another human being.
- Psalm 139 declares that God Himself "knits" us together in the womb. Abortion seeks to destroy the work of God and render Him irrelevant.

13

Blessed Are the Pure

S EXUAL ATTRACTION IS a powerful thing. Its lure can be overwhelming even to the point that one may stray from the marital commitment. But is the grass really greener over there? Apart from sex within marriage, will we find sex truly satisfying or beneficial? It has been observed that a person armed with no more than a strong sexual desire will go places and do things he or she ordinarily would not attempt even armed with a loaded shotgun. That person is a crisis waiting to happen. God's Word, as we will see in this chapter, warns us all to control our sexual urges. It does so with good reason, particularly in light of the potential for an unwanted pregnancy.

Keep the Marriage Bed Pure

In Chapter 1 of this book, God's plan for the family was presented in considerable detail. Recall Genesis 2:24:

> Therefore a man shall leave his father and his mother and hold fast to his wife, and they shall become one flesh.

Through this verse, we saw that it was God's plan that there be one man and one woman, unified in every way, including sexual relations, all in harmonious marriage. Marriage between a man and a woman is the only context in which God intended mankind to have sexual relations and the only circumstance in which He will honor it. All other sexual relationships fall short of His perfect plan. This is made clear by numerous biblical passages. For example, in Hebrews 13:4 we find:

> Let marriage be held in honor among all, and let the marriage bed be undefiled, for God will judge the sexually immoral and adulterous. (Heb. 13:4)

Sex outside the "marriage bed" is also forbidden by the commandment, "You shall not commit adultery" (Ex. 20:14). "Adultery" or "fornication" are both very broad terms and are used to denounce sexual relations outside marriage with anyone or anything, including a close relative, a parent, a step-parent, a sibling, a grandson or granddaughter, a step-sibling, an aunt or uncle, an in-law, a neighbor's spouse, another person of the same sex, or an animal (see Lev. 18:6-23). Modern interpretations of the Bible sometimes refer to such acts as "sexual immorality" and specifically label it as "sin." For example:

> Flee from sexual immorality (fornication). Every other sin a person commits is outside the body, but the sexually immoral person sins against his own body. (1 Cor. 6:18)

> I fear that when I come again my God may humble me before you, and I may have to mourn over many of those who sinned earlier and have not repented of the impurity, sexual immorality, and sensuality that they have practiced. (2 Cor. 12:21)

Furthermore, we are told specifically that it is God's will that His people be sexually pure:

> But sexual immorality and all impurity or covetousness must not even be named among you, as is proper among saints. (Eph. 5:3)

For this is the will of God, your sanctification: that you abstain from sexual immorality; that each one of you know how to control his own body in holiness and honor, not in the passion of lust like the Gentiles who do not know God. (1 Thess. 4:3-5)

The Greek word, *porneia*, is the word used in these New Testament passages. It is an all-encompassing word that relates to all forms of sexual immorality. It is the root from which we get our English word "pornography." In 1 Thessalonians 4:3, recited above, we are told to "abstain" from sexual immorality, that is, literally avoid it. Don't touch it! Keep away from it! This is God's will for all of us.

Sexual purity is not a popular doctrine, even among some Christians. It is viewed by many as being outdated and old fashioned. The sexual revolution is here and many refuse to be left behind. Yet the Bible leaves no doubt where God stands on this issue. Until we are married, God intends that we abstain from sex, and after marriage, the marital union must be kept pure. Whether married or not, we are all to flee from sexual immorality of any kind. We are to have nothing to do with it. Marriage is God's intended outlet for our sexual desires, an escape from sexual immorality. The Apostle Paul wrote:

Now concerning the matters about which you wrote: "It is good for a man not to have sexual relations with a woman." But because of the temptation to sexual immorality, each man should have his own wife and each woman her own husband. The husband should give to his wife her conjugal rights, and likewise the wife to her husband. For the wife does not have authority over her own body, but the husband does. Likewise the husband does not have authority over his own body, but the wife does. Do not deprive one another, except perhaps by agreement for a limited time, that you may devote yourselves to prayer; but then come together again, so that Satan may not tempt you because of your lack of self-control. (1 Cor. 7:1-4)

Sex is a good thing. Why should we deprive ourselves? Why not seek all the pleasure we can get? The answer is that it will lead us into more trouble than we can imagine. King Solomon wrote numerous proverbs about the lure of sexual immorality and its dangers. Though he ordinarily uses the terms "adulteress" or "prostitute," his intent is to steer all of us away from sexual sin. He says, for instance:

> For the lips of a forbidden woman drip honey,
> and her speech is smoother than oil,
> but in the end she is bitter as wormwood,
> sharp as a two-edged sword.
> Her feet go down to death;
> her steps follow the path to Sheol;
> she does not ponder the path of life;
> her ways wander, and she does not know it. (Prov. 5:3-6)

Sexual temptation drips with honey. It looks so good—so good that we rationalize and ask ourselves what possible harm could be done. We are walking a tight-rope without a net. The end of it all is disaster.

Biblical Illustrations

Having declared that sexual immorality travels a crooked path to certain destruction, the Bible then provides numerous examples from which we can learn much. Even wise King Solomon succumbed to temptation and took seven hundred wives and three hundred concubines, who, we are told in 1 Kings 11:3-4, led him astray "and his heart was not wholly true to the LORD his God, as was the heart of David his father." In the New Testament, we find in 1 Corinthians 5 that a member of the church was having sexual relations with his father's wife. His actions were soundly denounced. But none of the biblical illustrations are more instructive than the adultery of David and Bathsheba. King David fell victim to sexual temptation and paid tremendously, not only for the rest of his own life, but also through the resulting dysfunction of his children's lives for whom he was to be an example.

In 2 Samuel, Chapters 11 and 12, we follow the king's downward spiral from the initial temptation through his sexual encounter with Bathsheba and eventual disaster. This is followed with his attempted cover-up and the premeditated murder of Bathsheba's husband, all of which ended in utter catastrophe, both for himself and for his wives and children.

The sordid story begins with David abdicating his responsibility as commander-in-chief of his army, staying behind as his men went into battle, and leaving David with far too much time on his hands. While taking a leisurely walk on the roof, his eye was drawn irresistibly to the sight of a beautiful woman, naked and bathing below. With no other pressing matters that required immediate attention and no one there to whom he was accountable, he yielded to the temptation to study her lovely form and his fantasies soon began to develop into full-blown lust. He could have looked away, but he didn't. He was caught. He was a voyeur, and he knew he was enjoying it much more than he should.

He had to know more about her. He immediately sent one of his men to discover who she was, and he began the plot which eventually led to perhaps his greatest personal failure. Very soon he learned that her name was Bathsheba and that she was the wife of one of his own trusted soldiers, Uriah the Hittite. That knowledge alone should have been sufficient to dissuade any further thought of an encounter with her. But instead of honoring her marriage, and putting his unwholesome thoughts away, he allowed his desire to proceed unchecked and took the next step downward. Sending messengers to bring her to him, David took her to himself without another cautionary thought. Not long after, he was given the disturbing news that Bathsheba was pregnant with his child.

What could be done? He had to think quickly or his entire kingdom would learn of his awful sin. He would lose respect. His reputation would be ruined and his hypocrisy would be found out. His standing as Israel's spiritual leader would be seriously damaged, perhaps irreparably. There had to be a way out of this mess, and whatever it was, it had to be taken right now.

David was descending faster and faster down the slippery slope of his own making. He wasted no time in sending messengers to bring Uriah home from the battlefront. Once Uriah arrived, the king strongly encouraged him to go home to his wife. After Uriah had been with Bathsheba, no one would have reason to suspect that David was the child's father. The king's indiscretion would remain secret and his reputation kept intact. It was an ingenious plan, but there was one major flaw: Uriah was a man of impeccable honor and he refused to lay with his wife, knowing that the Ark of God and his fellow soldiers and officers were on the battlefield waging the king's war. He could not enjoy sexual relations with his wife while others were fighting for Israel's honor. Uriah determined to return to the war front without the pleasure of his wife's intimacy.

David panicked. His scheme had failed miserably. Uriah would now have to die so that Bathsheba could become David's wife without anyone uncovering his sin. The final stage of his spiral downward was now set. David commanded that Uriah be placed at the battle front where the fighting was fiercest, knowing for certain that he would be killed.

This tragic account illustrates well the lesson from James 1:13-15:

Let no one say when he is tempted, "I am being tempted by God," for God cannot be tempted with evil, and he himself tempts no one. But each person is tempted when he is lured and enticed by his own desire. Then desire when it has conceived gives birth to sin, and sin when it is fully grown brings forth death.

After the death of Uriah, David took Bathsheba for his wife and she bore him a son. But then we find this indictment: "But the thing that David had done displeased the LORD" (2 Sam. 11:27b).

Just as Cain's murder of Abel could not be hidden from the Lord, David learned all too soon that nothing escapes God's notice, even things done secretly and in privacy. Judgment was announced through the prophet Nathan, and David was made to acknowledge his awful sin and discover the consequences that would follow. Chapter 12 continues with the Lord's judgment through Nathan:

"Why have you despised the word of the LORD, to do what is evil in his sight? You have struck down Uriah the Hittite with the sword and have taken his wife to be your wife and have killed him with the sword of the Ammonites. Now therefore the sword shall never depart from your house, because you have despised me and have taken the wife of Uriah the Hittite to be your wife.' Thus says the LORD, 'Behold, I will raise up evil against you out of your own house. And I will take your wives before your eyes and give them to your neighbor, and he shall lie with your wives in the sight of this sun. For you did it secretly, but I will do this thing before all Israel and before the sun.'" (2 Sam. 12:9-11)

The punishment was bad enough already, but the Lord was not finished. Even though David repented earnestly and sought and received the Lord's forgiveness, the consequences of his sin would go even farther. The Lord announced further judgment:

And Nathan said to David, "The LORD also has put away your sin; you shall not die. Nevertheless, because by this deed you have utterly scorned the LORD, the child who is born to you shall die." (2 Sam. 12:13)

Bathsheba's child died on the seventh day despite David's continual fasting and prayer. From that day forward, things were never the same in the royal family. In Chapter 13, we learn that Amnon, one of David's sons, brought more disgrace upon the family by raping Tamar, one of David's own daughters. Two years later, Absalom, another of David's sons, killed Amnon to settle the score. Chapters 14 and 15 then recount the rise in power of David's son, Absalom, who then forces his father David to flee Jerusalem, and once gone, Chapter 16 brings us the fulfillment of Nathan's prophecy: Absalom having sexual relations with David's wives on the rooftop of the palace in full view of all Israel, much to David's disgrace.

Not long thereafter, as reported in Chapter 18, Absalom is caught by his hair in the branches of a tree during a battle with David's men, and Joab,

David's nephew and one of David's own generals, thrust Absalom through with three javelins. Joab's armor-bearers then sealed his fate. Absalom was dead and David mourned him greatly.

This biblical account of David, God's chosen servant-king for His people Israel, presents a vivid portrayal of the awful consequences of sexual sin. David knew what he was doing was horribly wrong, but failed to listen to his better instincts. His story is there for our instruction and for the purpose of emphasizing our responsibility to remain sexually pure. Its message comes through loud and clear: the physical pleasures of sin last for a moment, but the consequences can be enormous, not just for the adulterer, but for all those closest to him or her. David's entire family was made to pay the price. David and Bathsheba suffered the loss of their son. David's other sons witnessed David's example and committed their own foolish sins, which, in the end, brought disgrace to Tamar and death to Amnon and Absalom. These events, in turn, brought tremendous grief upon their mothers and all of David's extended family.

> Do not be deceived: God is not mocked, for whatever one sows, that will he also reap. For the one who sows to his own flesh will from the flesh reap corruption, but the one who sows to the Spirit will from the Spirit reap eternal life. (Gal. 6:7-8)

What about "Safe Sex"?

There is much talk these days about "safe sex." The truth is there is no such thing apart from the marriage bed. The safe sex message is another deliberate distortion championed by those who have no wisdom.

What is safe sex? Does it mean that we can indulge ourselves as we please so long as we take necessary precautions to prevent pregnancy or sexually transmitted diseases? Are the precautions fail-safe? Does safe sex insulate us from emotional ties that cause such pain when they are eventually broken? Does it avoid a broken heart? Can it revive a broken spirit? Does safe sex bring us closer to God and give us lasting fulfillment? The Proverbs provide some answers:

For the commandment is a lamp and the teaching a light,
    and the reproofs of discipline are the way of life,
to preserve you from the evil woman,
    from the smooth tongue of the adulteress.
Do not desire her beauty in your heart,
    and do not let her capture you with her eyelashes;
for the price of a prostitute is only a loaf of bread,
    but a married woman hunts down a precious life.
Can a man carry fire next to his chest
    and his clothes not be burned?
Or can one walk on hot coals
    and his feet not be scorched?
So is he who goes in to his neighbor's wife;
    none who touches her will go unpunished. (Prov. 6:23-29)

And:

One who wanders from the way of good sense
    will rest in the assembly of the dead. (Prov. 21:16)

Is God unreasonable when He demands sexual purity? Are the sayings of Solomon mere foolishness in our modern times? Or could it be that God sincerely wants the best for our lives? He created us to be happy, fulfilled people. What would happen if everyone lived by His standards of sexual morality, where the marriage bed is kept absolutely pure and husbands and wives were truly committed to one another? Would we have an AIDS epidemic? How many rapes would take place each day? How many children would be subjected to incest and other forms of abuse? How many murders would be avoided that are now being committed because of infidelity? How many divorces would leave children in broken homes, unable to understand why dad or mom cannot be there?

With a loving atmosphere in the home sustained by devoted husbands and wives, how many children would grow up without hope only to turn to drugs, alcohol and sex as a way to escape their pain and loneliness? How many of our daughters would search for love in basements and back seats of cars, only to find themselves pregnant, ashamed, and frightened with no one to whom they could turn? How many millions of babies would they find a need to abort each year? How much heartache, agony, guilt and regret could be avoided?

God knows what is best for all of us. His wisdom is perfect. He knows what makes us truly happy and He wants us to be happy. The problem is that we continually look for happiness and fulfillment in other ways—ways designed to avoid God and His righteous will for our lives. We make a habit of choosing the wrong path, unwilling to yield to His leading. As the prophet Isaiah said:

> All we like sheep have gone astray;
> we have turned – every one – to his own way; (Isa. 53:6)

Our "own ways" have brought us anything but true happiness or fulfillment. Our sin draws us further away from God and leaves behind a huge void which nothing else can fill. Jesus Christ came to save us from sin, to lead us, to instruct us, to help us find happiness in this life and for eternity, happiness that comes from only one source: the One through whom all things were made. He said it plainly, so there could be no doubt:

> The thief comes only to steal and kill and destroy. I came that they may have life and have it abundantly. (John 10:10)

The thief comes in many forms, but always to steal, kill and destroy lives. He is deceitful, preying on the unexpected, leaving behind devastation. It is only by the grace of Jesus Christ that one may have life and have it to the full. His Spirit that resides in the hearts of believers is what brings true fulfillment to their lives:

> But the fruit of the Spirit is love, joy, peace, patience, kindness, goodness, faithfulness, gentleness, self-control; against such things there is no law. (Gal. 5:22-23)

Abstain from sexual immorality. Practice God's way and see that His promises are kept. Teach these things to your children. Instead of "safe sex," a Christian's goal must be a holy life, obedient to God's will, and reliant upon Him to fill every void. True fulfillment comes from no other source but His Son, Jesus Christ. A godly life is a beacon of light to those in darkness. It is God alone who gives us every good and perfect gift. Do as Paul encourages us:

> I appeal to you therefore, brothers, by the mercies of God, to present your bodies as a living sacrifice, holy and acceptable to God, which is your spiritual worship. Do not be conformed to this world, but be transformed by the renewal of your mind, that by testing you may discern what is the will of God, what is good and acceptable and perfect. (Rom. 12:1-2)

In Summary

- The Bible teaches that the marriage bed must be kept pure and undefiled by adultery or fornication (sex outside of marriage). God has sanctified marriage as the only relationship in which we are to enjoy sex.
- Adultery and fornication bring disaster upon the lives of those who practice them and for their families. The biblical illustration of King David demonstrates this abundantly.
- There is no such thing as "safe sex."
- God's will is perfect and His commands to us are for our own good. Failing to abide in them will bring heartbreak and pain.

14

And Who Is My Neighbor?

THE PRECEDING CHAPTERS have concentrated on the many individual aspects of the abortion issue. As we have seen, the abortion issue is truly one of many distinct facets, each of which is vital to our understanding. In this final segment of our study, we will attempt to see the global view of the matter, particularly from a biblical perspective. Our goal in this chapter is to effectively summarize the message of the Bible and its bearing on abortion.

A Missing of the Mark

The word "sin" is actually an archery term that means "a missing of the mark." When one has missed the very center of the spiritual target, he or she has "sinned." In the biblical sense, sin is the failure to meet God's standard and a failure to measure up to the divine benchmark for perfection. When the word "sin" is used in the Bible, however, it is not simply referring to a missing of the bull's eye; the sin spoken of is more a matter of our failure to even attempt to hit the target. For many of us, sin is often rooted in the uncontrolled desire to do exactly as we please, free from all restraints imposed upon us by anything or anyone else, particularly God Himself.

Sin carries with it dire consequences for the human race. In Romans 6:23, the Apostle Paul makes clear that "the wages of sin is death." Fortunately, Paul immediately reassures us that our sin does not have to end the matter. He promptly adds that, for those who will accept it, "the free gift of God is eternal life in Christ Jesus our Lord."

Sin commonly results from the "I want," which consciously or unconsciously overwhelms consideration for others around us or the will of God that might deny us the fulfillment of our selfish desires. According to the words of Christ, the entire Bible was written for the purpose of helping us conquer this bent toward self-centeredness which we acquired as a result of the fall of mankind from grace as recorded in Genesis 3. In response to the question of which commandment is the greatest, Jesus answered:

> "You shall love the Lord your God with all your heart and with all your soul and with all your mind. This is the great and first commandment. And a second is like it: You shall love your neighbor as yourself. On these two commandments depend all the Law and the Prophets." (Matt. 22:34-40)

Jesus' advertence to the Law and the Prophets is a reference to the totality of Scripture. In a technical sense, the "Law" refers to the *Torah*, or the five books of Moses: Genesis, Exodus, Leviticus, Numbers and Deuteronomy. The "Prophets" refers to the *Nevi'im*, the prophets section of what is called the *Tanakh* (Joshua, Judges, I & II Samuel, I & II Kings, Isaiah, Jeremiah, Ezekiel) and the 12 minor prophets (Hosea, Joel, Amos, Obadiah, Jonah, Micah, Nahum, Habakkuk, Zephaniah, Haggai, Zechariah and Malachi). The *Ketuvim* section (which includes Psalms, Proverbs, Job, Song of Songs, Ruth, Lamentations, Ecclesiastes, Esther, Daniel, Ezra-Nehemiah, and I & II Chronicles) is not explicitly mentioned by Jesus in this passage, but by tradition is assumed. In short, by His allusion to the Law and the Prophets, Jesus has declared that the two commandments He references are a complete summation of all Scripture.

Do these two things, says Jesus, and you will be perfect, sinless: love God and love one another. This is easily said and humanly impossible to do in accordance with God's standards. Jesus Christ alone was able to conquer sin and live a truly righteous, sinless life. By His words, Jesus was giving His audience a succinct summary of the Ten Commandments (the first four being corollaries of "love God" and the remaining six being corollaries of "love one another").

Adam and Eve sinned, but not differently or to any greater extent than would any one of us. In other words, their sin typifies the human condition. As Paul taught, "No temptation has overtaken you that is not common to man" (1 Cor. 10:13). Even though God had created for mankind the perfect environment, providing everything needed for the abundant life, the human appetite required more. Throughout the first two chapters of Genesis, set in time prior to Adam's fall from grace, we find a close personal interaction between God and man.

God provided everything for man's good. He made Adam and Eve the beneficiaries of Creation's riches and the ones having full authority over all Creation. God talked directly with them. God made woman from the man, a helper suitable for him and designed to be an indescribable blessing.

In the middle of that magnificent garden, God placed what was called the tree of life for their great benefit. But the tree of knowledge of good and evil was also available. Adam and his wife were encouraged to eat freely from any of the trees in the garden, except of the tree of knowledge of good and evil. The tree of life was available to them without limit, along with the fruit of every other tree, except the one God had forbidden.

God gave them a choice: they could obey and live with God in perfect harmony while He supplied their every need, or they could disobey and attempt to become autonomous. The final verse of Genesis Chapter 2 informs us that so long as they obeyed, theirs was a relationship of complete harmony with one another and with their Creator.

And the man and his wife were both naked and were not ashamed. (Gen. 2:25)

Verse 25 combines the report of their nakedness with their lack of shame. But their lack of bodily covering is not intended to explain their lack of shame.

Rather, it is in spite of their nakedness that they had no shame. The absence of shame and guilt was the direct result of the intimate fellowship they shared, not only with each other, but with God Himself. They had no cause for shame because they had done nothing to hinder the relationship between themselves or, more importantly, with God. They had been made in the image and likeness of God, capable of fully comprehending and appreciating all that God created them to be and do. Unlike all of the rest of creation, the plants and animals, Adam and Eve were designed for divine fellowship with Almighty God. They had no cause for shame and every reason in the world to rejoice in their circumstances and their exalted position in all of creation.

When we come to Genesis Chapter 3, we are immediately introduced to the crafty serpent that set the trap for their terrible fall from grace. Although God had warned that the tree of knowledge of good and evil must not be eaten or they would die, the serpent planted a seed of doubt and mistrust.

> But the serpent said to the woman, "You will not surely die. For God knows that when you eat of it your eyes will be opened, and you will be like God, knowing good and evil." (Gen. 3:4-5)

No one can know for certain just what thoughts crossed Eve's mind at that point and why the temptation was so powerful that she was willing to disobey God's specific instruction. It is possible that she truly believed God had intentionally withheld knowledge from her and Adam and that the tree of knowledge of good and evil held untold promises of great things, or Eve could possibly have felt that fellowship with God could be wonderfully enhanced by eating from that mysterious tree since the serpent had promised that it would make them more like God, thereby heightening her ability to relate with Him on a more equal level. What she did know, however, was that to partake of the forbidden fruit was unquestionably disobedient.

Very little encouragement from Eve was required for Adam to also take the bait. Genesis 3:6 recounts that "she took of its fruit and ate, and she also gave some to her husband who was with her, and he ate." As a result, both of them experienced their awful fall from the height of God's grace.

The serpent knew well the awful consequences of his suggestion. This was a very similar temptation to that which Satan himself had surrendered and that had brought about his own downfall. In Isaiah 14, we find the following description of Satan's own attempt to disobey and usurp God's throne:

> How you are fallen from heaven,
>   O Day Star, son of Dawn!
> How you are cut down to the ground,
>   you who laid the nations low!
> You said in your heart,
>   'I will ascend to heaven;
> above the stars of God
>   I will set my throne on high;
> I will sit on the mount of assembly
>   in the far reaches of the north;
> I will ascend above the heights of the clouds;
>   I will make myself like the Most High.'
> But you are brought down to Sheol,
>   to the far reaches of the pit. (Isa.14:12-15)

Just as Satan was brought low, the consequence of Adam and Eve's disobedience was very swift. The death they had been warned about was immediate in the sense that the spiritual union between man and God was promptly severed and they would eventually be returned to the ground from which they had come.

> Then the eyes of both were opened, and they knew that they were naked. And they sewed fig leaves together and made themselves loincloths. (Gen. 3:7)

There has been much written as to what is meant by "the eyes of both were opened," but however that phase is interpreted, one thing is very clear: the fellowship between them and their Creator was changed forever. In addition, the relationship between the man and woman was likewise altered for the worse. By partaking of the forbidden tree, they learned the difference between good and evil, and the result was awful. Immediately following their sinful act, verse 8 informs us that the man and woman hid themselves from God. Now they felt shame, not only because of their nakedness, but because of their rebellion and disobedience to the One who had provided them with everything good and pure. By virtue of their guilt, they found themselves unable to look into the face of their loving benefactor. The trust was broken and the perfect fellowship destroyed.

The harmony and love Adam and Eve had previously shared with one another was also changed dramatically. When confronted with their sin, the man and woman did their best to deflect the blame, pointing fingers at each other, even at God Himself. The man said, "The woman whom you gave to be with me, she gave me fruit of the tree, and I ate."[287] It was God's fault for putting Eve with him in the Garden and it was Eve's fault for encouraging him to eat the forbidden fruit. The woman blamed the serpent for deceiving her. And wasn't it God who had created the serpent? Neither of them was willing to accept responsibility for their actions. Nothing would ever be the same again. The birth of the wayward human ego, with all its bent toward self-gratification and indulgence, had altered every aspect of life. Partaking of the forbidden fruit destroyed the innocence that was vitally necessary for the perfect fellowship they had once enjoyed.

Thus, in verse 23, we find them banished from the garden and all its blessings. Hard work, struggles and pain were now to be a significant portion of their lot and ours. In the end, they would return to dust from which they had come. Thanks to the grace of God, however, the banishment is not for eternity. For in John's Revelation, we once again find our way reopened to the tree of life[288] after Jesus has crushed the head of the serpent and accomplished all for the benefit of mankind.

---

287 Gen. 3:12
288 Rev. 2:7 and 22:2

There can be, and has been, perpetual debate as to the consequential extent of the original sin. Having "died" spiritually, Adam and Eve were incapable of either renewing their own innocence or reproducing in their offspring that which had been destroyed. They had lost their innocence and purity, having traded their previous glory for a weakened and sickly and carnal substitute, unable to fully appreciate the things of God they had once known. Flesh gives birth only to more flesh.

> For the mind that is set on the flesh is hostile to God, for it does not submit to God's law; indeed, it cannot. (Rom. 8:7)

Having set aside the spiritual things of God and having elevated the human ego above all that is holy, there is little in ourselves about which we can truly boast. What is left behind is not commendable.

> Now the works of the flesh are evident: sexual immorality, impurity, sensuality, idolatry, sorcery, enmity, strife, jealousy, fits of anger, rivalries, dissensions, divisions, envy, drunkenness, orgies, and things like these. I warn you, as I warned you before, that those who do such things will not inherit the kingdom of God. (Gal. 5:19-21)

> They were filled with all manner of unrighteousness, evil, covetousness, malice. They are full of envy, murder, strife, deceit, maliciousness. They are gossips, slanderers, haters of God, insolent, haughty, boastful, inventors of evil, disobedient to parents, foolish, faithless, heartless, ruthless. Though they know God's righteous decree that those who practice such things deserve to die, they not only do them but give approval to those who practice them. (Rom. 1:29-31)

To this list can be added the sins of pride, arrogance and insolence:

> When pride comes, then comes disgrace,
>   but with the humble is wisdom. (Prov. 11:2)

By insolence comes nothing but strife,
>   but with those who take advice is wisdom. (Prov. 13:10)

Pride goes before destruction,
>   and a haughty spirit before a fall. (Prov. 16:18)

One's pride will bring him low,
>   but he who is lowly in spirit will obtain honor. (Prov. 29:23)

It is the human ego that bears much of the blame for this awful bent toward sin. It is from the ego that pride comes, a pride that leads us in the direction of self-indulgence and ruin. It is this leading, evidenced by a prideful and haughty spirit, that prevents us from following the Lord's teaching and reaching our full potential.

A Plan for Regaining the Abundant Life

God is all in all, the first and last, the beginning and end of everything.[289] He cannot be anything else and He cannot fail in His plans. Despite our fall from grace and our attempts to re-create God in our own image and likeness, God has provided the means for renewal and reconciliation. Immediately after the sin of Adam and Eve, God announced His plan for our redemption. Speaking to the serpent, God said:

>   "I will put enmity between you and the woman,
>   and between your offspring and her offspring;
>   he shall bruise your head,
>   and you shall bruise his heel." (Gen. 3:15)

This is our first scriptural glimpse at the Messiah who would eventually come, the one who would triumph over Satan and provide the means for

---

289 Rev. 21:6 and 22:13

mankind to be reunited with its Creator. Although the serpent would bruise the heel of the woman's offspring, her offspring (the Christ) would conquer and overcome with a deathblow to the serpent's head. The death that the serpent carefully engineered for Adam and Eve would be annulled and the sting of death would be swallowed up in victory.[290] The sacrificial death of the Messiah would become our deliverance from the penalty of death.

> For the wages of sin is death, but the free gift of God is eternal life in Christ Jesus our Lord. (Rom. 6:23)

> In him [Christ] we have redemption through his blood, the forgiveness of our trespasses, according to the riches of his grace, which he lavished upon us, in all wisdom and insight making known to us the mystery of his will, according to his purpose, which he set forth in Christ as a plan for the fullness of time, to unite all things in him, things in heaven and things on earth. (Eph. 1:7-10)

Our Faith Should Produce Good Works

James, the brother of Jesus, presents the Gospel of Christ in very practical terms. Because of the grace God gives to the believing Christian, James argues that our faith should produce good works toward our fellow man.

> What good is it, my brothers, if someone says he has faith but does not have works? Can that faith save him? If a brother or sister is poorly clothed and lacking in daily food, and one of you says to them, "Go in peace, be warmed and filled," without giving them the things needed for the body, what good is that? So also faith by itself, if it does not have works, is dead. (James 2:14-17)

---

290 I Cor. 15:54-55, citing Isaiah 25:8

This is just another way of illustrating the commandment that we must love one another as we love ourselves, the second greatest commandment. Speaking of the evil that comes from a man's tongue, James then points out:

> With it [the tongue] we bless our Lord and Father, and with it we curse people who are made in the likeness of God. From the same mouth come blessing and cursing. My brothers, these things ought not to be so. (James 3:9-10)

Abortion misses the mark in every possible way. Contrary to Jesus' teaching that we must first love God and then our fellow man, abortion fails to honor either God or man who is made in the image of God. Abortion is, very literally, the antithesis of love for either God or mankind. Nothing good can come from it.

When Jesus teaches that we must love both God and man,[291] He means far more than mere lip service and appreciation. The word "love" used by Jesus in this connection is the Greek word *agapao*. This is a surpassing love, deeply rooted in a desire for the other person's welfare. It is a sincere, intensely strong love, complete to the point that nothing more could be added for its enhancement. To love the Lord with all our heart, soul and mind is to do so with every fiber of our being: our will, our intellect and our affection. To love our neighbor as ourselves is to make our neighbor's well-being as important, even more important, to us than our own.

We have seen throughout our study that it is God who works the miracle of reproduction. Psalm 139, for example, declares that it is God who forms our inward parts and knits us together in the womb.[292] Jeremiah acknowledges that even before God set about to form his body in the womb, he was consecrated and appointed as a prophet of God.[293] It was God who closed Sarai's youthful womb, only to open it in her old age to allow her to bear her

---

291 Matt. 22:34-40
292 Ps. 139:13
293 Jer. 1:5

son, Isaac.[294] And it is God alone who causes the life-giving spirit to enter the body being formed in the womb, and He alone who knows how such a miracle takes place.[295] God is our maker.

> Shall the potter be regarded as the clay,
> that the thing made should say of its maker,
> "He did not make me";
> or the thing formed say of him who formed it,
> "He has no understanding"? (Isa. 29:16)

He is God. We are not God, even though we were made in God's image. Our desire must be to love Him unconditionally and to do His will with joy. Scripture asserts that we are not our own. We were bought with a price and we must, therefore, honor God with our bodies.[296]

To love God with all our heart, soul and mind is to submit in all things to Him, allowing Him to have dominion over every aspect of our lives, even the very personal issues like the decision to bear a child. Our desire must be to glorify Him in every possible way. We cannot serve two masters. Just as Jesus taught that one cannot serve both God and money,[297] so it is impossible for us to love God with all our heart, soul and mind while at the same time seeking our own way.

When a proponent of abortion declares, "It is my body and I'll do with it as I please," we are hearing the complaint of the ages and witnessing firsthand the turning to one's own way as acknowledged in Isaiah 53—the very same assertion of a right to autonomy and freedom from God. It is an attempt to either ignore or usurp the authority of the Almighty, and it is the very reason that Christ was offered as a sacrifice in the place of fallen mankind. Abortion is the absence of love. It is anti-God. It is totally self-centered.

---

294 Gen. 21
295 Ecc. 11:5
296 I Cor. 6:20
297 Matt. 6:24

What of our *agape* love for others? Jesus said that the commandment to love one another is the second greatest of all, second only to the commandment that we love God. This is why the cross is the perfect symbol for Christianity: the vertical axis (the love of God) and the horizontal axis (the love of our fellow man). To be a Christian is to embody the example of Christ, practicing perfect love toward God *and* all of humanity. The Apostle John records the words of Christ that summarize the central message of the Gospel concerning our duty to love our fellow man:

> A new commandment I give to you, that you love one another: just as I have loved you, you also are to love one another. [35] By this all people will know that you are my disciples, if you have love for one another. (John 13:34-35)

With this passage, our command to love one another is given additional clarity. With it we also find just how deep and wide this commandment is meant to be. It is hard enough to love our neighbor as ourselves, but here Jesus adds that we are to love one another "just as I have loved you." His love is and was true *agape* love, a sacrificial love that is unparalleled in all of history because He had done no wrong, yet He loved us even to the point of offering up Himself and receiving in His body full punishment for the sins of humanity, though He was entirely innocent.

> But God shows his love for us in that while we were still sinners, Christ died for us. (Rom. 5:8)

That is the standard by which we must judge ourselves. To love one another as Christ has loved us requires that we be willing to humble ourselves and love our fellow man, even to the point of denying ourselves. Consider Philippians 2:3-11:

> Do nothing from selfish ambition or conceit, but in humility count others more significant than yourselves. Let each of you look not only

to his own interests, but also to the interests of others. Have this mind among yourselves, which is yours in Christ Jesus, who, though he was in the form of God, did not count equality with God a thing to be grasped, but emptied himself, by taking the form of a servant, being born in the likeness of men. And being found in human form, he humbled himself by becoming obedient to the point of death, even death on a cross.

Therefore God has highly exalted him and bestowed on him the name that is above every name, so that at the name of Jesus every knee should bow, in heaven and on earth and under the earth, and every tongue confess that Jesus Christ is Lord, to the glory of God the Father. (Phil. 2:3-11)

Others are to be considered more significant than ourselves. Obedience to the commandment to love as Jesus loved requires exceptional humility and dedication, and it can be very costly. If we are to love our "neighbors" as ourselves, what can be said of the decision to abort an unborn child? Is there anything selfless and loving to be found there?

The Good Samaritan

In a parallel passage concerning the greatest commandment and Jesus' exhortation that we must also love our neighbor as ourselves, an expert in Jewish law challenged Jesus with the question: "And who is my neighbor?"[298] In answer, Jesus told the parable of the Good Samaritan.[299] This parable was the story of a man who was stripped of his clothes by robbers, beaten and left on the side of the road for dead. First a priest, then a Levite, and finally a Samaritan passed by and saw the injured man. Neither the priest nor the Levite offered to help. Instead they moved to the other side of the road and went on their way. But the Samaritan bandaged the man's wounds, put oil on the man's

---

298 Lk. 10:29
299 Lk. 10:25-37

head, placed the injured man on his own donkey, and took the man to an inn, ordering the innkeeper to care for the man at the Samaritan's expense.[300]

To fully appreciate this parable, we must first understand that Jesus was sharing this story with a Jew, an expert in Jewish law. Jesus implies that the one beaten by the robbers was also a Jew since he was traveling between two Jewish cities, Jerusalem and Jericho. The first two men who passed by and who refused to help were fellow Jews, one a priest and the other a Levite. But clearly, these first two men were less concerned with the wellbeing of the injured man than with their own self-interests. They lacked compassion, and there can be no true love without compassion.

Because the wounded man was a Jew, the listener might naturally assume that help would come from a fellow Jew. For certain, the Jewish expert to whom Jesus told this story would have made that assumption. But the lesson to be learned by this simple story was radical. The man that helped, the one who showed mercy, was not a Jew but a Samaritan, a mixed race of people who were highly despised by Jews. This one, the one scorned by the Jewish people, had true compassion for the man in need. He, unlike the first two men who passed by, set his own interests aside, ignored the social and religious status of the victim that was so greatly averse to his own, and loved the man as he loved himself. This, Jesus insists, was a true fulfillment of the commandment that we love our neighbors as ourselves.

To complete the lesson, Jesus then asked his challenger, "Which of these three, do you think, proved to be a neighbor to the man who fell among the robbers?"[301] Notice that Jesus did not ask if this injured man was a neighbor to the three who passed by. Instead, He demanded to know which of those who saw the injured man acted like a neighbor to him. Being a neighbor is a personal responsibility for each of us. And our neighbor is the one right there in front of us.

When this young man asked the initial question, "And who is my neighbor," he was looking for an answer that would find a limit. He was asking

---

300 Lk. 10:30-35
301 Luke 10:36

who, in the context of that important commandment from God, could he eliminate as a neighbor he must love. Jesus turned the tables on him and demanded an acknowledgment that everyone is a neighbor to everyone else, even those we despise.

Note also that in response to Jesus' pointed question concerning which of the three men proved to be a neighbor, the expert in the law was unwilling to admit that it was the hated Samaritan who had done well. He could only reply, "The one who showed him mercy."[302] To which Jesus said, "You go, and do likewise,"[303] acknowledging the right judgment in this man's grudging admission.

A neighbor is our fellow man or woman, any fellow human being, regardless who he or she might be. It is because they are created by God and in the image and likeness of God that they deserve our love and mercy, the same as they may receive from God. That they are of a different race, religion, ethnic background, makes no difference. Neither does it matter whether they are perceived as good or bad, rich or poor, young or old, or whether they have shown mercy or not. According to Jesus, our neighbors include even our enemies.

> "You have heard that it was said, 'You shall love your neighbor and hate your enemy.' But I say to you, love your enemies and pray for those who persecute you." (Matt. 5:43-44)

How much closer can a neighbor be than the small one who is quietly developing within a mother's womb? Since the Bible clearly teaches, as we have seen in the earlier chapters of this book, that the unborn is on equal footing with those born alive so that both are simply one's offspring, can we deny their status as our neighbors? If to love with an *agape* love means to be humble and treat others as more significant than ourselves, sacrificing our own desires to the needs of others, can we fail to show mercy to the tiny, defenseless child that grows inside the womb? Can we assert our right to control our own body

---

302 Luke 10:37
303 *Id.*

and fail to acknowledge that separate, small heartbeat? The ageless commandment is that we *be* a neighbor to others, having mercy and showing true, selfless love—just as Jesus has loved us.

If all of Scripture can be summed up in the commandments to love God with all our heart, soul and mind and our neighbors as ourselves, how then can we justify abortion? We simply cannot. We cannot claim to love God while we destroy those being formed by the hand of God, created in the image and likeness of God. Neither can we claim to truly love our fellow man, our neighbor, while we curse the tiny human struggling to live and move and bring glory back to Almighty God by his or her mere existence. Try as we might, God's Truth, as revealed in Scripture, will bring it all to light. Abortion is a direct challenge to the majesty of Holy Scripture and the authority and sovereignty of God Himself and cannot be justified, nor should it be rationalized.

In the final analysis, God has put before us a choice, for certain. He says in Matthew 11:28, "Come to me, all who labor and are heavy laden, and I will give you rest." His offer is given freely and invites us all, even those who face an unplanned or unwanted pregnancy, to enter into His rest. The alternative leads in the direction of disobedience, away from what we know in our hearts is right, and the end of that is not good.

> And since they did not see fit to acknowledge God, God gave them up to a debased mind to do what ought not to be done. (Rom. 1:28)

Choices come with consequences. God's admonition to the Israelites through Moses is just as applicable to us in this day:

> "I call heaven and earth to witness against you today, that I have set before you life and death, blessing and curse. *Therefore choose life*, that you and your offspring may live, loving the LORD your God, obeying his voice and holding fast to him, for he is your life and length of days." (Deut. 30:19)

THEREFORE, CHOOSE LIFE.

In Summary

- The word "sin" is actually an archery term which means "a missing of the mark." When one has missed the very center of the spiritual target, he or she has "sinned."
- Abortion misses the mark in every possible way. It fails to honor either God or man who is made in the image of God. Abortion is, very literally, the antithesis of love for either God or man.
- The Greatest Commandment is a summary of all Scripture. To love God with all our heart, soul and mind is to submit in all things to Him, allowing Him to have dominion over every aspect of our lives, even the very personal issues like the decision to bear a child. To love one another means that we must love others as Christ has loved us and that we be willing to humble ourselves and put the other person first, even to the point of denying ourselves.
- We cannot claim to love God while we destroy those being formed by the hand of God, created in the image and likeness of God.
- To obey the commandment that we love our neighbors as ourselves, we are compelled to Choose Life for the unborn.

51519420R00155

Made in the USA
San Bernardino, CA
25 July 2017